HISTORY OF UNIVERSITY EDUCATION

History of University Education

Evolution and Development

Edited by
William James

ANMOL PUBLICATIONS PVT. LTD.
NEW DELHI - 110 002 (INDIA)

ANMOL PUBLICATIONS PVT. LTD.
4374/4B, Ansari Road, Daryaganj
New Delhi - 110 002
Ph.: 23261597, 23278000
Visit us at: www.anmolpublications.com

History of University Education

First Published, 2005

ISBN 81-261-2135-1

PRINTED IN INDIA

Published by J.L. Kumar for Anmol Publications Pvt. Ltd., New Delhi - 110 002 and Printed at Mehra Offset Press, Delhi.

Contents

Preface

Evolution and growth of university education has had a chequered history. These centers of higher learning developed with teachers of eminence. Before Christ, we have evidence of the existence of the universities of sort in India—Nalanda and Taxila to count a few. It is said, around one hundred teachers and ten thousand pupils were there in Nalanda. Famous Chinese traveller Hieun-Tsang also visited there and studied Buddhism. Back in Europe, the unorganised group of students and teachers was called a stadium generale, a name indicating either that a generality of studies was here pursued, or that the students were drawn from the widest territorial limits. 'Scholasticism' is the term given to the type of intellectual life, and hence of education, that prevailed from the eleventh to fifteenth centuries inclusive, that was largely responsible for the origin of universities. Politically, ecclesiastically, and theologically, the universities were the bulwark of freedom during the centuries from dark ages to the Reformation.

Here in this book we have presented an authoritative and categorical account of evolution and development of university education. We have selected eight essays encompassing the valuable information on the topic. Definitely this will prove a veritable mine of information to one and all.

—Editor

1

Middle Ages: Education as Discipline

In order to understand the attitude of the early Church of education, and the conception of education that developed from these early conditions and prevailed throughout the Middle Ages, it is necessary to have in mind some of the characteristics of the thought life and of the concrete social activities of the pagan life surrounding the early Church. Into the life of Greek culture and intellectual activity of the cosmopolitan period, modified, supplemented, and extended as it had been through adoption by the Romans, and into the life of Roman activity at its height of power, though past its prime in vigor and positive virtues, Christianity was introduced in the first century to spread with great rapidity, to modify this foreign world both in regard to thought and to conduct, and, on the other hand, to be itself profoundly modified as well.

The Greek mind had developed a versatility that probably has never been equalled, a power of dealing with abstract thought and an interest in philosophical questions that is as remote from the interests of society at large to-day as it was in ages preceding the time under consideration. Schools were very numerous and flourishing in both the East and the West; culture had never been so disseminated, nor the intellectual life so fostered. In very many point indeed, it can be shown that Christianity was influenced and modified by this solvent of Greek thought. These changes are, however, of more interest in Church history; here only a few points of contact can be indicated as of vital importance in the history of education.

Christian vs. Greek Solution of the Problem of the Individual and Society

The highest reach of pagan thought, its solution of the problem of the individual and society, was in the thought of Aristotle that found the perfection of the one and conserved the welfare of the many in well being and well doing. The solutions offered by Plato, Aristotle, and by the various schools of thought found their ideas in the intellectual nature of man and were necessarily aristocratic since possible only to the few. Opposed to this, Christianity offered its solution found in the moral nature of man which, since it is common to all alike, was universal in its application. It was in no ideal of immediate happiness or of any activity of the rational nature that Christianity discovered its solution of the world problem. It was in the idea of Christian charity or love that expression of personality which is most individual and most complete, and which at the same time from its very nature finds its expression in objects or personalities external to itself. Thus in the moral nature, which pagan religion had so slightly affected and which Greek philosophy had but dimly apprehended, a new basis of life was found and a new solution of the fundamental educational as well as ethical problem was secured. However different in its solution, the problem stated and the general principle sought were so identified with that of the highest thought of the pagan schools that a community of interest was immediately discovered, and a fusion of Greek philosophical thought and Christian teaching was attempted. The unknown god that the Apostle declared unto the Athenians was but a symbol of this declaration of the hitherto unknown truth for which the Greek thinkers for generations had been groping.

Points of Conflict between Greek and Christian Thought

Though there was this one point of contact of fundamental importance, there were divergencies too great to be bridged without compromises on both sides. The intellectual and aesthetic elements so essential to the Greek ideal, were wholly wanting in the opinion of the early Christian teachers. This led to an indifference on the part of the Christians to those features and characteristics of the Greek and the Greco Roman education and culture. Further strengthened by the fact that Christianity offered the greatest boon to classes wholly neglected in the economy of pagan society and Grecian culture, and by the additional fact that paganism found its strongest intrenchment for resistance against conquest by the new religion in its literature, its culture, and its schools, there grew up in time a general hostility between Hellenistic culture and Christianity that had not at first been evident. Especially when the old culture had degenerated into a more form without vivifying principles of the real search for truth that had characterized the early Greek philosophers or the later Stoics at Rome, Hellenism became identified with paganism.

Influence of Greek Thought upon Christianity

The extent to which Christianity was influenced in its thought life by Grecian intellectualism is evidenced by the growth of heresies, many of which were attempts to interpret Christian teachings in the light of the varying schools of Greek philosophy and in the formation of the orthodox Christian creed as well. Contrasting the Sermon on the Mount with the Nicene Creed (A.D. 325) one sees at a glance the difference between Christianity in Semitic form, and Christianity when cast in Grecian mold. This influence of the Grecian thought world on early Christianity can be seen in various aspects. Contrast, for instance, the methods of teaching. In the Grecian schools the method was that of formal selection of a theme or texts from the teaching of a philosophical school, of logical analysis, of careful choice of words, of discrimination in phrases and fine shades of meaning, and of formal delivery; the method of the Hebrew synagogue was that of informal comment and expiation; the method of instruction of the early Christian was that of prophet saying or impromptu exposition and exhortation. In a similar manner the allegorical method of interpretation so long in vogue among the Greek philosophers in the explanation of their literature, whereby trivial, irrational, or immoral acts were given a moral or rational meaning, was adopted by the Jews, under the leadership of Philo, in the justification of the *Old Testament* to Greek thought. Finally this same method was adopted by the Christian teachers, and the Church subsequently imposed these interpretations upon coming generations as a test of orthodoxy.

Influence of Roman Thought

The point of contact between Christianity and the Roman thought world was found in its relation to the Stoic philosophy. Peculiarly appropriate to the Roman character, and prepared for by all of their early historic experience, the Stoic philosophy, as formulated by a few leading exponents among the Romans and held by a large and saving element among the better members of society, expressed the highest attainment in moral thought reached by the ancients. According to this philosophy, virtue in itself was made the highest pleasure attainable. Conscience was exalted into the rule of life; good deeds, charity, and sympathy for the less fortunate were commanded not on the score of ostentation or for the approval of man, but because such actions were a duty. Duty, in its legal, institutional and parental form had always been exalted by the Romans as the highest expression of their moral life; they now found in the philosophical formulation of this ethical truth the highest expression of their cosmpolitan life and of their world empire. This represents the perfection of pagan philosophy in its ethical bearing. Conscience was defined into the sole arbiter of life; for in the Stoic philosophy of the Romans though it was otherwise with earlier teachings of the Grecian Stoics, there is no firm belief in a life after death, and little attempt to connect the duties of this life with any rewards and punishments in the hereafter. Says one of these teachers: "The wise man will not sin, though both gods and men should overlook the deed, for it is not through the fear of punishment or of shame that he abstains from sin. It is from the desire and obligation of what is just and good."

It is a striking fact that as it nears the period of the ascendency of Christianity, pagan philosophy, as illustrated by Seneca, Epictetus, and Marcus Aurelius, directs its attention more and more to the attempt to influence the conduct of men through ethical teachings, in recognition of the fact that this was the supreme need of the time. In this, again, Christianity had one great feature in common with the thought life of the times. Yet the differences here were very great. Both aimed to regulate the life of society, or at least the daily conduct of the individual, so as to secure the happiness, immediate or ultimate, of the individual and the security and stability of society. But while it aimed at the regeneration of society, philosophy could affect only a few. Attached, as they were to the great families of Rome in the capacity of moral advisers, the minor Stoics would seem to be in a position to exercise an influence, great though limited to a class. Their position, however, was little above that of a menial one; for the patronage extended to them was quite as much an ostentatious display of power as was that shown to the court scholar during the Renaissance, while the ease and influence attaching to the position called forth a great number of impostors, greedy of wealth and given over to the gratification of every whim and passion.

Limitation of Stoicism and Other Pagan Philosophies

The reason for the slight extent of the influence of Stoicism compared with that of Christianity is to be seen on the very surface. Both exalted virtue; but while virtue to the Stoic was to be obtained only through the development of reason, Christianity would obtain the same result through the emotional nature. The virtue of the Stoics could be obtained only by the few in whom the intellect was developed and the rational nature controlled; Christianity rendered the attainment to virtue a possibility for all. It appealed to emotions that were universal; to that which was noble, to the affection for an ideal human character that in itself is an expression of the divine, to sympathy for fellow-men, to fear of external retribution, and to the entire gamut of human feelings.

This limitation of Stoicism was a limitation of all ancient philosophy. The appeal of stoicism could be made only to minds already noble. It affected but a limited few in society, and those of the best. However nearly its ethical teachings approximated Christianity, there was no similarity in the extent of its influence, and hence in its educational character. The ancient philosophy did very little to improve mankind, to regenerate the society of the times. Unless, as in the impossible scheme of Plato, philosophers should be kings, it could do nothing to check vice among men and evil in society.

If philosophy did little to check vice and gave an ethical creed to but the intellectual few, the religion of pagan society did far less to effect any moral improvement in life. As a matter of fact, the religions of the ancients had little influence on morality. The grosser form of Asiatic religions were but the cloaking of every human instinct and passion, even the grossest, under the guise of worship. That of the Greeks was a refinement upon these through its clothing of aesthetic form and later through its content of philsophical truth. But the polytheism of the Greeks had long ceased to have any influence on the lives of thinking men, among the multitude it was little less than a subject for jeering. The ethical teachings of the Greeks were embodied in the writings of the dramatists and the philosophers. Of the latter, Plato most conspicuously took a position of open hostility to the Homeric and other early poetry embodying their mythology. The later philosophers inclined, on the one hand with the Epicureans, to the view that the gods were wholly indifferent to human affairs; and on the other with the Stoics, to the making of a clear distinction between the popular gods of their mythology and the one god of nature, possessing personality and exercising a providential care over man. The old Roman religion had fostered many social and individual virtues, which in this latter period, however, had lost all of this beneficial influence save on activities of a political and legal nature. As the Roman religion culminated in the deification of the emperors, who more often than not were the very embodiment of vice, the absurdity of this political religion became apparent to all. Though the religion of divination and of oracles persisted until after the conversion of the empire, it had long been scoffed at as mere fabrications for the unintelligent. Even as early as the second century B.C., Cato had wondered that two augurs could meet with sober countenances. Neither religions nor philosophies had taught any doctrines concerning the future life, and consequently had no means of enforcing any moral teaching upon the unintelligent masses.

Effects of Christianity upon the Thought Life

The contact of Christianity with this thought world had great results. Religion became disassociated from the state and ethics from philosophy: in religion, ethics and morality were given a new basis and a hold, altogether unprecedented, upon the masses of mankind. With this reassociation of religion, ethics, and politics, there came other readjustments of vital interest to education. Religion lost its previous relationship in aesthetic culture and to literature, philosophy its intimate connection with the practical life through ethics. For many centuries education took upon itself a moral and religious character to the neglect of the aesthetic and intellectual phases so essential to the education of the classical world.

CONTACT OF CHRISTIANITY WITH THE WORLD OF ACTION

Some of the leading political and moral characteristics of Roman imperial society, as these bore upon the formation of classes and the determination of the nature of the education of the upper class. There remain to be mentioned a few more striking moral characteristics of all classes of both the Eastern and Western Empire, of both the Greek and the Roman, that reveal by contrast the nature and value of the early Christian education.

The virtues of the Greek and Romans were largely civic. In all stages of their history the types of virtue held highest in general estimate were those of patriotism, bravery, and of service of any kind to the state. The personal virtues of sympathy for the unfortunate, of regard for fellow-man, of charity were seldom dwelt upon and never very highly regarded. Now with the imperial period even these civic virtues rapidly disappear. The emperor assumes to him, self and his subordinates all power; even municipal government disappears save as a machinery for tax gathering, and there is no demand upon the individual citizen for political services or opportunity for such activity other than through personal abasement to an absolute and irresponsible power. The army is filled with mercenaries, and the old Roman bravery, dignity, and sobriety give way to love of ease, to indulgence and to sensuality. Consider what must have been the results.

This large free population had for generations come to look upon themselves as the lords of the earth. They now had few political and military obligations or opportunities for activity; they were shut out from all mercantile and industrial pursuits by the immense class of slaves; they were supplied at Rome and the immediate vicinity with all necessities by the lavish distribution of food and even of money by the emperors. Their religion offered no restraint to their vices and no belief in a future life that would bring retribution or reward for conduct in this; on the contrary, it furnished occasions for the grossest scenes of public sensuality. They had before them a court and an aristocracy often given to unimaginable excesses and debauchery. The theatre furnished amusements which had little resemblance in their degeneracy even to those of the present time which are most reprehensible; and in public Spectacles thousands of their fellow-men and of animals were slain amid all the refinements of cruelty and bloodthristiness. One of the most difficult features of Roman society to comprehend is the importance and the extent of these gladiatorial shows. They met with little condemnation from even the moralists of the times, and practically the only restrictions placed upon them by the empire were the prevention of the enrolment of senators among the gladiatorial class, and the prohibition of the slaughter of an excessive number of men, though that at the accession of Trajan more than ten thousand men thus fought for public amusement was not considered excessive. The most refined women of the period were devoted to these public spectacles; even women descended to fight in the circus; there were connoisseurs in the expressions of men dying in torture; at private banquets men were torn to pieces by wild beasts for the entertainment of guests. It was said of one of the emperors that he "never supped without human blood." These facts indiciate how decadent beyond all modern standards was this society; how impossible it is for us now to comprehend those times; and also what was the task before the new Christian education.

Tacitus said of imperial society, even in his own times "Virtue is the sentence of death;" and Mr. Lecky, commenting on this statement says, "In no period had brute force more completely triumphed, in none was the thirst for material advantages more intense, in very few was vice more ostentatiously glorified."

CHRISTIANITY IN REACTION AGAINST THIS WORLD OF ACTIVITY

Early Christian Life: a Schooling

In its reaction against this corrupt society of the last pagan centuries, life in the early Christian Church was a schooling of very great importance; to be sure, this was not a schooling of an intellectual character, but we have previously seen how formal and how futile was the intellectual education for some centuries of the new era. Education now for a thousand years is to possess very little of the intellectual element. It was during this period that the character of the education dominant for the thousand years after the Christianization of the Roman Empire was shaped. As a type of education - the religious education that has existed quite as long as any other - and as an element that enters into all education, it is important for the student of educational history to comprehend it.

The early Church was concerned in the moral reformation of the world, in the destruction of the state of society already described; for this reason it turned its attention wholly to the moral education of its own membership and thus to the regeneration of society. The gladiatorial shows, which had extended their demoralizing influence throughout the empire, were put down by the Church, though not without a long struggle; divorce, which had become such an evil that it was said that men changed their wives as easily as their clothes was forbidden or at least strictly regulated; infanticide which was universally practiced and had been largely responsible for the great shrinkage of population and had been combated, when at all, by philosophers and by government only on political grounds and hence ineffectively, was now opposed on moral grounds and rooted out of the Church and finally out of society at large; in a similar manner, the exposure of children was definitely treated as murder, and through the teaching of the early Church and the large sums of money which it spent for the care of such children, the standard of public opinion was raised from the incomprehensibly low one of the entire classical period; the immoral public ceremonials and the lacivious practices of private worship of the pagan religions were of course denied all communicants of the new Church and werein time driven from public tolerance. In these respects, and, above all, through the high standards of personal morality, as expressed in the Mosaic law and in the Sermon on the Mount, standards altogether unknown among the masses of population, the early Church enforced a moral education that was entirely new in the history of the world as well as in the history of education. If one will compare the simplicity and purity of character of early Christian worship with the ceremonials of the pagan religions; the character of the Christian priesthood with that of the pagan cults; the morality inculcated in the one with the habit fostered in the other; the sacrifice entailed in the one with the indulgence granted in the other; the humanitarian sentiments in the one with the cruelty and brutality, however refined, in the other; the charity and generosity of the one with the selfishness of the other; if these comparisons be made, the importance of this education will be readily understood.

It is the unanimous testimony of historians that for the first two centuries, and for a large part of the third, the life upheld by the Christian Church, with its purity yet unsullied and its ambitions yet untainted, furnished one of the most remarkable phenomena in history; and that this purity of life was largely responsible for the rapidity and thoroughness of its conquest of the Roman world. This high ideal of moral life was exacted from all its membership, and since during this time, the body of church membership was sharply marked off from the rest of society, delinquent members could readily be returned in disgrace into the body of population whence drawn. Since it was neither honorable, popular, nor profitably in the worldly sense to live this Christian life, those adhering to the new ideal were more genuinely devoted to its teachings than was true in a later age when the whole Roman world became Christian. In this sense early Christianity was a schooling.

Catechumenal Schools

In the early Church there grew up, as a matter of necessity, a process of instruction for those who desired to become members of the Christian community but who lacked the requisite knowledge of doctrine and the requisite moral stability. In general these were divided into two groups, - those who had merely expressed a desire to become members of the Church, and those who were thought by the Church to be worthy of full admission. Only after candidates had undergone some instruction and discipline were they received into full communion through the sacrament of baptism. The tendency in this early period was to postpone this rite of baptism for a longer and longer time until eventually the custom gave origin to great evils. These catechumens included children of believers, Jewish converts, and the adult converts of the heathen population. Though to a certain extent the discipline entailed was intellectual, in that it had to do with doctrines, it was for the most part a moral discipline and a moral oversight. In one other respect, in music, this instruction possessed significance. The psalmody of the early Church, especially in the East was of conspicuous importance. In regard to moral training this use of music was probably of an importance comparable with the function of music in Greek education. At stated periods in the week, in some places every day, the catechumens met in the porch or in some other specific portion of the church for church for instruction and moral training. This custom of catechumenal instruction was universal and through it, supplemented by the oversight of the home which was far more rigid than that of the contemporary Roman or Grecian home, the children of the Christian population received whatever education they obtained.

Catechetical Schools

From their method, and from their use of the catechism as the basis of their instruction in subject-matter, the catechumenal schools were also called catechetical schools. But by way of distinction this term is better applied to a development of these schools in a few localities into institutions carrying on a higher grade of work. As the Christian leaders at Alexandria and other Eastern centres came in conflict with the Greek schools of thought, it became more and more necessary to equip the leaders and the ministers of the Church with a training similar to that of the Greeks. For some centuries Alexandria was the center of this intellectual and theological activity. In 179 A.D. Pantaenus, a converted Stoic philosopher, became head of the school for catechumens at Alexandria. Bringing to the service of Christian instruction the learning of the Greek philosopher and the eloquence of a rhetorician, through him and his successors both philosophy and rhetoric-in fact all the Grecian learning - was brought to the service of the Church. Pantaenus was succeeded in turn by the two most noted of the Greek Church Fathers, Clement and Origen, from whom came the earliest formulation of Christian theology. Such schools, though of less importance grew from the catechumenal schools elsewhere. In 231 Origen, compelled to leave Alexandria, established a similar school in Asia where he taught philosophy, rhetoric, logic, astronomy, and practically the entire round of Grecian learning. Here literature, history, and science were studied as in Grecian schools, though from a different point of view. Though to this school came scholars of all classes, it became a school especially for the training of the clergy under the direction of the local bishop.

Episcopal and Cathedral Schools

Thus there grew from this rather indefinite institution, termed the catechetical school, the very definite type, that developed all over Europe, constituting throughout the Middle Ages a class of schools as important in some respects as those of the monasteries and persisting until the present time. Other schools such as that of Origen at Caesarea, though less thorough, were established throughout the East by other bishops for the training of their clergy and for the general institution of converts. It was but natural that in a population well educated and much given to philosophical and theological discussion such schools should flourish. Calixtus, Bishop of Rome, during the opening year of the third century established there a similar institution, which developed rapidly into a flourishing school patronized by emperors and possesing a large library under the charge of skilled librarians whose names are preserved to us from the fifth century. Promotion in the ranks of the clergy soon came to depend somewhat upon studies carried on in this or similar institutions. Such schools developed rapidly because, as the identity of the words pagan and countryman indicates, the spread of the gospel occurred through the large cities. As the life of the priests gathered in these central places was brought into subjection to regular rules or canons, as was done first in 354, it became posssible to regulate the work of such schools more definitely. During the fifth and sixth centuries the Church councils legislated that children destined for the priesthood should early be placed in these training places under the charge of the bishop. As the result of this and similar legislation of the growth of powerful episcopal estates, of the need for the erection of appropriate buildings, and of the need for a larger body of clergy under the direction of the bishop such schools became attached to practically every bishopric in the West. In the West they were more commonly called cathedral schools from the building where located. With the overthrow of Roman culture by the barbarians, when education fell into the hands of the Church completely, these schools with those of the monasteries remained the only ones of the West. From the eighth to the twelfth centuries it is probable that the monastic school were of far greater importance than the cathedral schools; but with the expansion of knowledge and the greater tolerance of inquiry, the rigidity and the narrowness of the monastic schools resulted in the renewed growth and revived importance of the schools under the immediate direction of the bishop.

EARLY CHRISTIANITY IN REACTION AGAINST THE WORLD OF THOUGHT

Opinions concerning the relation between Christianity and pagan learning and culture divided the leaders of the early Church into two quite well-defined groups. One held that this ancient learning contained much that was valuable for Christians and for the Church; that much of it confirmed the teachings of the Bible; that philosophy was a search for truth as Christianity was; that all philosophies contained some valuable truth, though not the highest and not complete; and that Christianity should include all this ancient learning and should build upon it. The other group, recalling the scorn of the Greek philosophers, the insults and the atrocities heaped upon them by the representative of this heathen culture, and the immoralities contained in their literature and sanctioned by their religions, held that there could be no compromise between the truth and the world; that philosophies when connected with Christianity produced only heresies; that literature and culture in general represented merely the seductions and the pleasures of the world; that those who were instructed in the legends of Homer, in the myths of Zeus and the gods, got from them nothing but lessons of impurity and, hence, that such literature was unworthy of acceptance by the Christian Church; and consequently that the Church should reject all of this ancient learning a hostile to the interest and the purposes of Christianity.

In general the view friendly to this learning prevailed in the earlier history of the Church and especially in the East among the Greeks; the view hostile to this learning became more general in the West and even before the overthrow of the old social structure by the barbarians, prevailed among the Christians of those parts. And it was but natural that the

Christians of the West should identify heathenism with this ancient culture, for the chief hold which the old religion retained upon the people was through this literature: for most forcible opposition to the progress of the Church came from the class most conversant with this literature, and the chief stronghold of the pagan regime was, in the schools. On the grounds that a Christian could not appreciate, certainly could not teach Homer, Virgil and similar works, the apostate emperor, Julian, forbade all Christians teaching in the rhetorical and grammatical schools. While this proscription implies the presence of many Christians in these schools, it is probable that they were merely nominal Christians, as was Augustine in his earlier years. That this attitude was fully reciprocated is indicated by the action of one of the synods of Carthage. In 398, long after the Church was completely triumphant in the empire, even long after there was any specific danger to be apprehended from this pagan influence hiding in the old learning, this synod forbade all bishops to read any of the pagan literature. This had come to be the attitude typical of the Church. With such a hostility it is not to be wondered that learning almost ceased to exist, and that there followed for some centuries the period commonly termed "the dark ages".

Since this attitude of the Church explains to a large extent the condition of education for a thousand years, some further leasons in extenuation or explanation of it should be given. One of the most important of these has been mentioned; it is the fact that the great mission of the Church as well as the great need of the times was a moral one. Added to this was the belief prevalent throughout the early Church that the second advent of Christ was near, and that consequently, learning, culture, and in fact all mundane affairs were of trival importance. The persecution and the exile which many Christians in the first three centuries were compelled to undergo deprived them of all opportunity for the acquisition of pagan learning had they desired it, and destroyed all inclination to attain to the most distinctive possession of their persecutors. In the section following, that on monasticism is discussed more fully one other great reason for this indifference. This is asceticism or the opposition to all worldly interests and to all that gives satisfaction or pleasure of a human of natural character. Two other reasons, one operative in the earlier centuries, the other in later times, explain in part this indifference of the Church to learning. In the early period its success was largest with the lower class of people to whom its message brought a wonderful deliverance. They were disinclined, through nature, through sympathy, and through tradition to take any great interest in the culture that had been made possible only by their debasement. In the later period, the strength of the Church was found in the new Teutonic peoples, whom, it is true, the Church raised out of barbarism, but to whom at the same time it wa impossible for many generations to impart the graces of culture. Again the unification of the Church in the West and its reputation and desire for orthodoxy acted as a check upon learning and upon the spirit of inquiry, that, after a manner, was fostered or permitted in the East long after it had disappeared in the West.

As a foundation for the study of the subsequent ages a more concrete view of this difference in the attitude between the early and the later, the eastern and the western Church is desirable.

Attitude of the Greek Christian Fathers towards Learning

Though the Apostle Paul remarked that "not many wise are called," by the second and third centuries many trained in all the learning of the Greeks had accepted Christianity. Among these Justin Martyr, Clement of Alexandria, Origen and Basil, and others of the Greek Fathers were the most prominent. It is but natural that these men, who were primarily Greek philosophers and most of them teachers as well should aim to bring all of this learning to the service of the Church.

The earliest of importance was Justin Martyr, whose life covers approximately the first three quarters of the second century. A converted teacher of philosophy, he continued throughout his life, to follow his profession, to wear his philosopher's garb, and to retain his belief in Platonism. He claimed that Plato, Socrates, and Heracleitus were Christians before the time of Christ, and that philosophy was an attempt, though falling short, after the same end as Christianity. Consequently, he held, the teachings of philosophy were included in those of Christianity, and so far as they were correct, harmonized with it.

Clement (c. 160-c. 215) was the successor of Pantaenus as head of the catechetical school at Alexandria. Holding that the Gospels were perfected Platonism and, with early Christian philosophers in general, that "Plato was Moses Atticized," Clement taught that pagan philosophy was "a pedagogue to bring the world to Christ." Another one of his doctrines was that God had made three covenants with man,—the law, the Gospel, and philosophy. Most of his teachings and writings were directed toward the reconciliation of faith and reason, of Christian revelation and pagan philosophy. To such a degree did he find this true that to him Christianity became for the most part, a philosophy. His citations from writings of the Greeks show a familiarity with many hundred different works in every field of literature.

His pupil and successor, Origen, the most learned of the Christian Fathers (c. 185-c. 254) when speaking of the sciences of the Greeks, wrote: "They are to be used so that they may contribute to the understanding of the Scriptures; for just as philosophers are accustomed to say that geometry, music, grammar, rhetoric, and astronomy all dispose us to the study of philosophy, so we may say that philosophy, rightly studied, disposes us to the study of Christianity. We are permitted when we go out of Egypt to carry with us the riches of the Egyptians wherewith to adorn the tabernacle; only let us beware how we reverse the process, and have Israel to go down into Egypt and seek for treasure; that is what Jereboam did in old time, and what heretics do in our own." This allegorical use of the despoiling of the Egyptians occurs over and over again in later times as by St. Augutine himelf. A the founder of systematic theology, the formulator of most of the dogmas of the Church, the earliest scientific critic of the Scripture, Origen exerted the most extended influence of any of the Father except possibly St. Augustine. Especially through his teachings concerning the harmony of the pagan sciences with the doctrines of religion, of Greek culture with Christian faith, he reconciled the Greek world to the new religion and aided in its dissemination.

By the time of St. Basil (c.331-c.379) and Gregory of Nazianzus (c.325-c.390), the opposition of the Christians to pagan learning and especially to Greek philosophy had become more pronounced; but both these Fathers unite in the protest of the earlier ones against this prejudice and in the effort to show that Greek literature is full of both principle and event, of both precept and example, helpful in instruction and leading to the higher life. Speaking of the closing of the pagan schools to Christians by Julian Gregory wrote: "For my part I trust that every one who cares for learning will take part in my indignation. I leave to others fortune, birth and every fancied good which can flatter the imagination of man. I value only science and letters, and regret to labors that I have spent in their acquisition. I have preferred and shall ever prefer learning to all earthly riches, and hold nothing dearer on earth, next to the joys of heaven and the hopes of eternity." However, the opinions of these later Fathers is not so unqualified as that of the earlier. It is only within limits that learning is recommended. Later Chrysostom (c.347-411), though not in condemnation, it is true, yet with greater disparagement, writes, "I have long ago laid aside such follies, for one cannot spend all one's life in child's play." And Basil, writing on the education of children, thus sums up his judgment, expressed fully in a much longer discussion: "Are we then to give up literature? you will exclaim. I do not say that; but I do say that we must not kill souls... In fact, the choice lies between two alternatives: a liberal education which you may get by sending your children to the public schools, or the salvation of their souls which you secure by sending them to the monks. Which is to gain the day, science or the soul? If you can unite both advantages, do so by all means; but if not, choose the most precious."

Attitude of the Latin Church Fathers

By the fourth century, especially among the Roman Christians, Hellenism had become almost synonymous with hostility to the Church. Most of the Latin Fathers - Tertullian, Arnobius, Lactantius, Gregory, Augustine - had been teachers of oratory or of rhetoric. Tertullian was primarily a lawyer; Jerome and Augustine were saturated with the pagan learning. All were skilled in the science, if not the practice, of Roman learning and education, and some had written treatises upon these subjects.

Tertrullian (c.150-c.230), the earliest of the Latin Fathers reveals the attitude of the West in a most characteritic manner. To him all Grecian learning was bound up with heresies and, as he was especially engaged in the conflict against Gnosticism, he sought to widen the breach between philosophy and the Church. In his Prescription against Heresies, he writes:

"These are `the doctrines' of man and `of demons' produced for the itching ears of the spirit of this world's wisdom; this the Lord called `foolishness,' and chose even the foolish things of this world to confound even philosophy itself. For philosophy is the material of the world's wisdom and rash interpreter of the nature and dispensation of God. Indeed, heresies themselves are intigated by philosophy. From this source came the aeon and I know not what infinite forrr s, and the trinity of man in the system of Valentinus, who was of Plato's school, (etc.) ... The same subject-matter is discussed over and over again by the heretics and the philosophers; the same arguments are involved. Whence comes evil? Why is it permitted? What is the origin of man? and in what way does he come? ... Unhappy Aristotle! who invented for these men dialectic, the art of building up and pulling down; an art so evasive in its propositions, so far fetched in its conjectures, so harsh in it arguments, so productive of contentions - embarrassing even to itself - retracting everything and really treating of nothing! Whence spring those `fables and endless genealogies' and `unprofitable questions' and `words which spread like a cancer'? From all these, when the apostle would restrain us, he expressly names philosophy as that which he would have us be on our guard against... What indeed has Athens to do with Jerusalem? What concord is there between the Academy and the Church? What between heretics and Christians? ... Away with all attempts to produce a motled Christianity of Stoic, Platonic, and dialectic composition!"

In his work On Idolatry in the chapter On schoolmaster and their Difficulties, while he absolutely denies that a Christian can be a teacher of this ancient learning, he is somewhat more tolerant toward the study of it since thus one might be able to refute its errors.

To St. Jerome (331-423), the translator of the version of the Bible for centuries accepted by the Church, this conflict between the classical learning and the Christian faith became most clearly defined. Perhaps no single event of this general conflict had so great an influence upon succeeding generations, by which it was repeated over and over, as that of his famous vision (374). Dreaming that he was dead and dragged before the judgment seat, he was asked the question, "Who art thou?" Upon answering, "A Christian," he heard with the stricken conscience that repeated its awful warning to many successive generations, the terrible judgment, "It is false: thou art no

Christian; thou art a Ciceronian; where the treasure is, there the heart is also." Jerome was also chiefly responsible for the introduction of monasticism into the West. The love of learning and the ascetic idea were the two conflicting motives appealing to him throughout his life. As is shown by his constant quotation from classical authors, he could not entirely give up his love for pagan learning, though after this vision he turned his scholarship entirely to scriptural study and religious writings. While he could no longer favour an education in the old literature, he could not bring himself absolutely to condemn it. As he shows in his Letter to Laeta (CVII) he believed that if such studies were to be permitted at all, it should be "rather to judge them than to follow them."

In the case of St. Augustine the same retrograde movement in respect to appreciation for the old learning is to be found as in the case of Jerome. Augustine (354-430), until middle life a teacher of rhetoric and oratory, had begun a cyclopedia on the liberal arts, of which he completed the portion on grammar, a part of that on music, and the introductions to the other parts. His treatise on dialectic, either original or epitome from Aristotle, had considerable influence in the later Middle Ages. Not so thorough a scholar as Jerome, he yet was a man of broad interests and sympathies and one passionately fond of Latin literature. Being intellectually the most active and the most active and the most brilliant of the Fathers of the western Church, and exerting the widest, the deepest, and the most far-reaching influence of them all, he called into service his extended learning in combating the many heressies in the Church through polemic and expository writings. Thus, while in his earlier years he sanctioned "the spoiling of the Egyptians," at a later period of his life his sympathy for classical learning was much restricted. He discountenanced its use and is supposed to have been personally responsible for the prohibition of philosophical and literary study made by the Council of Carthage.

Monasticism, Education as a Moral Discipline

Monasticism and monastic education and topics so large that even were it necessary it would be impossible to give a complete view of the educational importance of monasticism within the limits of a few pages.[1] In the period of time covered, it reaches from the fourth to the sixteenth, even to the eighteenth, century; in the types of life represented it includes the anchorite in the desert, the cenobite in his cell, the friar in his wanderings, and the Jesuit in his schoolroom or on his political or ecclesiastical mission; in the territory influenced it extends from the valley of the Nile to the highlands of Scotland; in the diversity of types of intellectual life represented, it includes the fearfulness of the hermit, the indifference of many a cenobite, the enthusiasm of the friar, and the brilliancy of the followers of Loyola. Without pretense of giving any adequate account of the history or of the educational activity of monasticism, it needs to be here presented only as a type. Yet as a type it is of great importance, historically, if not in the present. In monasticism the education of the early Church finds its culmination and perpetuation. From the sixth century to the thirteenth, save for the cathedral schools, - which during the greater part of this period were in a state of but minor activity and even then taught for the most part by monks, - there was in Western Europe no other education containing any intellectual element. Again, since in the activities of the frairs the work of the early universities is largely included, for three additional centuries this type of monasticism continued to be the most important single educational institution.

In this discussion little or no attention is given to the constant tendency to decline in the character of the monastic life, and to the general decay that occurred throughout the monastic organizations after the fervor of the friar movement had expended itself, and that had much to do with the origin and violent character of the Reformation movement. Such topics are aside from educational interests of a narrower character, and discussions of them are rendered impossible by the scope of the work.

The term "monasticism," in its original significance, could be applied to the hermit alone. It is frequently used in a sense that would exclude the mendicant orders of the thirteenth century, the canonical clergy that live, as do also the Dominicans, under the rule formulated by St. Augustine, and the teaching congregations of the post-Reformation period. Yet the term is here used, as it is commonly, in its most general significance, to include all these forms. Through these various stages and changes, of working conception as well as of rules, we cannot for lack of space trace the monastic development. As our interest is primarily in monastic education as a type, and especially in its ideal of education as a moral discipline, our interest in its schools is confined for the most part to that period preceding the thirteenth century. Then other types of schools and other conception of education arose. But from the sixth to the sixteenth century the history of monasticism is the history of education.

ORIGIN OF MONASTICISM

The primary idea of monasticism is asceticism. In its original significance, the word asceticism indicates the training or discipline of the athlete in preparation for the physical contests; in its figurative use it connotes the subjection or the disciplining of all bodily desires and human affections that the mind and soul may be devoted to the interests of the higher life. Found in some degree in all types of religious beliefs, it was given a speical prominence in many of the types of beliefs—the Jewish, Persian, the Egyptian, and several of the Grecian philosophical sects - with which Christianity early came in conflict. In all of these the highest ethical thought was that of rising to spiritual excellence and insight through the mortification of all natural and material wants; through fasting, through penance, through flagellation, through prolonged and enervating physical exercise or, better still, through inducing a quiescence of the physical nature and the complete eradication of natural desire and temporal interests. Thus the Christian ascetics united in themselves the Stoic virtues of contempt of pain and of death and the indifference to the vicissitudes of fortune, the Pythagorean customs of silence and of submission of the physical nature, and the Cynic neglect of the obligations and the forms of society. In the teachings of Christ also, in his command to take no thought for the morrow, to sell all one's goods and give to the poor, to forsake father and mother, wife and children, and, above all, in the frequent exhortations to world-renunciation and to the devotion of one's self to the service of spreading the Gospel, the ascetic idea found support.

Similar to the idea of asceticism, though not quite identical with it, for it formed but a part of the larger thought, - was the more prevalent motive of world-renunciation. A part of the root idea of asceticism was the belief - held also by Gnosticism - that God no longer ruled in the world of matter, or more especially, in the corrupt social life around the early Christians, and that consequently the true Christian life was to be obtained by a renunciation of this world - an isolation from the affairs of everyday life. To this extent monasticism was merely an expression of the desire to save one's self by leaving one's fellows to their sins and their just punishment. This motive prevailed to the greatest extent in the old classical society; for when the new Teutonic peoples came into control, world-renunciation was replaced by the motive of world-conquest.

One other important condition, which if not a cause of the origin, was at least the great cause of the development of monasticism, was the changed character of the Christian Church from the third century on. By the middle of the third century the Church had become largely secularized; by the opening of the fourth, with the conversion of the empire (312, 322, etc.), Christianity was identified with society; the customs and manners of the world were the customs and manners of Christendom; the Christians were no longer marked-off or distinctive people. It happened then that the clergy, or more especially the monks, became a body of separated people, as before the entire Church had been, living according to a higher code of morality, possessing distinctive marks of their profession, and abstaining from the common interests and activities of society.

Two other causes of the development of monasticism need but to be mentioned. One was the persecutions that drove many Christians to the wilds of the deserts and the mountains; and the other was the belief - almost universal in the early Church - that the second advent of Christ was at hand, and consequently no interest in the affairs of everyday life were to be considered in comparison with the spiritual preparation for the new life near at hand.

Out of these ideas and practices of the religious sects of the East and the philosophical schools of the Greeks, Christian monasticism developed naturally upon the soil where at this time both religions and philosophies found their most ardent devotees, - that is, in Egypt. However, early this movement may have begun, its coming into prominence was first due to Anthony, who in 305 fled to the desert, and there near the shores of the Red Sea subjected himself to a series of physical penances - tortures one might almost say - that were the first of a long line of exacting, ingeniously devised, and heroically endured practices for the mortification of the flesh. His example begot many imitations, and soon one of his followers, Pachomius, had collected fourteenth hundred followers who desired to imitate this life of effacement for the sake of spiritual benefit. The ideal in the East ever continued to be that of isolated life as a hermit or anchorite. Monasticism was transferred to Greece by Basil and to Rome by Athanasius (341) and Jerome. But throughout the West neither nature nor the human mind was favourable to this life of isolation and quiesence, so life in communities - the cenobitic life - was preferred to that of the anchorite. Such communities during the fourth and the fifth centuries became very numerous. Each was controlled in its independent existence by its own rules. Some of them, it is true, adopted the rules of St. Basil, the only ones ever introduced at all generally in the East; but in 529 Benedict, a Roman patricias who had fled from the scandals and corruption at Rome to find in the solitary life relief from such wickedness and such temptation, and who had drawn around him many attracted by his own life of spiritual devotion, organized a community under a set of rules. While these were designed only for his own group, they soon became of universal influence throughout the West.

Ideals of Monastic Life and Education: Asceticism, an Ideal of Discipline

The rules of monastic life might present the greatest variation; its ideals were everywhere the same. In all places and in all ages its dominant ideal was that of asceticism. The virtue of the monk was often measured by his ingenuity in devising new and fantastic methods of mortifying the flesh through fasting, through eating insufficient and inappropriate foods, through taking insufficient sleep, through wearing insufficient clothing, through assuming unnatural postures of extreme dicomfort and maintaining them sometimes for months, through uncleanlinesss of body, through binding the limbs with ligatures, through loading the body with chains and weights, through every means which would reduce or even destroy the natural wants or would produce suffering from insufficient care for them. That at the same time this regime might also destroy or weaken the mind, and in any case make it subject to abnormal visions, which but increased through the terror of such temptations, the irrational regime that produced them seems seldom to have been noticed. All these forms of discipline were for the sake of the spiritual growth, the moral betterment of the penitent; all these, as the very significance of the word "asceticism" indicates reveal the dominant conception of education which prevailed through out this long period - the idea of discipline of the physical nature for the sake of growth in moral and spiritual power. The ideals of monasticism were usually summed up in the three ideas of chastity, poverty, and obedience, or more technically, conversion, stability, and obedience.

Chastity. - The idea of celibacy went far beyond the rigid restrictions of the early Church; far beyond the provision of celibacy for the clergy. The ideal was the condemnation of the family and of all human relationhip and affection. These were now to be completely effaced and their places taken by religious relationship, established through the monastic rule and life, and by spiritual interests, realized through a life of silent isolation and of continuous devotion and worship. It was because the ties of relationship - the love of father, or mother, or child, or sister - represented the most powerful and least readily severed influence of "the world" that monasticism exerted its greatest strength to destroy them. Not only the lives of the saints, but also the writings of such a great and noble churchman as Jerome, are filled with incidents or counsels that appear to us now almost in human, holding, as they did, that "in this matter cruelty is only piety."

Poverty meant the rejection of all the material interests of the world; for after Christianity became the state religion, the ordinary Christian could continue to be a merchant, a civil or military officer, or have part in any vocation devoted to the pursuits of earthly interests. Upon entering the monastic life one must give up all his property and all claims upon the rights of inheritance. Except on consent of his superior he could never receive anything as his own - not even a letter. Within the monastery all things were held in common, and this life was held to be the nearest approach possible to the commands of the Savior and to the life of the early Christian Church. It was through the influence of this monastic ideal of poverty that during so many medieval centuries the virtue of charity, or rather of mere giving, was exalted to the position of the highest Christian virtue, one that would cover the absence of almost all others.

The Ideal of Obedience was the distinctive characteristic of the cenobitic life as opposed to the hermit life. In the West, with few exceptions, the community monastic life prevailed. In entering this community one gave up all rights of personal choice, of disposal of his own time, of determination of his own interests. His will was completely subjected to the will of his superior, and in this last surrender and effacement was found the perfection of moral and spiritual growth. The entire routine of life and of its activities and interests was determined by minute precepts formulated in the rule of the house. Since one gave up all allegiance to other institutions, such an ideal was the surrender of the last evidence of personality and the negation of all political organization of society. This self-effacement was to be complete, and in the rules most generally adopted, minute regulations pursued him in his most secret moment. "Submission had to be prompt, perfect, and absolute. The monk must obey always, without reserve, and without murmur, even in those things which seemed impossible and above his strength, trusting in the succor of God, if a humble and seaonable remonstrance, the only thing permitted to him, was not accepted by his superiors; must obey not only his superiors, but also the wishes and requests of his brethren."[2]

Social Significance of these Ideals. - Thus, in a manner, the monastic ideal had its negative as well as its positive significance. In its three great ideals it negated the three great aspects of social life, - the family, industrial society, and the state; among the anchorites and in many cases in the western monasteries which rejected the oversight of the bishop, it tended to negate even the Church. Certainly it represented a type of disciplinary education which left out of account these three great classes of needs of society and emphasized and developed those moral virtues that, in a restricted sense, find expression largely through the Church and religion.

On the other hand, monasticism became in the larger sense an educational force of very great importance to society as a whole. Each one of these monastic ideals introduced new factors into social development. For example, the habit of obedience, with its accompanying virtue of humility, presented as great a contrast as can be imagined to the strong individualism of the barbarian and the arrogance of the Roman. The ideals and habits of the monks entered into the reorganization of society in the institution of feudalism, revealed themselves in the crusade movement, and probably did more than any other single factor in the subjection of the rude Teuton to the restrictions of civilization and culture.

THE MONASTIC RULES

The details of these three great ideals are expressed in a code of rules, in the earlier days formulated and adopted by each individual monastery, but after the sixth century almost univerally patterned in the West after the rule of St. Benedict.

It is proper to speak of the spread of these rules as being by adoption, for there was no general organization of monasteries under Benedict's rules, but each remained independent as before. Nor were these rules exclusive; they were to be supplemental to rules already adopted, and individual monasteries might add to them, as they did very generally after the eleventh century. These rules were seventy-three in number: nine relating to the general duties of abbots and monks; thirteen to worship; twenty-nine to discipline, errors, penalties; ten to the administration of the monastery; and twelve to various topics, such as reception of guests, conduct of monks while travelling, etc. The distinctive feature of the Benedictine Rule was the insistence upon manual labor of some kind added to the implicit obedience which the monk must render the abbot in the performance of this work. In very great divergence from the ideas and habits of the monk of the East, indolence was termed the enemy of the soul. To provide against this, at least seven hours a day must be given to some kind of toil. Thus at one stroke were eradicated from the monasteries of the West many of the evils that had come into monastic life, both through the surrender to temptation coming as a result of idleness and to the more subtle evils of a subjective kind arising from enforced solitary confinement and a brooding over imaginary evils by minds little adapted to profit from such a course. The Benedictine Rule is the first recognition of the value of manual labor in education; and though the conception of education and the value placed upon the manual activities in this moral training were both very different from those in our own time, they were a great step beyond the position of the Greeks and Romans. From this provision came most of the social benefits of monasticism in the West,— for in the broadest sense of the term monasticism was an education. In the cultivation of the soil the monks furnished models for the peasantry; they introduced new processes for the craftsmen in wood, metal, leather, and cloth; they gave new ideas to the architect; in a way they stimulated and fostered trade among the mercantile class; they drained swamps and improved public health and public life in almost every way; and besides offered asylums to the poor, the sick, the injured, and the distressed.

The rules also provided that two hours of each day should be devoted to reading; indicated the portion of the Bible and of the Fathers to be read; provided for the reading of the Bible during the meal hours; and through minute rules saw to it that these times for reading were not to be wasted in idleness, in sleep, or in talking. Naturally the greatest care was given to minute specifications concerning worship the occasion, duration and number of prayers throughout the day and night; the song services, etc.

To the rules of Benedict, these were very generally added during the eleventh and twelfth centuries more rigid rules by a variety of new monastic orders. The most notable of all was the Cistercian Order (founded 1098), which carried asceticism to a greater extreme than any other body. It enjoined absolute silence, provided for the solitary life so far as possible, simplified worship, and in their churches and ceremonials applied the most rigid ascetic rules as no other order ever had done. Common among these provisions of the eleventh-century reforms was that permitting the admission to monastic orders of lay brothers exempt from the duties of religious service but devoted to the rough work of the monasteries. Though these formed a distinctly uneducated class, their presence permitted a greater devotion to study and to literature upon the part of the more educated. The general effect of this provision was to improve the literary character and the educational work of the monasteries.

MONASTICISM AND LITERARY EDUCATION

As we have seen, monasticism was not primarily a scheme of education in the library or school sense; its conception of education was of a wholly different types, - one relating to the formation of moral and religious character alone. Many, consequently, have resented any criticism of the learning or the educational efforts of the monks as altogether invalid, on the grounds that an institution or a class of people is not to be held responsible for that which it does not explicitly undertake. It is true that until the organization of the teaching orders in the sixteenth and seventeenth centuries, the monastic orders did not make education a controlling aim. On the other hand, it is also true that from the seventh to the opening of the thirteenth centuries, there was practically no other education but that offered by the monks, and that the Church and the monastic institutions were responsible for the fact that no other conception of education existed and that no other educational institutions were tolerated. As we have seen, the Church through its hostile attitude and monasticism through its new and revolutionary ideals were largely responsible for the complete disappearance of the old cultural ideas, for the neglect of the study of the old literature, and for the substitution of a radically different type of educational institutions in place of a rejuvenation of the old. Our need, however, is to appreciate exactly the character of the education that monasticism offered to the world for some six centuries in lieu of all others.

The historical evidence concerning life during the Middle Ages is such that, together with our diverse emotional natures and conflicting religious bias, it permits two interpretations of most point connected with medieval education and thought life. Adhering as closely as possible to the facts, and omitting partisan bias, let us look at both sides of the question under the topic of.

Study in the Monasteries

One must ever hold in mind the fundamental idea of asceticism, previously referred to as given in the literal meaning of the word, - that of discipline or training. St. Benedict, whose ideas were adopted throughout Western Europe by all of monasticism that comes within our view, did not believe that the mind or soul should be allowed to work simply upon itself to produce evils quite as great as those fled from, but that it should ever be kept busy. Hence he provided for seven hours of labor, chiefly manual, though it might be literary, and for from two to five hours, of reading each day. Some similar provisions had been made before by St. Basil in the East. It was in all probability Cassiodorus, the great statesman, - who, as prime minister to several successive barbarian rulers of Italy, preserved so much of the ancient customs and who, in his old age, turned monk, - that formulated this idea and gave it to the Benedictines. From these provisions, imposed as matters of discipline for the monk, not for any external results, came most of the indirect social benefits of monasticism. If the monks must read, they must be taught to read, they must have books, and they must in turn teach the novices to read and copy manuscripts. Hence, without any word in the rules concerning schools with but the briefest reference to the training of the youth accepted for the monastic life, without any direct reference to the copying of manuscripts or to the study of literature or to the preservation of books, all of these things followed.

But there were other causes contributing to make the results of this one provision so great and so far-reaching. In those restless ages of rude culture, of constant warfare, of perpetual lawlessness and the rule of might, monasticism offered one opportunity for a life of repose, of contemplation, and of that leisure and relief from the ordinary vulgar but necessary duties of life essential to the student. Hence the youth who came at the age most impresionable and most given to the pursuit of ideals, was influenced toward the life of reflection and of study; those bereft of family and of protection found in the monastic cell a retreat and in study a consolation; while those worn out with a life of toil, or shocked by the brutality and callous indifference about them, found here a natural resting place and in the pleassures of a life of reflection and study a legitimate reward for the burdens they had borne.

Thus it happened that the monasteries were the sole schools for teaching; they offered the only professional training; they were the only universities of research; they alone served as publishing houses for the multiplication of book; they were the only libraries for the preservation of learning; they produced the only scholars; they were the sole educational institutions of this period. In each of these line their activities were, to be sure, meager; but the opportunities were meager and however great the needs, the conscious social demands of the times were more meager still.

Every monastic rule - and they were much more numerous than this brief account would seem to indicate - either authorized indirectly or commanded directly the study of literature. The earliest of all rules, those of Pachomius, required specifically that every monk should read and write, and provided for the instruction of those admitted who could not. In the East this intellectual requirement was, of course under the dominance of Greek ideas. The latest great monastic movement, of the post-Reformation period, was specifically an educational one. The supplementary rules added from time to time by the Benedictine institutions laid more and more stress upon this literary aspect of their life. The most famous monasteries in every country were those noted for their learning and for the training they afforded. Typical of these were those of Fulda and Hirschau in Germany at Tours, Corbie, Bec, and Clugny in France; at St. Gall in Switzerland; at Glastonbury, Malmesbury and Canterbury in England; at Monte Cassino in Italy. While these were exceptional institutions, there were many that adopted as their motto, "Love the study of Scriptures and you will not love vice." Some of the monasteries, especially those of the type mentioned above, carried their study much further and included the study of the Greek classics. At St. Gall, in the latter part of the tenth century, lectures were given on Cicero, Quintilian, Horace, Terence, Juvenal, Persius, Ovid, and Sophocles.

Let us now turn to the other side of the question and consider the meagerness of the learning of the monks. We may disregard such careless judgments as are founded presumably upon isolated cases. Such is the argument respecting the probable rarity of books as evidenced by the extravagant prices paid for occasional ones; the argument that many monasteries were without book, because mention is made of an occasional monastery in a dilapidated condition possessed of only one missal (meaning probably several copies of the same work); that all monks were densely ignorant, or vicious because occasional ones might be. There are, never the less, certain general conditions that must be borne in mind. In the first place, it was the study of the Scriptures only that was commended and though the term *Scripture Sacre* indicated more than we understand by the term Holy Scriptures, including as it did all religious writings, it did not go beyond this. Then, again, study was never an end in itself but simply a disciplinary means or an occupation for otherwise idle moments; the instant study became an end or a pleasure in itself, the very purpose of its introduction into the monasteries was negated. Further, it is just as erroneous to argue from a few exceptional cases, such as St. Gall, or Monte Cassino, that "to the monk of the tenth century no knowledge was unfamiliar," as to argue from other occasional instances that they knew nothing. It is quite evident that many monks were entirely ignorant; that many monasteries gave practically no attention to learning; and that those which gave attention to secular literature were comparatively few. Considering the opportunity for study afforded by their leisure time, their freedom interruption, their knowledge of the language, their possession of the few books existing, it is surprising that the monks made so little advance in the knowledge of the ancients and created so little literary material.

In explanation of this situation two further considerations are to be borne in mind. To most of these monks, save those in the intellectual centers, the study of ancient literature, disapproved as it had been by the Church for several centuries, represented distinctly the interests and the temptations of the world, and a desire for such study was indulged in only at a distinct risk or as a positive sin. Such study was a gratification of human desires, a satisfaction of the tastes that was distinctly hostile to the idea of asceticism. The uncertain or changing attitude toward the ancient classics of such leaders is Jerome and Augustine would lend emphasis to the idea that all such learning was a temptation.

The other consideration is most fundamental of all, and applies to the intellectual of the entire Middle Ages. Quite as prominent in its early history as now were the many divisions within the Christian Church. Even as late as the period of St. Augustine, these numbered eighty-five according to his own enumeration. As a result of this, both error of judgment and the state of intellectual doubt came to be looked upon as sinful. One of the most commendable traits of ancient society within the polytheistic period of Greece or Rome or in the later skeptical cosmpolitan period, was toleration or beliefs. To this fact Christianity itself in its early days owed very much. But to the Christian, tolerance of a belief that might mean external damnation to those enslaved by it was no virtue but a distinct evil. Hence the very basis of all intellectual progress, the spirit of inquiry and the desire for truth or reality, irrespective of its effect upon emotional states or religious beliefs held as a matter of faith, was wanting to these ages. Doubt concerning any belief or an interpretation of a fact or incident established by the Church or suggested by its relation to the welfare of the Church and the further development of this age of faith came to be considered of as great demerit and evil as error itself. The validity of any statement, the actuality of any alleged instance, came to be determined, not by any application of rationalistic principle not by inherent plausibility, not by actual inquiry into the facts of the case, but its agreement with religious feelings or beliefs, its effect in furthering the influence of the Church or the reputation of a saint - in general by its relationship to matters of faith. Thus it happens that the chronicles of the monks and the lives of the saints, charming and interesting as they are in their naivete, their simplicity, their trustful credulity, and their pictures of a life and an attitude of mind so remote from ours, are filled with incidents given as facts that test the greatest faith strain the most vivid imagination, and shock that innate respect for reality that it is the purpose of modern education to inculcate.

Schools in the Monasteries

Aside from the training of novices, wholly religious, and this provision for reading, there is no mention direct or indirect of schools or of instruction in the rules of St. Benedict. However, Benedict himself had accepted youth to train, and the monastery of Cassiodorus, which had great influence over the Benedictines, laid much greater stress upon intellectual training. Except for the training of the monks themselves or of the youth offered for monastic life, the monasteries made little provision during several centuries for schooling of any kind, and that given was chiefly of a religious character. The arts of reading and of writing, of singing and of calculating the Church calendar were, of necessity, given though probably this latter was reserved for but a few. Rules supplementary to the original ones of St. Benedict were later adopted by the monasteries of the order. Those affecting the school required a novitiate of two years, and stipulated that no member should be received into the order under eighteen years of age. As boys not yet in their teens were often accepted, a prolonged schooling and discipline were provided.

Previous to the later portion of the eighth century such schools throughout Western Europe, save in the British Isles, were very rudimentary, and the character of learning in all the monasteries was very meager, with no opportunity for education of boys not destined for monatic life. Especially in Ireland, and thence transported to the monateries and cathedral foundations of England and Scotland, a knowledge of classical literature, even of the Greek tongue, was kept alive. This learning and interest in intellectual activity, and a breadth of view that was wanting during this time to the Continent as a whole, had been inherited by the Irish monks from the monasteries of the Romanized Celts of the Continent and of Britain, whence St. Patrick came.

During the latter part of the eighth century, through a movement headed by the Emperor Charles the Great and his minister Alcuin, - a movement to be discussed later - monastic schools became much more numerous and of better grade, and generally provided an education for youth not intended for monastic life. Though there was decline during the ninth and the greater part of the tenth centuries, nevertheless, the monastic schools so dominated the realm of education that the eleventh century is known as the Benedictine Age. This term is also frequently applied to the entire period from the seventh to the eleventh centuries. It was not until the eleventh century that there was any education to speak of outside of monastic schools, and not until the thirteenth century that there occurred marked change in the character of education given in any intitutions, for until then practically all of these schools were taught by monks. During all of this period it might be said that every monastery was a school, and that all education was either in the monasteries or under the direction of monks.

We have spoken of the meagerness of this learning; it may be well to notice it at its broadest. Alcuin tells of the work in the school of his master Albert, as follows:-

"The learned Albert gave drink to thirsty minds at the fountain of the sciences. To some he communicated the art and the rules of grammar; for others he caused floods of rhetoric to flow; he knew how to exercise these in the battles of jurisprudence, and those in the songs of Adonia; some learned from him to pipe Castalian airs and with lyric foot to strike the summit of Parnassus; to others he made known the harmony of the heavens, the courses of the sun and the moon, the five zones of the pole, the seven planets, the laws of the course of the stars, the motions of the sea, earthquakes, the nature of men, and of beasts, and of birds, and of all that inhabit the forest. He unfolded the different qualities and combinations of numbers; he taught how to calculate with certainty the solemn return of Eastertide, and, above all, he explained the mysteries of the Holy Scriptures."

For the fact that schools were not more numerous, and that the character of their work was not a higher grade, the Church and the monastery must not be held altogether responsible. It must be remembered that the masses of the people of these centuries were little more than barbarians, and that they certainly took much more naturally to warfare and destruction than they did to schooling. That learning and the scholastic traditions should be preserved at all in the midst of a society not settled and of a people devoted largely to repelling invasions or engaging in similar excursions for depredation, was no inconsiderable service.

The Copying of Manuscripts and the Preservation of Learning

Through the provision requiring a certain amount of reading each day, and the inclusion under the head of manual labor of the copying of manuscript for those who were physically unable to perform heavier tasks, or because of inclement weather, the monasteries came to perform quite as great a service to learning as that involved in the establishment of schools. This activity of the monks continued from the earliest formulation of the Benedictine rules, for the conduct of religious services depended upon a supply of the missals, of the Scriptures, and of the writings of the Fathers for daily reading. An architectural feature of every monastery was the *scriptorium*, or general writing room. In many monateries special cells for copyist were later added and also in many instances, a library and a schoolroom. That this work of the copyist was not merely mechanical, but was designed to have an intellectual and a moral effect as well, is indicated by the words used later at the consecration of the *scriptorium*;

"Vouchsafe, O Lord, to bless this room of the servants, that all which they write therein may be comprehended by their intelligence and realized in their works." As we have hitherto seen, this dedication would indicate that the monks were expected to deal with religious writings but it was true also that the classics of Rome and a few of those of Greece, cheifly in Latin form, were also copied. If this had not been true, we should not have many of the classics that remain to us to-day.

Montalembert goes so far as to claim that the knowledge of the classics was more general in France in the thirteenth century than it is at the present time, but this seems a great exaggeration. While it is not true of the period we have especially in mind in this discussion, - that from the sixth to the twelfth, - it is certainly true of the centuries immediately preceding and immediately succeeding this period that Church Fathers and Schoolmen who wrote treatisess intended for general circulation, depended upon the monastic copyist to give these wide circulation.

It should be noted that many of the nunneries were quite as famous as were any of the monasteries for their manuscript, and some for their schools also. This work of copying was peculiarly adapted to the abilities and inclinations of the female recluses.

Another aspect of this relation of the monasteries to the literature of the past is to be noted. Many of the extant manuscripts devoted to the chronicles of the monastic foundation, to wearisome comment on some older sacred writings, or to the disquisitions of the Schoolmen, are written on parchment from which a previous writing, usually of some classical texts, has been removed by chemical or mechanical process. In this way, undoubtedly many classical texts were destroyed. They were chosen for destruction with the distinct feeling that they were unworthy of preservation. Possibly in this way some ancient text have been irrevocably lost for all time. This destructive and from our point of view somewhat barbarous, custom is not now believed to have been nearly as general as once supposed. It is thought to have flourished only after the thirteenth century, by which time duplicate manuscripts were common. Then the destruction of ancient writings was due to the increased demand for parchment consequent upon the rise of universities and to the interference of the source of supply in the East by the Saracen conquests.

The Monasteries as Depositories of Literature and Learning

One service which monasticism performed by learning cannot be gainsaid. Whatever of ancient learning and literature we have preserved to us to-day is largely owing to the monks. Though the Arabs added much during the later Middle Ages, even then such additions were given into the possesion of the monks. These conservators of learning were very often ignorant of that which they preserved from obliteration; but if it had not been for such places of retirement and of protection, it is difficult to see how more than the merest rudiment of the classics would have survived from the seventh to the twelfth century. Through all this long and tumultuous period of barbarian aggression, when the remnants of classic civilization, along with the fundamentals of social structure, were being transferred to a people no farther advanced in the stage of culture than were the American Indians, the monasteries served as the safety deposit vaults of learning, whose monkish keepers were all unaware of the precious jewels within their charge. Occasional glimpses of a rare gem but convicted them of sin for yielding to the temptation offered by the riches or the pleasures of a wicked world.

While in the early Benedictine rules there is no mention whatever of the care of books, such mention appears in the later modifications of Clugny. Special rooms for libraries did not appear until much later, probably during the university period, but special provision for their care in cloister of cell had appeared long before. A monk of the twelfth century expresses clearly the attitude assumed toward learning by monasticism long before his own time: "A monastery without a library is like a castle without an armory. Our library is our armory. Thence it is that we bring forth the sentences of the Divine Law like sharp arrows to attack the enemy. Thence we take the armor of righteousness, the helmet of salvation, the shield of faith, and the sword of the spirit, which is the word of God."

While the majority of monasteries possessed but few books, probably none outside of a strictly religious character, there were yet many that possessed hundreds and some few whose volumes mounted to the thousands. As early as the tenth century, that of Novalese, in Italy, was said to have had a library numbering sixty-five hundred volumes at the time it was destroyed by the Saracens. The few monasteries especially noted for their learning had large libraries, and gave particular attention to the collection of books through the exchange of duplicates made by the monks. Among these more noted foundations there existed a very definitely regulated system of exchange, and several of the later orders made special provision in their rules for this interchange and for the requisite work of copying. Some few made it a means of financial support. This was first definitely accepted as the chief means of support by the Hieronymians very late in the Middle Ages. During the later centuries, in cathedrals, in royal palaces, even in the castles of the nobility, collections began to be made that soon were to rival those of the older foundations. But with the founding of the universities and finally with the invention of printing, the monasteries, now that their great service had been performed, ceased to give as much attention to this activity; or at least with changed conditions, the literary character of their service no longer appeared conspicuous.

The Monks as Literary Producers

Though the range of their interests was not broad, yet until the general appearance of vernacular literature in the eleventh and twelfth centuries, the monks produced practically all the literature of this period. This included the lives of the saints, the short moral tales or sermons, - such as are collected in the Gesta Ramanorum, Biblical or patristic comment, and monastic chronicles. The Schoolmen appeared about the same time as any considerable production of vernacular literature, and during all the later half of the Middle Ages the literary importance of the monks was overhadowed by the work of these classes. To be sure, the greater number of Schoolmen were friars, whom we have included in this discussion with the monks. It is in the early half of the Middle Ages - the dark ages - that the monks had this unique position of including all learning within their organizations.

Unhampered by any restrictions upon their faith or their credulity, with the tendency to doubt and the faculty of criticism atrophied, with imagination vivified by ascetic discipline and the horrors of the life of their times, the content of many of these writings, whether ostensibly historical or biographical, is limited only by the fecundity of their imagination. History was ostensibly written for the glory of God and the advancement of the interests of the Church; hence the accuracy of fact, the assignment of motive, the judgment of results, were all determined from this one point of view. As a result while much of our knowledge of the political history of the times comes from these monastic chronicles, and while some of them, such as those of the Venerable Bede for England, are most excellent and furnish the chief source of information for particular periods or people, most of them are so full of inaccuracies or misinterpretations that their statement, must be rigidly verified by cross reference before being accepted. However, in this respect as in others, these monastic chronicles are probably superior to the few which emanated from the courts, for the monk was free for the most part from the motives of personal aggrandizement, being led astray by motives of a wholly different character; namely, those of adding influence to the Church or reputation to its secular defenders. The importance, however, of such writings as the biography of Karl by Einhard and of the chronicles of Paulus Diaconus, subject as they are to many of these limitations, can be better estimated when we remember that it is said no records were kept at Karl's court because of the difficulty of finding persons who could write, and when we recall the character of the Carolingian myths that grew up to be accepted as history in the centuries following. Regarded, then, as exact annals of the times, these chronicles are more important as sources of information concerning the institutions, manners, laws, and ideas of these ages. The list of these chronicles from the monasteries of Italy, of France, of Germany, of the Low Countries of the British Isles, as well as of the minor European countries, is a long one in each case, and it is from these that our knowledge of these few centuries is largely reconstructed.

The one other class of secular writings besides the chronicles is that devoted to the discussion of the Seven Liberal Arts or of one of the component subjects. This needs to be discussed from another point of view.

The Literary Heritage of Monasticism: The Seven Liberal Arts

In outline the Middle Ages possessed all the knowledge of the few preceding and the few succeeding centuries; in its content this knowledge was immeasurably more meager than that of either the preceding or the following era. It is desirable to note briefly the actual character and content of the secular learning that these Middle Ages preserved from complete barbarian neglect and destruction.

The knowledge of the ancients possessed by the Middle Ages was far from being in its ancient form, for most of these writings had disappeared; it was the knowledge of the ancients organized in a much abridged form by a few learned men chiefly of the fifth century. At this time the expression, The Seven Liberal Arts, as inclusive of all learning, came into vogue. Long before the fifth century, however, practically all these differentiations into subjects had occurred; it was reserved for the ecclesiastical and symbolical tendencies of the Middle Ages to limit the sciences definitely to seven. Plato had shown the distinction between what now came to be called the trivium, including grammar, rhetoric, and dialectic, and the quadrivium, including arithmetic, geometry, music, and astronomy. Varro, the most learned of the Romans, wrote, in the last pagan century, upon the liberal arts of studies which included all of these, together with architecture, medicine, and philosophy. In his treatise on education, Quintilian omitted from the liberal studies two of them, dialectic and arithmetic. St. Augustine wrote a treatise on two of these, and stated that he intended to write on five others. Writing in the same period, Capella completed his treatise on the seven in which all knowledge was presumed to be summarized. It is said by Professor Davidson, however, that the first actual use of the numeral seven in connection with the liberal art was by Rabanus Maurus in the ninth century. It is certain, however, that Cassiodorus, in the sixth century, and Alcuin, in the generation preceding, had justified the study of secular subjects recognized by Rabanus Maurus, by identifying them with the seven pillars of the temple of wisdom.

Martianus Capella, mentioned above, was one of the best representatives of the pagan culture in North Africa, and wrote (between 410-427 A.D.) a treatise entitled De Nuptiis Philologiae et Mercurii (The Marriage of Philology and Mercury), which, throughout the first half of the Middle Ages, was used more widely than any other book as a text of the ancient learning. The god Mercury desires to marry, and all the machinery of the pagan heaven is set in motion, first to determine to whom, and then to celebrate the consummation of the marriage to the most learned maiden, Philology. The seven bridesmaids, or handmaidens, presented by Phoebus, are the Ars Grammatic, Ars Dialectica, Ars Rhetorica, Geometrica, Arithmetica, Astronomia, Harmonia, and each, as led forward in the ceremony, gives her parentage and expounds to the assembly the substance of the art typified. These speeches contain in the driest of text-book form practically all of the learning of the schools of these centuries. While Capella follows the order and arrangement of Varro, the substance of his works is borrowed from Cicero, Pliny, and Solinu, and from less important writers.

Boethius (c. 480-524). Though no more prominent than Capella through the use of his books in the schools, Boethius was the most influential of all the learned men of the early Middle Ages. His chief service was to give to several succeeding centuries the little knowledge of the Greek writers, especially of Plato and Aristotle, that they preserved. His purpose was to translate all the writings of these two philosophers into Latin; he accomplished, however, only a small portion of his task, and of that but little was known during these centuriess of darknes. While some of his briefer treatises gave impetus to the early scholastic movement, his more important works were not known until the twelfth century. He gave to the Middle Ages logic and ethics or the basis of the entire dialectic element in their education, and also wrote on arithmetic, geometry, and music. These works of his were extensively used as text-books; the one on music continued to be employed in some universities until well into the eighteenth century. His most widely read and influential work was the Consolations of Philosophy, written during his imprisonment just preceding his martyrdom by the Emperor Theodoric, whom he had served so long and well. Through this, the most widely read secular work during all the Middle

Ages, the early half of this period received most of its ideas of the ancient philosophers and moralists. Though his writings afford practically no evidence of his avowal of a Christian faith, he was accepted by the medieval Church as a Christian, and thus his writings, the last product of pagan culture, were incorporated into the traditions of the Church.

Cassiodorus (c. 490-585), the prime minister of at least four of the early barbarian emperors, or Gothic kings and thus to them the interpreter of Latin culture as well as the exponent of their will to the conquered Romans, derives his chief importance from his political activities; but the latter half of his long life was spent in a monastery which he himself had founded. Here he wrote for his monks commentaries, text-books and an educational treatise containing a presentation of the seven liberal arts. For the world, he wrote his chronicles. Cassiodorus laid great emphasis upon study by the monks, urged them to give great attention to classical writings, directed that those without interest in letters should devote themselves to agriculture, but should read Cato, Columella, and other writers on agriculture. Much of his wealth he devoted to the collection of manuscripts, and through his influence the custom of copying these as a specific part of the work of the monasteries became established. There is much basis for the view that the preservation of learning in the monasteries was due more to Cassiodorus than to Benedict. To the influence of Cassiodorus was largely due the dissemination of the custom, begun by one of his monks in 562 A.D., of dating from the Christian era. While the lives of Boethius and Cassiodorus, often described as the great twin-brethren, ran in similar channels, had similar objects and resulted in similar influences, yet the interest of the former was in the learning of the past, that of the latter in the learning that was to be in the future. Hence, while the former is most often described as the last of the Romans, the latter becomes the first of the new type of scholars who would devote all learning to the advancement of the interests of the Church.

Isidore (c. 570-636), Bishop of Seville, is the distinctive representative of the medieval learning. For his monks and clergy he composed an encyclopedia called Origine or Etymologies, which purported to be a summary of all knowledge worth knowing. Its general content is of interest as giving some idea of the learning time. Books I-III are on the liberal arts; IV is on medicine and libraries; V, on law and chronology; VI, on the books of the Bible; VII, on the heavenly and earthly hierarchies; VIII, on the Church and on sects (sixty-eight in number); IX, on languages, peoples, etc., X, on etymology; XI, on man; XII, on beats and birds; XIII, the world and its parts; XIV, on physical geography; XV, on political geography, public buildings, land surveying, and road making; XVI, on stones and metals; XVII, on agriculture and horticulture; XVIII, on vocabulary of war, litigation, and public games; XIX, on ships and houses, dress and personal adornment; XX, on meats and drinks, tool and furniture. This seems a broad outline capable of including a wide scope of learning; but it must be remembered that many of these books are little more than catalogues of names; that many are filled with odds and ends of information or error; that most of the contents is drawn from ancient authors, and this not at first hand; that its dreariness is about as far from inspiration as possible; and that though including, as it did, all knowledge, it was yet in one volume. Though familiar with portions of the writings of the Greeks and Romans, Isidore forbade his monks to make any use of them whatever, and his book, through the excellency it possessed, partially prevented monks or students in general from going any farther. Such, indeed, was the general influence of this entire class of books, of which numerous others, by the few learned monks, followed in subsequent centuries.

Content of the Seven Liberal Arts. - Another aspect of these intellectual possessions of the Middle Ages is to be considered. One can hardly estimate the extent and the value of their learning until the content of these liberal arts is noted.

Geometry, for example, always included the rudiments of geography; astronomy included physics; grammar included literature; rheotric including history. The actual extent to which the literature of the ancients found any place whatever under grammar and rhetoric is a question to which very diverse anwers are given and which is very difficult to decide.Isidore and Cassiodorus knew Greek and possessed a small library of Greek Classsic; but during the following century the knowledge of the Greek language almost disappeared from Western Europe. It is believed that this knowledge was kept alive throughout the entire Middle Ages by the Celtic monks of the British Isles; but, while a general knowledge of Greek was undoubtedly preserved there much longer than on the continent, it only in rare instances survived these centuries of the dark ages. Alcuin had some knowledge of the language but little of the literature; though some of his predecesors and successors had more. Even the indirect knowledge of Greek literature, through Latin translations or rather summaries or extended references by such writers as Boethius was very meager, as, indeed was that of Latin literature. Some of the writings of Virgil and of Cicero were well known. For the most part, however, monasteries possessed but very few of the works of classical authors. In the book list of the library of York, Alcuin mentions Boethius, Pliny, Aristotle, Cicero, Virgil, Lactantius, Lucan, Donatus, Priscian, together with all of the important Church Fathers and several minor Latin authors. It is stated moreover, that this catalogue shows the library at York in the eighth century to have been greater than that of any other in either France or England until as late as the twelfth century. The extensive use of the pagan literature in the monastic schools at St. Gall during the tenth and eleventh centurie has been mentioned and in many monastic records, the mention of their possession of certain classical works, usually those of Virgil, Ovid, and Cicero, is to be found frequently.

Nevertheless, the general attitude toward this literature and its study was distinctly hostile. Alcuin tells his pupils at Tours, "The sacred poets are sufficient for you; there is no reason why you should sully your mind with the rank luxuriance of Virgil's verse." Showing a certain devotion to their studies on the part of some monks and the general attitude toward the classic writers, Peter the Venerable, head of the Clugny house (during the twelfth century), writes as follows: "See, now, without the study of Plato, without the disputations of the Academy, without the subtilties of Aristotle, without the teaching of philosophers, the place and the way of happiness are discovered. You run from school to school, and why are you laboring to teach and to be taught? Why is it that you are seeking through thousands of words, and multiplied labors, what you might, if you pleased obtain in plain language with little labor? Why, vainly studious, are you reciting with the comedians, lamenting with the tragedians, trifling with the metricians, deceiving with the poets, and deceived with the philosophers? Why is it that you are now taking so much trouble about what is not in fact philosophy but should rather (if I may say it without offense) be called foolishness?"

One minor regulation in the rules of this same great house (Clugny) which dominated monasticism for two or three centuries possesses a similar significance. It was customary, as with all monastic organizations wherein silence was enjoined, to indicate one's wants by signs: thus the desire for a religious book was expressed by extending the palms of the hands and then making a movement to imitate the turning of the leaves of a book; but if a copy of one of the classical authors was wanted, the wish was indicated by imitating the motion of a dog scratching his ear, thus showing the proper disposition toward the work of the unbelieving. Significant also is a very common attitude during the Middle Ages toward Vergil as the most prominent and most seductive of these ancient writers, wherein he is portrayed as a minion of the evil one, representative of all the temptations and wiles of this world. In fact, there arose during these centuries a very extensive Vergilian demonology that gives peculiar significance to the office of the poet as guide of the nether world, as portrayed by Dante at the close of this great historic period.

THE REVIVAL OF LEARNING UNDER CHARLES THE GREAT (r. 771-814)

The one important aspect of educational history from the seventh to the twelfth centuries that was not wholly monastic was the revival of learning under the Emperor Charlemagne. The task of this great emperor was to unify the work of the Teuton and that of the Roman, to adjust the barbarian Frank to the Roman culture, to transfer to the German who was hereafter to build upon it, the structure of modern society, the foundations of social organization. Through the Holy Catholic Church the transfer of the religious element had been made and the barbarians were now orthodox Christian; through the Holy Roman Empire, established by Charles in 800, the political and legal structure of society was finally accepted by the Teuton. There remained to be added to these forms of external unity that internal unity which consisted in a community of ideas, of language and of the cultural elements of social life. To bring about this union, this adoption of the Latin language, and the learning of the Church and of such of the Roman culture as survived, was the ambition of Charles.

Naturally, he used as his instruments the only educational institutions of his times, - the monasteries. The old Roman schools, if they survived at all in the chief centres of provincial learning, were of the most rudimentary sort, and had been assimilated into the episcopal or monastic schools. But this movement instigated by Charles was of more than monatic significance. It is practically the only one by a sovereign for the fostering of education among his people, between the last of the Roman emperors and the period of the universities. The work of Alfred of England and a few similarly inclined rulers was purely personal and local.

In 1782 Charles called Alcuin from the cathedral school at York to the Continent, to assist him in his attempt to revive an interest in learning. For a century or more preceding this time Irish monk had been largely instrumental in missionary and educational activities on the Continent, and the chaplains of the court of the Merovingian kings had in a way attempted to foster learning. But by Alcuin this school of the palace was developed into a definite institution, patronized by Charles himself, by other members of the royal family and by the youth of the nobility. From it Charles drew many of his assistants in the administration of his great empire. While the work of the school was very meager in its literary character, yet its importance was great from the influence which it exerted as an examaple. In 787 Charles issued his capitulary upon schools, which has been accounted by some, though in a somewhat figurative sense we believe, as the foundations of modern education,—"the charter of modern thought." It commanded the study of letters both by the clergy and by the monks; by the former, since it had come to his notice that great numbers could not even read, and hence simply repeated the church services by rote, and since many of the educated showed through their correspondence with him that their education was mot faulty; by the monks, that there might again be "a regular manner of life and one conformable to holy religion." Two years later, the first capitulary not having produced the desired effect, he issued another, prescribing in greater detail the study appropriate to the monks and the clergy. Several capitularies of the same year are devoted to raising the standard of character of the clergy, both morally and intellectually and one directs the bishops that clerics should be sought for, not only from among the servile class, but also from among the sons of freemen. One of these (that of 789) directs that "every monastery and every abbey have its school, where boys may be taught the Palms, the system of musical notation, singing, arithmetic, grammar; and let the books which are given them be free from faults, and let care be taken that the boys do not spoil them either when reading or writing." Karl's officials, the missi dominici, were empowered to visit all monasteries, to enforce the provisions of these edicts, and to see that the monks lived according to their rules. At least in one bishopric, that of Orleans, there was an attempt to carry out similar provision in regard to the parish churches, and thus to form system of elementary schools. This gives basis to the extravagant claim that elementary education for the lower classes was more general in France in the eighth century than in the early half of the nineteenth century. On the other hand, Gibbon summarizes the whole movement by saying that "the emperor strove to acquire the practice of writing, which every peasant now acquires in his infancy." That rapid advances in learning were made by the clergy and the monks during Karl's time is evident; that these efforts were not altogether satisfactory even to Alcuin is evidenced by his great desire to withdraw from the court on account of the corrupt life of the members and the rude, almost barbarian, character of society, whose constant occupation was warfare. In 794 this desire culiminated in the withdrawal of Alcuin to the abbacy of the monastery at Tours. Meanwhile, the educational movement furthered from this and other monasteries, as well as from the court, continued to thrive under difficulties. Of quite as great importance as the edicts of Karl himself, was one by the successor of Karl issued in 817. This reactionary edict restricted the work of monastic school to those boys who were destined for the monastic life (oblati).

Alcuin (735-804), who, on account of his influence upon Karl, as seen through these various edicts, is generally regarded as the most important educator during the first half of the Middle Ages, deserves some further notice. The position which Karl, in 794, bestowed upon Alcuin was the most important ecclesiastical office in France. The monastery of Tours was the richest in France, its possessions were almost a department in extent, and it was offered as a reproach to Alcuin that he was master of twenty thousand slaves. This monastery Alcuin made the center of learning in France as well as the center of influence in the Church. To him flocked the youth desirous of learning, and from the monastery went out an ever increasing stream of influence in the work of his pupils and disciples found in numerous monasteries throughout the land. Alcuin's ideas of education grew rather more restricted than broader; he rejected the study of the classical literature, to which as a youth he himself had been addicted; emphasized the ascetic aspect of the monastic training; and limited his pupils and the monasteries in general to the study of the sacred writings. On the other hand, while emphasizing the importance of the study of the liberal arts, within these limits, he took pains to build up a great library at Tours, sending copyists to England for this purpose, and encouraged a like activity and interest in the other monasteries. Though his learning was probably as great as that of any one of his century, yet his scholarship was limited. His great service was to bring learning to the support of the Church, and with Karl to demonstrate that intellectual training was quite as essential to the welfare of society as efforts at purely religious and moral betterment. He writes: "Despise not human sciences [the liberal arts] but make of them a foundation; so teach children grammar and the doctrines of philosophy that, ascending the steps of wisdom, they may teach the summit, which is evangelical perfection, and while advancing in years they may also increase the treasures of wisdom." Thus following Cassiodorus, with whose writings he was familiar, and from whom he borrowed in his own writings on the liberal arts he identifies these latter with the seven pillars of the temple of wisdom and thus gives this study Biblical sanction. He himself wrote on Grammar, on Rhetoric, on Dialetic, on Arithmetic, and on The Seven Liberal Arts. The treatises on the special subjects are in the catechetical form, - that of question and answer,—so familiar for centuries to come. Some of them are almost puerile in character. The arithmetic consists of fifty-three propositions of which forty-five are in simple reckoning. Many are in arithmetical and geometrical proportion, with little or no idea of principles involved. Several are trivial catch questions of modern almanac variety, such as "After a farmer has turned thrice at each end of the field, how many furrow has he drawn?" Alcuin's reputation as a scholar depended upon his several works on grammar.

Rabanus Maurus (776-856) was the ablest and most noted pupil of Alcuin. As the abbot of Fulda, the first and most important monastery and school in North Germany, he exerted an influence in this region similar to that of Alcuin in Frankland. His chief work was an encyclopedia similar to that of Isidore, upon which it was founded. Like Alcuin, he had some slight knowledge of Greek, but being of more virile mind his chief interest was in dialectic instead of in grammar. Dialectic he terms the science of sciences, which teaches us how to teach and how to learn. Another important work upon The Education of the Clergy contains a treatise on the seven liberal arts and hence covers the entire field of education of his day.

Joannes Scotus Erigena, or John the Scot (c. 810-c. 875), the most noted successor of Alcuin in the palace school was called by Charles the Bald, about 845, from the British Isles as Alcuin had been Karl. Of greater scholarship than either Alcuin or Rabanus, he introduced the study of the Greek language and brought a wider knowledge of the ancient learning, and especially of the Greek fathers, than had hitherto been found among the Teutons. With a much more liberal attitude toward the pagan authors, with whom he had a fairly wide acquaintance, he made the work of Capella the chief text in secular learning in the monasteries. Of more vigorous mind than any of his predecessors, he laid more emphasis upon the study of dialectic than had any before him, and being somewhat heretical in his views, he stimulated an unprecedented activity in theological discussion. With John begins the long conflict between realism and nominalism, though there followed what might be termed an intellectual interregnum of more than a century. The work and influence of Rabanus Maurus and John Scot lead directly to the great revival of intellectual interest in the later eleventh and the twelfth century, which will be discussed under scholasticism.

MYSTICISM, EDUCATION AS A SPIRITUAL DISCIPLINE

One other type of education is of importance, in that it supplements the other aspects of the disciplinary conception of education. Since practically all mediaeval mystics were monks, as far as its personnel is concerned, this type of education bears a close relationship to the monastic. Since, through its very nature, mysticism can have influence upon but few people, its importance is far greater in the history of philosophy and of religion than in that of education. While its presentation need concern us but briefly, it is desirable to have at least a general conception of its meaning in order to appreciate the intellectual life and the conception of education prevailing in the Middle Ages. As a type of life, mysticism differed from the ordinary unreflective life religious or secular, from monasticism the organized religious life, and from scholasticism the organized intellectual life; it possessed an education peculiar to itself. For an age such as our, educated from the most realistic point of view, it is all but impossible to do justice to the tenets of mysticism; it is impossible for one not sympathizing with these views to understand their full meaning; it is probably impossible for any one adequately to define this type of thought in simple terms. Mysticism was the belief that the aim of life was to attain to perfection of the soul, to the highest knowledge and to spiritual satisfaction by means of appropriate training. This was to be accomplished through the elimination of all that comes through the senses, by the withdrawal of the mind within itself, and through the identification, in the world of spirit, of the individual with the infinite reality or whole. Mysticism is defined by a modern scientific critic as "a state of mind in which the subject imagines that he perceives or divines unknown and inexplicable relations among phenomena, discerns in things, hints at mysteries, and regards them as symbols by which a dark power seeks to unveil, or to indicate, all sorts of marvels." A more sympathetic way of stating the same idea is that "mysticism is the consciousness that everything that we experience is an element, and only an element in fact; i.e. that in being what it is, it is symbolic of something more." Philosophically, mysticism has been defined as "the filling of the consciousnes with a content (feeling, thought, desire) by an involuntary emergence of the same out of the unconscious." From the religious point of view, "Mysticism is the tendency to approach the Absolute morally and by means of symbols."

There is both a philosophical and a religious element in myticism: philosophically, it is an attempt of the finite mind to understand the ultimate nature of thing, to comprehend the divine essence or the spirit of God as it pervades and rules all matter; religiously, it is the effort to come into actual and immediate communion with the Deity. To the mystic, "God ceases to be an object and becomes an experience." By means of ecstatic experience the mystic seeks to become" a partaker of the divine nature." As a religion it becomes the most intense and extreme of soul experiences; as a philosophy, the most abstract and idealistic while at the same time possessing a strong rationalistic bent; as an education, it becomes the most extreme, though the least widely influential, type of the disciplinary conception.

The Origin of Mysticism can affect its educational bearing but slightly, so needs but to be suggested here. From the nature of mysticism, it will be seen that it is not a definite type, but rather a belief in various forms among different people and at different times. Less natural to the religion and the life of the West than to that of the East, it is a feature essential to both the religions and the philosophy of the latter. Both to the Buddhist and the Brahman, the phenomenal world is an unreality, and the mystical absorption of the soul with the divine the highest goal. To a less extent, in both the Persian and the Mohammedan religion mysticism finds a place. The very term come from the mysteries of the Greek religion, from which the idea of shutting in things not to be revealed was carried over to the idea of shutting out all thing of the sense in order that the revelation might be given. In Plato the idea of rising to the infinite through a series of related phenomenal existences, and the finding in this same phenomenal world a symbol or type of the spiritual, gave a basis for the belief of those who would seek reality in this world of ideas by fleeing from the world of phenomena. In the writings of St. John and St. Paul, relating to Christian doctrine and Greek philosophy, and full of the technical terms of the Greek mysteries, the Christian mystics found the basis for their beliefs. In the Alexandrian schools of Philo the Jew, and later in the works of the early Church Fathers, similar interpretations are found. Clement made knowledge - knowledge similar to the Socratic type, "the thinking of holy things" - greater than faith. This knowledge though aided by intellectual training, was in itself a contemplation. Christianity was looked upon as of two types; the popular irrational faith and the knowledge or spiritual Christianity gained through wisdom. Their resemblance to the dominant heresy of the times - Gnosticism - rendered these teachings somewhat dangerous. In fact, throughout the Middle Ages mysticism showed a tendency toward rationalism, certainly toward a greater freedom of thought, and hence toward heresy.

The mediaeval Christians drew their mysticism directly from Plotinus and the Neoplatonic philosophy of the later Alexandrian schools and from Dionysius, who, though writing in the late fifth or early sixth century, was supposed to have been a disciple of St. Paul. John Scot revived their teachings. In the eleventh century a new type of mysticism sprang up under the leadership of the monks of St. Victor, distinguished from the former type by its attempt to harmonize mystical thought with scholastic formalism and terminology.

While the type of education represented by the mystic was not of general application, it is the freest from the restraints of institutional authority; it lays peculiar stress upon reason in its development of the contemplative mind and gives a completeness and a peculiar interpretation to the mediaeval idea of disciplinary education.

The Education of the Mystic was based upon a psychology formulated largely by Plotinus. These peculiar doctrines appear not only in the writings of Christian mystics, but color most of the treatises on the soul written throughout the Middle Ages by numerous Churchmen, both mystics and Schoolmen. In these treatises their psychological ideas are found. The soul is immaterial and immortal because it belongs to the world of reality, that is, of ideas or spirits. Its nature is threefold, the lowest, or animal part is bound up with the body; the logical, or reasoning part of the soul is its peculiarly human aspect; the third the superhuman, or spiritual part is that by which or in which man is identified with the highest intelligence, that is, the divine. Hence there are three excellencies of the soul; three stages of experience.

The higher stages are reached by a withdrawal from the world of action and of sense into the world of thought. The world of action is but the shadow of the world of thought; hence the latter alone is reality. Action is the shadow of contemplation. "Action is coarsened thought," as a modern writer formulates it. God, reality as transcendent and infinite, is to be approached and apprehended by analysis and abstraction, through thought, through the shutting out of all impressions of sense and a sinking into one's thought-self. "The way to God is to descend into one's self" said Hugo St. Victor; and Richard of the same school puts the same thought in similar words, "If thou wishest to search out the deep things of God, search out the depths of thine own nature."

After the development of scholasticism the stages of mystical education were formulated somewhat more definitely. The first step was that of purification, or purgation, similar to Aristotle's idea of purgative education and to the asceticism of the monks. All obstacles to the vision of the divine, consequently all impressions of sense, all material and worldly interests, were to be eliminated. In this connection an elaborate ethical system was developed, often including the social virtues as well as the discipline of self. The second stage was the illumination of life; as the first stage was a struggle with the outer life, so this was a struggle with the inner life. Good works are now performed spontaneously and need no thought. The whole nature, will, intellect, emotions, was to be concentrated upon religious ideas, that is, spent in devotion. The third stage, the unitive or contemplative life, was the goal of the mystic, and was to be reached by no other. This life was a continual approximation to the life of God in which man beheld the divine and was assimilated in it. In his Eruditionis Didascalicae, probably the most direct and important educational treatise by a mystic, Hugo St. Victor indicates these three stages from the educational point of view as cogitation, meditation, contemplation. Above the ordinary unreflective life, and separated from it by a gulf, comes the life of thought, of cogitation, of Aristotelian analysis. Separated from this by a similar distance is the life of meditation, approximating the Platonic life of contemplation, and resulting in the knowledge of ideas through dialectic. Above this again, now Christianized and rendered more spiritual, is the stage of contemplation, wherein the vision of the divine is vouchasafed to the Christian mystic, and to him alone. It is not to be wondered that in comprehending or in presenting this conception of life and its appropriate education there arises some difficulty.

Aside from this philosophical mysticism there was a practical type, very similar in its stages, but attainable by the unlettered through devotion. The importance of philosophical and intellectual training is replaced by the corresponding emphasis placed upon symbolism, which was of minor importance in the more rationalistic mysticism. While it was this latter that was of greatest importance during the Middle Ages, it is only the symbolic mysticism, that which finds in each material entity a portion of the divine and a symbol of it all, that has any considerable influence upon modern education. Even then, as it appears in the teachings of Froebel, it has little connection with the disciplinary conception of education.

CHIVALRY, EDUCATION AS A SOCIAL DISCIPLINE

Origin and Nature of Chivalry

Chivalry represents the organization with in secular society of those recognizing the highest social ideals and attempting to realize them through definitely established forms and customs. Chivalry was to the secular life what monasticism was to the religious life. It did not necessarily include all of the nobility, but only those who definitely accepted the highest obligations of a social character, sanctioned, as these obligations were, by the Church. Knighthood and the chivalric character were not inherited as nobility was. They were not the gift of birth, though only the free born and those who possessed some land, and who consequently could command the support of some subordinates, could hope to attain to its distinctive characteristics. While toward the close of the chivalric period knighthood was sometimes conferred on youth, even in infancy in the case of the royal family, for the most part it could not be attained before the age of twenty-one and then only after a long period of training, through which the knightly traits of character were developed, and after some deeds of daring that revealed the most striking of these. As the institution of chivalry represents the education which secular society received, so this training formed the only education of the members of the nobility. Like all education during the Middle Ages, this education was a discipline, both for the individual and the social class, but one in which the intellectual element was even slighter than that in monasticim or mysticism. Says Cornish: "The consecration of the Teutonic soldier to a rule of life, a brotherhood and equality of noble service, a discipline of lifelong obedience, a sense of personal honor and rectitude, though inferior to the Roman conception of civic virtue, was an education of those who bore rule in the world, and made them more worthy of the position which they had won and maintained by force, than if they had never bowed to the yoke of the Church and learnt from her teaching the lesson of *noblesse oblige*."

The origin of chivalry is found in the character and customs of the Teutons, influenced as they were by the structure of Roman Society, upon which they built modern institutions and by the Christian Church, which directed their energies into particular channels and discovered to them in many of the teachings of Christianity a bond of sympathy between the Church and the worthier traits of character of the barbarians. In the centuries between the final overthrow of Roman society and the definite organization of society upon the feudal system in the ninth and tenth centuries, cavalry had come to be the dominant military force, and every king baron, lord, or freeman of estate who travelled or warred on horseback, and hence had subordinates to serve him, was a knight. Knighthood and feudalism were coextensive and in many features identical, for their origin was similar. Chivalry, however, as it was organized, and in the form in which it dominated from the opening of the Crusades to the sixteenth century, was a knighthood within a knighthood, an organized life recognizing definite ideals and rules and possessing a special training that represented all the education there was for the ruling classes until the formation of definite schools of another character in the early Renaissance movement of the fifteenth century.

The Ideals of Chivalry are those ever since accepted as the ideal of "a gentleman". This is a very different conception of personal virtue from that of classical society, and involves some radical modifications of the elements of the early Christian ideal. In speaking of the character of the leader of the first Crusade, Cornish describes the knightly character that in its weakness and its strength is not much less typical of the entire chivalric period than of the earlier century. "We observe in them [the knights] reckless courage, personal pride, and self-respect, courteous observance of the word of honor, if plighted according to certain forms, disregard of all personal advantage except military glory; and, on the other hand, savage ferocity, deliberate cruelty, anger indulged in almost to the point of madness, extravagant display, childish wastefulness, want of military discipline want of good faith alike to Christians and infidels." Under chivalry these ideals, constituting the character of gentleman, were very much more definitely formulated than in modern ages. As thus definitely organized, the knight summed up all duties of life, under his obligations to God, to his lord, and to his lady.

In one respect chivalry performed for secular life a service identical with that performed by monasticism for the religious life: it dignified the idea of service and held up to a rude and violent people, accustomed both to resent any restriction upon their liberty of action and to indulge in a most unrestrained manner temper and anger, the ideal of obedience to rule and to peronal command. While this organization of society had its demerits as well and led to or sanctioned a contempt for inferiors and a regulation rather than an eradication of evil, it is difficult to overestimate its value in ameliorating the crudities and the barbarities of the life of the times through the new attitude toward service and obedience.

This influence was probably the greatest or, at least, the most immediate that Christianity could exert upon the virile barbarism of the Teutons. And chivalry is largely, though indirectly, the result of the influence of the Church. Especially in the Crusades, - and with this movement chivalry first became definitely organized, - the Church consecrated the dominant militant interests and characteritics of the Teuton and secured their devotion to its interests. This ideal of a life of service substituted for one of lawless gratification, if it did not modify radically the character of their life, constituted a complete change in the direction and motive of their education.

Reverence for superiors, a consideration for inferior, a gentleness toward all weak and defenseless, a courtesy toward all women, were further ideal or amplifications of the ideal of service and obedience. A greater gentleness of manner, of consideration for others in deed and speech, in fact, a general amelioration of manner followed throughout all classes of society. While it is true that this courtesy and consideration were enforced by the constant threat of mortal combat if violated, and that this was a regulation of evils that sanctioned the violence of previous times, yet it was a great advance to have definite ideals of social conduct recognized by these classes of society. Such recognition implied a long course of training, a definite education upon the part of those professing to follow this new type of life.

The ideal of courage or bravery required no specific training to secure its development, but the use of arms necessary to follow this life did. The ideal of gallantry or courtesy in itself probably needed no formal instruction that it might be produced; but chivalric gallantry, the proper courtesy and demeanor in company, did require a prolonged training, for its forms were many and intricate and the entire chivalric life was one of most punctilious formal observance. The general ideals of chivalry, its effect upon society and the individual, and, by inference, the character of education demanded are indicated in this summary from Cornish; "Chivalry taught the world the duty of noble service willingly rendered. It upheld courage and enterprise in obedience to rule, it consecrated military prowess to the service of the Church, glorified the virtues of liberality, good faith unselfishness, and courtesy, and, above all, courtesy to women. Against these may be set the vices of pride, love of bloodshed, contempt of inferiors, and loose manners. Chivalry was an imperfect discipline, but it was a discipline, and one fit for the times."

Our concern is in the organization of this discipline into an education scheme, such as furnished to the free and especially to the upper classes in society their only organized education from the seventh to the fifteenth or even sixteenth century.

THE EDUCATION SYSTEM OF CHIVALRY

The education of a knight was divided into two distinct periods; that of the page, which covered approximately the period from the seventh to the fourteenth year, and that of the squire, which covered approximately the period from the fourteenth to the twenty-first year. Every feudal lord, of every rank, and the more prominent clerics as well, maintained a court that was attended by the sons and frequently by the daughters of the subordinate gentry of his realm. The greater gentry usually sent their sons to the court of the king or sometimes to that of one of their peers. Oftentimes the son of kings served in their own home. But it was the usual custom for all ranks of chivalry, a custom probably growing out of the earlier custom of taking hostages, to send their children from home. In some instances, though very rarely, schools were established. For the most part the training was given through a definitely organized household or court service. Obedience and service were thus dignified by having the noblest born conform to the same ideals. For during this training sons of knights even thus waited upon the table and performed similar menial offices. By the same process, gentleness and consideration were developed in those in authority, since they had also served, and since their servants, those in personal charge of the table, of the horses, the dogs, the hawks, the bed chamber, the stables, etc., were all persons of rank.

The page began with simple service about the castle, especially in attendance upon the ladies. As he grew older he waited upon the table. This duty he continued to perform as a squire; and in addition to these a great variety of personal services to his lord. All culminated in the office of "squire of the body," who was the immediate personal attendant upon his lord in battle and in tournament.

The page and the squire were supposed to learn "the rudiment of love, of war, and of religion." The "rudiments of love" were courtesy, kindliness, gentleness, pleasant demeanor, generosity, the knowledge of the very elaborate formalities of conduct, good manners, pleasant, even stilted speech, and the ability to turn a rhyme. Love was to protect the youth from the evils of anger, envy, sloth, gluttony, and excesses of all kinds. The rudiments of love were to be acquired through service to the ladies and through the teachings of the minstrels. It often happened that to these things the squire added the ability to play the harp and to sing. The squire had in particular to devote himself to the service and the amusement of the ladies of the court. He participated in their hunting and hawking expeditions, in the entertainment of the court, perhaps in the reading of chivalric literature and in the game of chess. Chaucer thus describes the squire:

"Syngynge he was or floytynge [playing], al the day;
He was as fresh as is the monthe of May.
Short was his gowne, with sleves longe and wyde.
Wel koude he sitte on hors and faire ryde;
He koude songes make and wel endite,
Juste and eek daunce and weel purtreye and write.

So hoote he lovede that by nyghtertale
He slepte namoore than dooth a nyghtyngale;
Curteis he was, lowely and servysable,
And carf biforn his fader at the table."

The ability to just, spoken of by Chaucer, was the chief of the rudiments of war. The justing in the tournament was the chief preparation for war; in time it became a substitute. For this the youth was trained from his earliest years in the ability to ride, to handle the shield, to wield the sword, to till with the lance, to cast the javelin, to exercise in armor, - in fact in every martial exercise. Tilting at a revolving target either in boats or on horseback, was much practiced. Hunting and hawking furnished training for warfare as well as the chief amusements of the nobility. The latter, which was chiefly the hunting of water fowl, was the peculiar privilege of the nobility. This training in the rudiments of war developed an ability to withstand all hardships of life in the open air, an indifference to pain, an ability to withstand hunger and fatigue.

As the period for knighting drew nigh the religious aspects of chivalry were emphasized. Throughout the ceremony, which usually required some weeks of religious service, the Church attached the nobility to it and sanctioned and directed their warlike activities. The prospective knight must go through ceremonies of purification, his sword was blessed by a priest, and in the ceremony, frequently if not usually held in a church, he swore "to defend the Church, to attack the wicked, to respect the priesthood, to protect women and the poor, to preserve the country in tranquillity, and to shed his blood on behalf of his brethren."

In all of this training there is little of the intellectual. In the earlier centuries of chivalry it was an effeminacy to know how to write; in the later centuries the knowledge of reading and writing both among men and women of the upper classes was quite common. The knowledge of the French language- the language of chivalry - was quite necessary. This study of French and the song and music of the minstrels were the only literary elements in this type of education. However, there were occasional instances of more marked attainments.

One of the early English texts gives this description of the aim of chivalric education: "To lerne them [the future knights] to ryde clenely and surely; to draw them also to justes; to lerne were their harenys; to haue all courtesy in wordes, dedes, and degrees, dilygently to kepe them in rules of goyinges and sittinges after they be of honor. Moreover to teche them soundry languages and other lernyings vertuous, to harpe, to pype, sing and daunce."[3]

Scholasticism: EDUCATION AS AN INTELLECTUAL DISCIPLINE

Nature of Scholasticism

Scholasticism is the term given to the type of intellectual life, and hence of education, that prevailed from the eleventh to the fifteenth centuries inclusive; that was largely responsible for the origin of universities, and represented the work of these institutions for three or four centuries; that produced a vast literature; and that possessed very distinct characteristics of its own which mark it off from modern intellectual life. Definite though narrow in its aim, restricted in its subject-matter, keen and subtle in its method, fruitful in its outcome in the development of certain mental traits and abilities, extremely limited in its social influences, scholasticism was a type of intellectual life that has been as grossly abused and as much underestimated during the centuries following its overthrow by the Renaissance movement of the sixteenth century, as it was overvalued by its own devotees. Scholasticism is not characterized by any common group of principles or beliefs, but is rather a peculiar method or type of intellectual activity: consequently it is very difficult to give any accurate definition of the term. Most attempted definitions merely give descriptions of its external features, its methods, its subject matter or of the time limits within which it prevailed. Without attempting a further definition, let us consider the purpose, the content, the form, the method, the defects, the objections to scholasticism, and its result from the educational point of view.

THE PURPOSE OF SCHOLASTIC THOUGHT

The dominant characteristic of the intellectual life of the early half of the Middle Ages was the attitude of unquestioned obedience to authority; of receptivity to all doctrines, statements or incidents sanctioned by the Church; of dependence upon the formal truths dogmatically established; of an antagonism to any state of doubt or of questioning or of inquiry as wrong ànd sinful in itelf. By the eleventh century a new attitude was necessary. Heretical views had crept in from the East, and had to be met by argument as well as by force; a few men of exceptional learning for the times, especially John Scotus of the ninth century, had suggested many questions that could not be ignored; the study of dialectic, which had received new and unprecedented emphasis from the time of Rabanu Maurus, had stimulated an interest in intellectual activity and in the logical formulation and statement of religious beliefs; and the Crusade movement, with its breaking down of the isolation and the rusticity of the people of the West through their contact with the variety of beliefs in the East—all these stimulated new intellectual interests and made it necessary to state religious beliefs in new forms. The purpose of scholasticism was to bring reason to the support of faith; to strengthen the religious life and the Church by the development of intellectual power, and by silencing, through argument, all doubts, all questionings, all heresy. Faith was yet superior to and anterior to reason. The credo ut intellegum ("I believe in order that I may understand") of Anselm was the dominant principle throughout the period.

But at the same time it was the belief that there was no conflict between reason and faith, and it was the constant purpose to show this harmony between reason, with its newly given liberty, and the doctrines so long accepted by the Church. Church doctrines had long been formulated; they were now to be analyzed, defined, systematized. As in the past, synods had declared that the sun turned round the earth, had determined the exact way in which the painter should represent the beard and the robes of a saint, so now in a similarly, minute manner authority prescribed the beliefs of the people. It was necessary that authority should be organized and present a systematic completeness. This was the purpose of scholasticism in its broader meaning. Since scholasticism includes the questionings raised by reason as well as the refutation of these doubts, or the solution of these problems, the entire period may be looked upon as a conflict of reason with authority; and scholasticism is often so defined. But the dominant attitude was not one of protest but of conciliation.

Educationally, the purpose of scholasticism was included within this broad purpose. Scholastic training aimed to develop the power of thus formulating beliefs into logical system, of presenting and defending such logical statements of beliefs against all arguments that might be brought against them, without at the same time developing an attitude of mind that would be critical of the fundamental principles already establihed by authority. In other word, relying upon authority it sought to avoid developing the attitude of inquiry, of hostility to the acceptance of any statement without a preliminary inquiry into its rational validity; it did not desire to stimulate the attitude of honest doubt, which in modern educational thought would be considered the only proper preparation of the intellectual soil for such sowing of the seeds of truth as promised fruitful returns. In a more general way the aim of scholastic education was to systematize knowledge, to give it scientific form. But to the scholastic mind knowledge was primarily of a theological and philosophical, that is, metaphysical character and the scientific form valued was that of deductive logic. In this, the aim of scholastic education was brilliantly successful; for there were elaborated most exhaustive systems of knowledge, compassing the whole range of their interest in a most effective manner, and in some cases of such profoundity that these systems have few rivals in more modern times and yet serve as the basis and content of the intellectual life of large portions of modern society.

The third aspect of the educational purpose of scholasticism was, then, to give to the individual a mastery of this systematized knowledge, now reduced to propoitions and syllogisms all united into a logical whole.

THE CONTENT OF SCHOLASTICISM

From the previous statement of the purpose of scholasticism, it follows that the content expressing the realization of this purpose was the complete fusion of theological and philosophical material. It constituted the complete reduction of religious thought to logical form. All other phases of knowledge were subsumed under these, for secular interests as such had no standing. Since this organization was furnished entirely by the logical writings of Aristotle, or by such portions of them as were known, scholasticism is often defined as the union of the Christian beliefs and the Aristotelian logic. All legitimate knowledge had to be sanctioned by religion, or the Church; it had to be given its place in the logical system of scholastic thought and reduced to the appropriate logical form. To do this was the task of the Schoolmen.

The primary interests of the times were in the great doctrines of the Church concerning justification, predestination, the Trinity, the freedom of the will, the doctrine of the eucharist, etc. To give these and similar doctrines their proper philosophical statement, to reduce all to a harmonized system, to present them with answers to all objections to the orthodox view and with refutations of all unorthodox interpretations, constituted the content of scholastic literature. Now it happened that at the same period in which circumstances emphasized the necessity of supporting by reason the beliefs of the Church, a certain superficial knowledge of the fundamental philosophical problems discussed by Plato and Aristotle became prevalent; hence in the very nature of the problem, the interpretation of the orthodox views came to depend upon the acceptance of some such view as that of Plato, and the heretical theological views became bound up with a metaphysical doctrine contradictory to that of Plato.

The early Schoolmen were not aware of the conflict between the views of the two great masters concerning the theory of knowledge, or at least with the general outline of Aristotle's view, for they possessed and were guided only by those portions of Aristotle's writings that related to the logical formulation of thought, more specifically the Categories of the Organon. Plato's views that ideas, concepts universals, constituted the only reality, became accepted by the orthodox Schoolmen under the name of realism. By the Schoolmen and the Church such general concepts were regarded as the archetypes in the Divine reason, and the various phenomenal existences and the species were regarded as but copies or reflections of these thoughts of the Deity. The view that such ideas or universals are only names, and that reality consists in the individual concrete object, - in the species of Aristotle, - was termed nominalism. The conflict between these two schools of metaphysicians continued long and loud, through four centuries and innumerable volumes, and constitutes the material product or the content of intellectual life we are studying. As the Carolingian revival of learning had attempted to bring the ordinary learning of the ancients, their grammar and rhetoric, again into the service of the Church so the scholastic revival was the reintroduction of ancient philosophy in the service of the Church. This philosophy was to remain under the control of ecclesiastical doctrine, already determined though not systematized, and in case of any discrepancy the latter was always the standard to which philosophical doctrine must be accommodated.

But these views were of more than metaphysical interest; they compassed all interests. Consider, for a moment, the application of the views to some of the fundamental doctrines previously suggested. At this period the doctrine of transubstantiation had peculiar practical importance, on account of growing heresies, especially the Manichean, which held, on account of the belief in the evil of matter, that Christ's life was only an appearance and that the true God was not the God of the Old Testament. If ideas of substances are realities, as the realist held, and are hence independent of the attributes or qualities which identify them in the concrete and which to the nominalist constitute the only reality, then it is possible to distinguish between the substance and the accident, and it is possible to conceive of a change in the substance without any corresponding change in the attribute. Only thus could the Church justify its belief in the doctrine of transubstantiation, or the actual change in the bread and wine of the sacrament of the Lord's Super. As in this sacrament of the Church, wherein this contact between Christ and flesh was demonstrated daily, was an answer to the heresy that the divine could not have lived in contact with a wicked world; so in the general doctrine of realism, with its distinction between substance and accidents, the general relation of finite and infinite was indicated. Other doctrines with their explanations are very similar. So these philosophical views furnished characteristic solutions to all theological problems. Almost every heresy, every divergence from the accepted view, found its justification in the nominal position, while to the realist, the orthodox view of the Church, representing as it did the universal, was the only reality, - was the truth; the view of the individual, any special interpretation which he might desire to give, was merely an "unsubstantial," temporal accident, not worthy of consideration or of toleration. To the nominalist this view of the individual was the reality; thus both his religion and his philosophy became heresy.

This is but one, though the fundamental, aspect of the philosophy of the times. It is sufficient to indicate the point in which we are here interested. The content scholasticism is this fusion of philosophy and theology, in which all theological questions - and all secular questions became theological - were given a philosophical form and a most formal and extended elaboration. On the other hand, the most abstract of metaphysical questions were given the form of a concrete theological problem.

The educational content of scholasticism consisted in the most noted of these systematized schemes of learning, with the innumerable comments upon them. During the twelfth and thirteenth centuries were constructed the two most noted of these: The Sententia of Peter the Lombard (c. 1100-c. 1160) and the Summa Theologia of Thomas Aquinas (1225-1274). The former of these was the most generally used text-book, and the most generally prized summary of scholastic knowledge of the remaining scholastic centuries; while the latter was and yet remains the most complete and thorough presentation of the knowledge of the times, or, to be more exact, of the theology of the Church, and was accepted as it yet is by the Roman Catholic Church, as the orthodox presentation of its beliefs. Preliminary to the mastery of such summaries of scholastic knowledge, scholastic education demanded the mastery of the science of logic or dialectic as a preparation for the practice of the art. Therefore, the earlier years of scholastic training, after a brief preliminary study of grammar, were devoted to this study. As the development of these studies is synonymous with the growth of universities, it will be further noted in connection with a subsequent topic. In general, the content of scholasticism and of scholastic education deals, with the abstract and immaterial; just as the tendency in current education is to reject all that is of this character and to deal only with that which is concrete and material in character. Hence, in respect to content, present education and present thought are so opposed to that of the period under consideration, that there is no tolerance for it at all, and hence it can be little appreciated.

THE FORM OF SCHOLASTIC KNOWLEDGE Logical perfection was the ideal sought for in the completed works; these perfected works constituted the texts. Even in more rudimentary phases of the study, logical arrangement was the sole aim. The idea of organizing knowledge according to principles derived from the mental condition or stage of development of the student is an idea of much later development. By this period of scholastic education the complementary principle, that of organization based upon the logic of the subject was fixed upon education for many centuries. Hence in the introductory subjects, such as grammar, which the child first attempts in his school work, the most formal logical arrangement was adopted. The subject was presented to the child for his mastery in the order in which it appeals to the most mature mind. Previous to this time, the catechetical arrangement, that of questions and answers, was much followed, even in treatises upon the seven liberal arts. During the earlier scholastic period, the dialogue form was yet much used. But with scholasticism the systematized, logical form prevailed almost to the exclusion of the other. A very brief statement of the form of Aquina's great work may serve as an example. The Summa is divided into four parts, each one of which is composed of a number of questions, each representing some great doctrinal truth, for example, the doctrine of the Trinity. The questions are divided into a number of articles, each representing some subtruth under the general truth. Following the statement of the problem under each article, the objections or the counter solutions of the problem are stated in order (1, 2, 3, 4 etc.) then follows the argument in favour of the true solution then the accepted resolution of the problem and finally seriatim answers to each of the difficulties raised. All this is given in condensed, abstract form, in a style without any ornament or attempt at literary embellishment, and that, too, in a work that fills several folio volumes. So far as form alone is concerned, the most exacting requirements of modern science could desire no more; for it is most rigidly scientific in form though wholly deductive in character.

THE METHOD OF SCHOLASTICISM In reality there were two distinct methods used by the Schoolmen and in the universities as well. The first of these, the one in most general approval, was that of the Summa just given. The entire subject, if a treatise by a Schoolman, or the entire text, if a course of lectures upon a text-book or subject in the university was divided into appropriate parts, then into heads, subheads, subdivisions, etc., down to the particular propositions of each sentence. Each topic was examined most minutely after the manner of Aristotelian logic, under the headings of formal, final, material and efficient causes; its literal, allegorical, mystical, and moral meaning. Thus with analyzed text and comment upon the basis of each division, the student was overwhelmed with a multitude of fine metaphysical distinctions.

The other and freer method was that of stating the proposition, then the several possible interpretations with the difficulties of each interpretation, and finally the selection of the favored one. The solution favored gave rise to other problems; these in turn suggested varying solutions with their appropriate answers and their subsequently suggested problems following as a consequence. So far as approaching a definite conclusion and giving order and system to knowledge, this method was inferior to the former, but in its stimulus to thought, to the freedom of inquiry, and to general progressiveness, it was far more beneficial in its influence.

According to this method some of the Schoolmen stated their theories in the form of questions instead of in propositions, thus provoking inquiry and stimulating independent thought rather than merely suggesting varying ways of stating an accepted proposition. Thus it was possible to propose almost any view. A few such questions from the Yea and Nay (Sic et Non) of Abelard will illustrate this tendency and the daring freedom of thought sometimes shown. Should human faith be based upon reason, or no? Is God a substance, or no? Is God the author of evil, or no? Can God be resisted, or no? Do we sometimes sin unwillingly, or no? Does God punish the same sin both here and in the hereafter, or no?

It became customary for the radical thinker to protect himself from opposition and persecution by stating that proposed views were true philosophically but not theologically, or vice versa; but this subterfuge fell into disfavor with the ecclesiastical authorities. While the customary attitude was one of complete dependence upon authority, and while a general view, accepted as orthodox, tended to prevail, yet there was considerable variety of opinion among the few. Though the prevalent view was that of realism, it is impossible to assign any given content of principles or dogmas as the philosophical content of scholaticism, for there can be found at least a suggestion of almost every phase of modern philosophical thought. In a similar way there are few modern theological views but found some exponent at some time within the scholastic period. Scholasticism then, is primarily a method; the systematization of all thought according to the principles of the deductive Aristotelian logic, the subjection of all intellectual interests to the restrictions of logical form.

DEVELOPMENT OF SCHOLASTICISM

Some of the causes immediately operative in the development of scholasticism have been enumerated. The liberal thought of John Scotus Erigena, who declared the identity of true religion and true philosophy rather than the subordination of the latter, produced little effect upon his age because he was so far in advance of it. It is true that the doctrinal disputes in dialectic form, especially those concerning transubstantiation, began with Scotus and his follower Beranger (d. 1088), but then the logical and philosophical interests were wholly subordinate. During the eleventh century this conflict between realism and nominalism became definitely formulated in the discussions between Anselm (c. 1034-1109) and Roscellinus (d. 1106). Anselm, called the father of scholasticism, first as abbot of Bec and later as archbishop of Canterbury (1070-1089), expounded in a number of writings the realistic position and its application to the doctrines of the Church, especially in his "Monologue of the method in which we may account for our faith." Roscellinus, a Breton canon, attacked these positions in regard to many of the doctrines of the Church, especially that of the Trinity, on the basis of the nominalist position. Roscellinus held that logic had to do only with the right use of words, and opposed all those views which made the traditional realism of Aristotle the basis of theological belief. These disputes were continued for a century or more in various places, especially in France, and by various Schoolmen of minor importance. The number of persons attracted by these disputations was so great that a chronicle states in regard to some "that if thou shouldst walk about the public places of the city and behold the throngs of disputants, thou wouldst say that the citizens had left off their other labors and given themselves over entirely to philosophy."

The fate of Roscellinus, who was martyred, discouraged those inclined to hold the nominalistic view, which consequently did not reappear in its extreme form until the latter part of the scholastic period. The critical work of Roscellinus was continued by one of his pupils, and one of the greatest of the Schoolmen, Abelard (Petrus Abelardus,) 1079-1142) who however, opposed the extreme nominalism of one of his teachers as he did the realism of William of Champeaux his other teacher. His philosophical position, strikingly similar to that of Aristotle - a fact then unknown - was the compromise view of conceptualism. According to this view universals are existent, though not independent of the phenomenal form in which they exist, save as conceptions in the divine mind before creation. Abelard's position regarding the great philosophical question was a conciliatory one; but his real influence, and his writings in general, were far from it. His most influential work, Sic et Non (p. 301), was a collection of passages from the Bible and from patristic writings on theological questions, designed to show the conflicting ideas or views of the religious and ecclesiastrical authorities. He gave no decision concerning the solution of the conflicting views, consequently inquiry was stimulated, the importance of research emphasized; but the general impression was that faith in the unanimity and hence the reliability of ecclesiastical authority was questioned. While the theological and philosophical positions of Abelard were less radical, his influence was far more critical and far more destructive of unquestioned obedience to authority. Reason, he held, was antecedent to faith, and much of Christian belief could be supplied by reason. At least the arrogance of ecclesiastical authority was shattered; and though the man and his writings were condemned, his life blighted by persecution, his views regarded as heretical, his influence continued to exist as one of the most powerful forces in scholastic thought during the following period.

The thirteenth and the fourteenth centuries constitute the period of the complete dominance of scholasticism. During this period philosophy and theology seem to be in complete sympathy; the widest extension is given to philosophical thought in its Christian dress; theological views are elaborated into most perfect and complicated systems; reason and faith are in fullest accord. The causes of this complete triumph of scholasticism, the perfection of its system, and the wide extension of its limits, were twofold. In the first place, most of the doctrines of the Church were formulated and established as a result of the previous controversy. Certain of these, wherein complete harmony with ancient philosophy or with reason was impossible, were held to be beyond the limits of philosophical discussion. It is in this respect that the bondage or subordination of philosophy to theology is seen; for within certain established limits, perfect freedom of discussion was given. The second of these causes was the recovery of most of the writings of Aristotle, possessed to-day. The largest number of them, however, came at that time through corrupted translations or in the form of Arabic commentaries. Of the most influential of these, the cheif work of Averroes, Renan remarked that it was "a Latin translation of a Hebraic translation of a commentary on an Arabic translation of a Syriac translation of a Greek text of Aristotle." Imperfect as were these texts, they at least allowed the Schoolmen to perfect their system, for they gave them the complete system of Aristotelian logic. Besides the metaphysics of "The Master," his physics, psychology, and ethics were now introduced to furnish new material for scholastic learning. Through the modification of some Aristotelian principles, the scholastic position concerning the harmony of faith and reason prevailed throughout this period. Its educational aspect is to be discussed in connection with the universities. Mention can here be made of the names of but a few of the greatest among a host of educational leaders and writers and intellectually powerful men.

THE GREAT SCHOOLMEN

The first of the Schoolmen to be acquainted with the entire philosophy of Aristotle and to employ it in the service of theology was Alexander of Hales (d. 1245), The Irrefragable Doctor, author of Summa Theologie. Vincent of Bauvais (d. 1264) was an encyclopedist. Bonaventura (1221-1274), The Seraphic Doctor, a Platonist rather than an Aristotelian in his philosophy, represented as did the Victorines of the preceding century the mystical tendency in thought and education. Albertus Magnus (1193-1280), called The Universal Doctor, was the first to reproduce the philosophy of Aristotle in systematic form and with constant reference to the Arabic commentaries that constituted so large a part of the new knowledge of the times. Thomas Aquinas (1225-1274), The Angelic Doctor, was the most influential of all. In his great work he represents the culmination of scholasticism, and is its authoritative exponent both in that period and in subsequent times Joannes Duns Scotus (c. 1271-1308). The Subtle Doctor, was famous as a founder of a school of theology rival to that of Thomas; his work, however, was rather of a critical and negative than of a constructive character.

The long line of great Schoolmen was closed by William of Occam (1280-1347). The Invinicble Doctor, who revived again the nominalist views. His work was rather an attack upon the entire realist system than a formulation of specific doctrines. In general Occam denied that theological doctrines could be demonstrated by reason, and held that they were wholly matter of faith. He held that particulars alone were real and that universals were mere conceptions of the mind. Thus, he prepared the way for the careful, concrete study of the objects of nature and of the mind. On the other hand, some more questionable results of nominalism were also evidenced in Occam's view. In opposition to the realists, who posited that the idea of right and wrong were eternal and unchangeable because copies of ideas of right and wrong in the Divine mind, he taught that right and wrong depended merely upon the arbitrary will of God, and that "moral evil was evil only because it was prohibited." He rejected the prevailing Aristotelian psychology, holding that the mind was a unity, and that the distinction between the faculties was only formal or logical. In many further details of his philosophy and psychology he foreshadowed the views of modern schools, especially those of Locke and the sensationalists, and is responsible for the oft-quoted and expressive summary of these views, -" There is nothing in the understanding that was not previously in the senses." Politically and ecclesiastically Occam represented a similar protest against the dominance of the authority of the Church, consequently with him scholasticism entered its last phase, the period of decline. Whatever was vital to the spirit of progress now lived in nominalism only, and soon passed over into the new spirit of the fifteenth century Reniasance. The old scholaticism persisted but it no longer represented the progress of intellectual life and developing educational ideas and procedures.

Criticism of Scholasticism

That scholasticism was a tremendous advance in intellectual life beyond that of the early Middle Ages is evident; that it possessed some decided merits peculiar to itself is at least suggested by the previous discussion; that it served as the only education of the higher or intellectual type for several centuries, and produced a succession of great men unsurpassed in their intellectual acumen, has been noted. For all that, by the fifteenth century scholasticism reached its limits, degenerated into mere form, and became an obstacle to further progress, so that it had to be cast aside as outgrown and useless by the Renaissance movement of that period. Though revived in Protestant form with but slight variations, scholasticism has been mentioned only with execration and derision by almost every writer, except those of Roman Catholic sympathies, during all the subsequent centuries, until the nineteenth, at least. This was especially true of the sixteenth and seventeenth century philosophers, who found it necessary to overthrow the methods of scholaticism before progress could be made. Hobbes held that "those who wrote volumes of such stuff were mad, and tended to make others so;" that "the common sort of men seldom speak insigni- ficantly and are, therefore, by those other egregious people [the Schoolmen] counted idiots." Bacon declared:-

"This kind of degenerate learning did chiefly reign amongst the Schoolmen: who having sharp and strong wits, and abundance of leisure, and small variety of reading, but their wits being shut up in the cells of a few authors (chiefly Aristotle their dictator) as their persons were shut up in the cells of monasteries and colleges, and knowing little history, either of nature or time, did out of no great quantity of matter and infinite agitation of wit spin out unto us those laborious webs of learning which are extant in their books. For the wit and mind of man, if it work upon matter, which is the contemplation of the creatures of God, worketh according to the stuff, and is limited thereby; but if it works upon itself as the spider worketh his web, then it is endless and brings forth indeed cobwebs of learning, admirable for the finenes of threat and work, but of no substance of profit."

Hallam said that their works consisted of "worthless mental abtractions, of axioms assumed at haphazard, of distinctions destitute of the smallest foundation, and with the horror of a barbarous terminology." Criticisms such as these could be found without limit.

A factor in all of these criticism is the scholastic use of terms; but this for the most part is but the same criticism that can be made against the philosopher or metaphysician at all times. Undoubtedly from the extent of their discussions, and the fact that these discussions contained all the learning of these centuries, this terminology was vastly extended; but there is no real criticism to be found in this. The criticism against their literary style and the corruption of the language induced has a basis in fact; but from the very nature of their interests any other style would have been out of harmony. A more fundamental criticism is that they dealt altogether with unrealities. But they dealt with the same material and used much the same methods as does the philosopher or theologian of modern times. Criticism against the one lie also against the other. The real objection here is found in the fact that this material constituted the sole intellectual interests of the time; this, however, is an indictment against the age rather than against the Schoolmen. The indictmént that their beliefs, their propositions, their problems, were without any foundation, that they possessed no reality, is again one that argues a limitation in the critic as well as in the criticised. The foundation of these beliefs was primarily in authority; the foundation which a modern student seeks for his beliefs is in experience but the Schoolmen sought to supplement the support of authority by that of reason, just as the modern student seeks to interpet experience; only, again, reason to the Schoolmen was discovered by introspective, deductive analysis; to the modern largely by objective experimentation or by comparative induction. The valid objections to .scholastic learning are not so much those pointing out its positive defects, as those revailing its negative limitations.

Merits and Demerits of Scholastic Education

The first great limitation of the Schoolmen, and the one sufficient to call forth the condemnation of the modern mind, was that they never stopped to inquire concerning the validity of the material with which they dealt or to ascertain whether they had all the data before attempting the conclusion. A second and related limitation was that the material they dealt with was abstract and metaphysical without being supplemented by any knowledge of the concrete and physical. Here again the scholastic attitude is wholly out of sympathy with the modern. The truths they reached possessed only formal value; they could affect primarily the thought life, and only indirectly and remotely the conduct of the people, and then of but few. They made no attempt to connect the two worlds of intellectual interests; hence they possessed no external test or criterion to judge the reality, or at least the value, of their principles. Their procedure was forever in a circle; no intellectual progress was possible until there came to prevail the nominalist position, - that the concrete, the individual, was reality. From scholasticism general principles, of formal value only, could be derived. By some keen minds of the time this limitation was realized. John of Salisbury (c. 1115-1180), a keen student, a famous teacher, a pupil of Abelard's and of other noted Schoolmen, a friend and supporter of Thomas a Becket, a Schoolman who, almost alone among the learned men of his time, is distinguished by his knowledge and love for the classics and his distaste for what he felt to be the futility of dialectic, has left in his Metalogicus - one of the very few detailed accounts of the educational methods and activities of the times,—a statement of the non-progressiveness of dialectic study. After a student life at Mount St. Genevieve at Paris, under Abelard and other famous masters, and after a study of theology in other schools, he returned to Paris and thus summed up his impressions of the activities of his fellow-students:-

"And so, it seemed pleasant to me to revisit my old companions on the Mount, whom I had left and whom dialectic still detained, to confer with them touching old matters of debate; that we might by mutual comparison measure together our several progress. I found them as before, and where they were before; nor did they appear to have reached the goal in unravelling the old questions, nor had they added one jot of a proposition. The aims that once inspired them, inspired them still; they only had progressed in one point, they had unlearned moderation, they knew not modestly; in such wise that one might despair of their recovery. And thus experience taught me a manifest conclusion, that, whereas dialectic furthers other studies, so if it remains by itself it lies bloodless and barren, nor does it quicken the soul to yield fruit of philosophy, except the same be conceived from elsewhere."

One further decided limitation of the Schoolmen was the fact that much of their discussion posessed no reality; not only no reality in the concrete world of everyday life, but no validity in thought as well. Much of it consisted merely of endless and profitless discussions about words and terms. Accurate terminology is usually necessary to the progressive formulation of truth for further discovery or investigation; but there may be endless disputations about terms, "hair splitting" niceties of thought, that have for their purpose nothing beyond the discussion. Even against the greatest of the Schoolmen such a criticism is often valid. On the other hand, much of the modern contempt for the Schoolmen in this respect is based upon a failure to apprehend their point of view and their interest. To them all questions must be given a philosophical form and a theological bearing. Hence such trivial or even sacrilegious questions as those so often quoted to indicate the puerility and utter worthlessness of scholastic learning are upon subjects yet considered of greatest importance in the thought world of our own times and yet productive of many volumes. "How many angels can stand on the point of a needle?" Can God make two hills without the intervening valley?" "What happens when a mouse eats the consecrated host?" - all such questions conceal beneath their simple form the profound inquiries concerning the relation of the finite to the infinite, the attributes of the infinite, the nature of reality. Give them a form that only the trained metaphysician can understand and they constitute the profundities of thought; give them the form such that the untrained adult or the youth just beginning his course of scholastic studies can comprehend and handle, and they form the "monstrosities" of the Schoolmen.

One decided merit of scholasticism was that it stimulated intellectual interests. In the development of the universities we are to see the immediate results of this. As a stage in educational evolution, scholasticism is worthy of strongest emphasis. The education of the early Middle Ages gave little or no place to purely intellectual concerns; the entire tendency was to eliminate these. While scholasticism represents a type of such interests that finds no parallel either in preceding or succeeding times, it is also true that there are few periods in history in which interests of a purely intellectual, even metaphysical character are prominent.

This legitimatizing of intellectual interests had a further profound result; it developed an intellectual ability no longer confined to rare and infrequent cases. The learned men of the early Middle Ages are few and widely scattered in time and place. From the thirteenth century men of learning are very numerous. As we have seen, the character of their learning is not very highly valued by subsequent ages, but no one denies the acuteness of their minds. The subtlety of their reasoning is such that the modern student, trained to deal with concrete material rather than with abstractions, finds it very difficult to follow their arguments with their fine distinctions and their multitude of accurately used scientific or logical terms. Even their discussions about words and subtleties of thought performed an extremely important function in the subsequent development of thought, because it produced a scientific and logical terminology so essential to all accurate thinking.

From the point of view of realism, scholasticism was the attempt to support authority by the intellect, to supplement faith by reason; it was the union of theology and logic, of religion and metaphysics. But from the nominalist point of view, scholasticism was the conflict of reason with authority, an attempt to overthrow religious despotism by philosophy, the desire to broaden religious beliefs by intelligence. Realism as seen in the earlier scholastic discussions concerning the doctrine of the eucharist was based upon the deceptiveness of the senses, the insufficiency of human experience as a source of truth; nominalism was based altogether upon the validity, the trustworthiness, and the sufficiency of experience. Truth was to be reached through the testimony of the senses; only thus was the validity of the general notion to be tested. To be sure, this view was rather implict than explicit in the teachings of the nominalists; they held it as a formal truth. Only very gradually did it work itself out; only in the course of time was it realized that this position was wholly destructive of the scholastic attitude; only with the close of the period was it seen that even if the nominalist position was true, it possessed only the formal value that might also be possessed by the realist position. Philosophically, the modern point of view was to reject both; the approach of modern thought is different from that of scholasticism. But the nominalist influence as it became stronger and stronger had this important result; the emphasis upon the importance of experience, not now in the formal sense, but in a more material sense, as the source of truth is peculiarly characteristic of the development of the Renaissance thought as formulated in the seventeenth and eighteenth centuries. Nominalism gradually worked toward this conception; and, with its triumph in the fourteenth century, the scholastic period shortly came to an end and a new educational, philosophical, and intellectual period began.

THE UNIVERSITIES

Origin of Universities

Under the stimulus of the interest in dialectic, a number of schools connected with the cathedrals and monasteries sprang into prominence in the later eleventh and early twelfth century. The most important of these was that at Paris under William of Champeaux (d. 1121). The success of Abelard in causing William to modify his dialectic statements the fact that Abelard took a position decidedly hostile to the dominant realism, and the resulting fact that unorthodox dialectic views thus found room for expression and a more genuine discussion concerning views was thus stimulated, soon made Paris the center of these intellectual interests. The statement that Abelard drew thirty thousand students around him at Paris is probably an exaggeration, though the other statement that from his students came twenty cardinals and fifty bishops receives greater support. Undoubtedly great numbers of students were so drawn and demanded a multitude of minor teachers to prepare them for the more profound discussions of the master. Thus the essential elements of the early university - the students and the teachers - were found at Paris before the middle of the twelfth century. With the eleventh century Western Europe, especially the Church began to throw off the incubus to enterprise and the obstacle to greater intellectual freedom that existed in the belief that the millennium was at hand. The fact that during the tenth and the eleventh centuries the Northmen, the last of the migratory Teutons, accepted a settled life and gave to France and England a period of comparative peace, rendered a development of the interests of a stable civilization possible. Though as yet they showed little appreciation for the cultural aspects of life, these same Normans, in fact the Teutons in general, were endowed with virile minds. Hence they were drawn to dialectic discussion, as they could not have been to a mere literary study of appreciation; and more and more as other lines of activity were reduced to the orderlines of a complex society, they turned their genius into intellectual lines. This new Teutonic blood affected Italy as well as England, France, and Germany. The papacy and the Church in general had recovered from a period of greatest degradation, and through the struggle with the Holy Roman emperors both had acquired new strength and new interests. This affected intellectual pursuits and stimulated to the study of dialectic, theology and canon law. The development of commercial enterprise and municipal government, especially in the Italian cities, stimulated secular interests and secular learning to a point such as they had never reached before. Meanwhile the Crusade movement had begun. The isolation of European society - which really under early feudalism had not been a society but a series of isolated groups - was broken down. The communication of ideas was stimulated and the intellectual horizon broadened immensely. The "barbarians" of the East were discovered, with reason, to consider in turn the people of the West as "barbarians." The attitude of inquiry and of doubt, of freedom of opinion, which belonged to the East began to affect the West. This contact with the East and with Saracen learning brought to Europe, not only a knowledge of Arabic culture and science (first looked upon as black art, later to be embraced as science), but it also furnished in the thirteenth century a completer knowledge of Aristotle and of Greek philosophy. These influences combined to varying proportions: no two universities were founded by the concurrence of exactly the same circumstances. Each had some causes peculiar to itself, and all the earliest ones were, in reality, special schools where one or two special studies were pursued. Only later did they offer in their curricula the entire range of higher studies.

The immediate cause of the origin of universities in Italy was not the same as that in France and England. In these latter countries they were the outgrowth of theological and dialectic interests both growing out of the Church. In Southern Italy, where the contact with the Saracens, with the Normans, and with the old population of Greek origin was intimate, and where a more direct acquaintance with Greek literature was preserved, there had grown up, in connection with the monastery at Salerno, an interest in the study and practice of medicine. The work and teachings of the monks along these lines were stimulated by the first Crusade and the fame of this school spread abroad by the returning knights. Under the shadow of the monastic influence there grew up a school for the teaching of medicine, which in a way became the first university. Salerno itself was never organized into a chartered university, though this distinctive teaching work of a secular character was well established shortly after the middle of the eleventh century. Later the school was united to that of the neighboring city of Naples which was chartered by Frederick II as the University in 1224. In the northern Italian cities, struggling as they were with the German emperor for their rights, a new and vital interest grew up in Roman law, a knowledge of which had been allowed to fall into destitude. The emperor based most of his claims to authority upon the rights of the old Roman emperors; the cities sought to check these claims by a knowledge of charter of edicts, and of legal limitation that had long been forgotten. The knowledge of Roman law had probably never been allowed to die out entirely, though it was long thought that the growth of this study dated from an alleged discovery of a copy of the Pandects of Justinian made in 1135 at the sack of Amalfi. However that may be, there grew up in several of these cities schools for the study of law. That at Bologna was made famous by the greatest of these early teachers. Irnerius (1067-c. 1138), in the same manner that Abelard raised Paris to distinction, and large number of students collected here. Thus Bologna became a centre for study, and as these students and teachers were given privileges, it became the first organized university.

Founding of the Universities

These definite privileges, given in the form of a written document from emperor or pope, thus became the character or charters of the institution. It was only much later that an institution was organized outright by conferring on it all desired privileges. At Bologna the first charter was given by Emperor Frederick I, in 1158. Paris received its first recognition from Louis VII in 1180 and was recognized by the pope at about the same time. Its full recognition came in 1200. At Oxford and Cambridge the date of the formal recognition by charter is yet more difficult to determine but was somewhat later. In all these cases the large groups of students and teachers had existed for some time previous to charter organization and schools had existed under monastic or Church control in all these centres for an indefinite period. Chartered institutions that is those possessing special privileges, quickly came to exert peculiar influence and were rapidly multiplied. During the thirteenth century nineteen of these institutions were created by popes and monarchs; during the fourteenth, twenty-five more were added; and during the fifteenth, thirty more. By the period of the classical Renaissance there existed some seventy-five or eighty of these institutions scattered over all the countries of Europe.

STRUCTURE AND ORGANIZATION OF UNIVERSITIE

No individual during the Middle Ages was secure in his rights, even of life or property, certainly not in the enjoyment of ordinary freedom, unless protected by specific guarantees secured from some organization. Politically, one must owe allegiance to some feudal lord from whom protection was received; economically, one must secure his rights through merchant or craft guild; intellectual interests and educational activities were secured and controlled by the Church. In the cases mentioned, groups of students are collected in centres made famous by earlier cathedral or monastic schools, but are now no longer governed by the narrow interests of the monastic or clerical aspirant and no longer controlled by the rigid rules of these institutions. It became necessary that these groups should organize in order to regulate their own conduct, to protect themselves from extortion by citizen of the community, to secure themselves legal rights, and to maintain their interests in the face of Church authorities. By the conferment upon them of these special rights, such groups of students, or of students and teachers, were recognized as distinct bodies.

The unorganized group of students and teachers was called a studium generale, a name indicating either that a generality of studies was here pursued, or that the students were drawn from the widest territorial limits. Since none of these new centers of learning, in the early period, taught all the university subjects, the wide origin of the student clientele is probably the primary characteristic indicated. Other features of the universities that distinguished them from previous schools were their government, democratic in its nature; their location in centres of population rather than in remote spots, such as those sought by the monasteries; their special privileges legal and pecuniary; and the fact that these privileges had to be conferred by general authority, and hence that universities were founded by pope or emperor or later by kings, but could never be founded by local patrons as were monastic or other ecclesiastical schools.

Privileges of Universities

These special privileges conferred by pope and emperor upon students and masters were the specific instruments through which the university protected itself and built itself up. In general, these charters conferred upon all masters, students, and even their attendants the privileges of clerks or of the clergy. Thus the privileges originally belonging to the teaching class and extended by the Roman emperors to the clergy of the Christian Church in turn, were again extended to the teaching class, and developed a new professional interest and a new class in society. Such privileges exempted students from official service, from military service, except under specific limitations (e.g. at Paris only when the enemy were within five leagues of the city wall); from taxation, especially the petty local exactions, from contributions, etc. One of the greatest of these privileges was that of internal jurisdiction. Just as the clergy had been permitted to absorb in their privileges the right of trying their own members practically in all civil and many criminal cases, so in turn the universities developed much the same power over their own members and their adherents. This custom first grew up in Bologna under the favour of the emperor, where since civil law was the chief study students and masters were particularly competent to exercise the right. The civil or at least police jurisdiction which the German university yet exercises over its student members and the special favor of a privileged standard of conduct which the American college student claims, are survivals of this once extended right.

The other important privilege is that of granting the degree, which was merely the license to teach. Previous to this time this important privilege had been granted only by the Church through the archbishop, the bishop, or one of their subordinate officers; and thus the Church had controlled the method and the content of teaching. Ordinarily, under authority conferred by the pope, the university diploma granted the privilege of teaching in any institution wherever the authority of the university - that is, of the pope delegated by his charter - extended. This practically meant entire Christendom; and though nominally sanctioned by the pope, the authority was exercised by the university direct, and thus one important monopoly of the Church over learning was destroyed. These privileges possessed a sanction in the "right", not granted by charter but developed by usage known as cessatio, the right of "striking" or of moving the university, consisting as it did of students and teachers only, if its privileges were infringed. Thus the importance of Oxford dates from a migration from Paris in 1229; the importance of Cambridge from a similar disturbance at Oxford in 1209.

Many petty privileges were developed peculiar to each university. These, such as the right to demand bread or wine from dealers on certain feast days, though all such are merely incidental, were held on to quite as tenaciously as these more important ones.

Nations and the University

These privileges had to be conferred upon definite bodies of people, and hence a more definite organization than the studium generale was necessary. The most natural division of these heterogeneous masses of students, drawn from all over Europe at a time when territorial lines were very indefinite and national distinctions were more those of a genetic than of a territorial and political character, was that of language and kinship. Hence students and masters organized into groups according to their national affiliations. And upon these nations singly or more often in group organization, charters containing privileges were granted. Such a body was called universites magistrorum et scholarium. The term universitas means primarily "all of us" or "some of us," and had the general significance of our word corporation or association or company. In time, but not until the fourteenth century, the one word came to be used instead of the previous more general term.

At Paris there were four nations, the French, the Normans, the Picards, and the English (after the Hundred Years' War began the latter was changed to German). In Bologna there were at first four universities; then two, the Cisalpine, consisting of seventeen nations, and the Transalpine, consisting of eighteen nations. Finally, all were amalgamated into one organization.

A most peculiar characteristic of the Southern universities was the fact that the nations, and hence the governing bodies were there wholly controlled by the students. Thus the students in the nations determined when lectures should begin, how long they should continue, whether the charges were legitimate, etc. In the North where the student were for the most part those of the arts instead of those of law and were consequently much less nature, the masters themselves constituted the controlling force in the nations.

The Faculties

The organization of the nations had to do with conduct, civil right, and ecclesiastical jurisdiction. It had little direct reference to the studies. In time, however, it became necessary to regulate studies and methods, - in fact scholastic procedure in general. The faculties were a somewhat later development than the nations. In Paris they took shape in the second half of the thirteenth century. The term itself, quite as indefinite as the term university, simply meant knowledge or science; but in time it was applied to a department of study, as faculty of law, theology, arts, etc., and finally to the body of men, previously termed consortum magistrorum, that had control of a particular department of study. This body, as it developed, obtained control of the granting of degrees and was originally composed of all who had taken.

Governing Body and Other Officials

The nations elected, usually annually, a procurator or councilor, each faculty a dean; and these representatives together a reactor of the university. This official head of the university possessed only delegated power, was usually elected annually, and in the South, at least, was usually a student. The real governing power of the university lay in the nations. By the sixteenth century these head official had become for the most part political appointees, and the nations had long since lost all material authority. In the earlier centuries the Church continued to be represented directly by the chancellor, who nominally represented the archbishop in the conferring of the license to teach. This right soon became restricted to the ceremonial of the public conferment of the degree.

DEGREES

The nature of the degree and of the entire work of the university can best the understood by a comparison with some simpler aspects of medieval life which the student life paralleled. Such, for example, is the chivalric education, with its seven years of training as a page and seven years as a squire preceding the acquirement of full kingthood. A similar parallel can be found in the making of a master in any craft or mercantile pursuit, where the youth had first to serve seven years as an apprentice; then a more or less indefinite period as a journeyman, - a further period under a master while yet working for an independent wage, - all before he finally became a master possessing full rights in the guild. In quite a similar way the youth of thirteen or fourteen who wished to study the liberal arts, or to prepare himself for teaching appeared at the university where he had to enroll himself with a master who was thereafter (for the first period at least) responsible for him. Here he served an apprenticeship of from three to seven years, until he learned to read the ordinary texts in grammar, rhetoric, and logic, to define the words and determine the meaning of phrases, the use of terms and classifications. When now he could define and determine and could demonstrate this to the satisfaction of masters other than his own, he was accepted, as it were, as a journeyman workman; he continued his studies under some master, no longer being rigidly held to the one as hitherto, and at the same time gave instruction to the younger boys under the direction of a master. After a further period of study, varying with time and place, in which he demonstrated his ability to carry on a logical disputation, and familiarized himself with the required texts, or the course of study, he was permitted to demonstrate this ability, as a journeyman workman does by making a "masterpiece," by defending in public a thesis against the masters of the art, that is, the members of the faculty or those who already possessed the degree. This having been done successfully, he was given the degree, the licentiate, the mastership, the doctorate - whatever it might be called. Master, doctor, professor, were synonymous terms in the early university period. These degree were all one and the same; they signified that he was able to dispute as well as to define and determine, and authorized him to teach publicly, that is, determine and dispute; thus he was admitted into the guild of masters or teachers, in other words, into the faculty. He was now on a parity with other members of the faculty, and could teach in the free competition into which they all entered, providing he could obtain students.

The preliminary degree, the baccalaureate, - a term which signified a beginner, an inferior, an apprentice in any field and was used in the Church, in chivalry, in the guilds, and in the country feudal organization, as well as in the university, was simply formal admission into candidacy for the license and was not originally a degree in itself. During the fifteenth century it became a distinct stage in the educational process and hence quite well defined as a minor degree. The mastership and doctorate, so far as there was any distinction between them, also indicated merely two aspects of the final conferment of the privilege, - one was the more private professional test, the other the public ceremonial. The one term came to be preferred in England, the other on the Continent. That there should be three successive degrees, as in an American institution, is an anomaly or at least a result of slow historical growth, not to be found in the medieval institution.

THE METHODS AND CONTENT OF UNIVERSITY STUDIES have been previously discussed under scholasticism. After the opening of the thirteenth century the course of study was determined by papal bull or university statute and was far more restricted than was the intellectual activity of the twelfth century. While it is true that the thirteenth century possessed far more of Aristotle than did the twelfth, this but resulted in making the work more formal and restricted. Peter the Lombard was a pupil of Abelard and held much the ame theological views; but the spirit of Abelard was that of free inquiry, of investigation of rationalism, while that of Peter was one of rigid scholastic orthodoxy. Abelard was condemned as a heretic; Peter became the master authority of the university for two centuries. The influence of the one was dangerous to the supremacy of non-rational ecclesiasticism; the influence of the other rendered it triumphant.

A brief statement of definite details will make more vivid our conception of the work of the early universities. In the school of arts were used the grammatical works of Priscian, a work on grammatical figures by Donatus, the logical works of Aristotle given through Boethius and Porphyry; the Categories and the de Interpretatione of Aristotle, and the

Isagoge of Porphyry, from which originated the realistic-nominalistic controversy, were known in the translations of Boethius; the remainder of the Organon was known only through summaries or other writings of Boethius. To these latter the greatest amount of time was given, and even much of the time aside from the long hours in the lecture room was spent in participating in or listening to the endless disputations. At Paris the statutes of 1215 introduced the Ethics of Aristotle, and in 1255 his Physics, Metaphysics, and his treatise On the Soul. These works of Aristotle, previously interdicted at Paris, had been introduced somewhat earlier in other universities. Elsewhere some other introductory works on logic might be read, but everywhere the study of logic consumed the greater part of the time. Up to the middle of the fifteenth century, Aristotle controlled the work of the universities. The study of logic replaced all others, and rhetoric was given no attention whatever. The study of geometry and astronomy had made some progress, especially in the Italian universities and in the University of Vienna. The work of the professional faculties consisted, likewise in the study of a few fundamental texts together with their innumerable commentaries.

The education of the early universities was wholly one of books, of a very limited selection of books in each particular field, but of books that were looked upon a furnishing in the written word absolute and ultimate authority. It was directed much more to the mastery of form and the development of power of formal speech, especially argumentation, than to the acquisition of knowledge, the pursuit of truth in the widest sense, or even to familiarizing the student with those literary sources of knowledge which, though lying within his grasp, were outside the pale of orthodox ecclesiastical approval.

THE INFLUENCE OF EARLY UNIVERSITIES

The reults of scholasticism may be taken as the results of the universities, as was true with content and method of work.

There are other influences, however, to be noted. The political influence of the universities, both direct and indirect, was marked. In the first place they furnished the first example of purely democratic organization. While in the monastery as well as the episcopal college a certain democratic freedom in the election of abbots prevailed, yet their government was essentially an absolutism. On the contrary, the officials of the early universities possessed only delegated powers and were under the immediate direction of the governing democracies. Freedom of discussion concerning political as well as ecclesiastical and theological matters here found its first home. While for the most part the sympathies of the universities would naturally be with the privileged classes, whose privileges they themselves had obtained, they often became the mouthpiece of the common people in opposition to king or priestcraft.[3]

The right of the university to a voice in the government, to a seat in the parliaments of France, England, Scotland, is a recognition of this political authority and of the fact that the univerity had become a great "estate." The influence of the University of Paris was unique, and as the parent and representative of all northern universities it came to represent the French nationality, as the Holy Roman Empire did the German and as the papacy did the Italian. It acquired almost as much influence in the thirteenth, fourteenth and fifteenth centuries, as did these other great institutions.

Question of State and of controversy between State and Church, such as the divorces of Henry VIII of England and Philip of France, were submitted to the arbitration of the universities. The university often became the mouthpiece of the nation in voicing an opposition to the papacy; and in one instance the king of France and the university compelled one pope publicly to recant his views and apologize, and in another secured the deposition of the head of the Church.

Largely through the influence of the University of Paris

the great schism in the papacy and the "Babylonian Captivity" were ended. Though most of their famous teachers of the thirteenth and fourteenth centuries were friars, the universities in general became representatives of the secular as opposed to the regular clergy and hence champions of the rights and interests of the people and the national clergy, as opposed to the encroachments of the papacy.

In a similar way the university became an authority in the settlement of disputed doctrinal points, and in the determination of questions of heresy. In holding this balance of power it tempered the extreme views of the papacy and especially of the papal representatives, - the friar bodies, - and thus mitigated if it did not entirely eliminate, the operations of the inquisition in the north of Europe.

Politically, ecclesiastically, and theologically, the universities were the bulwark of freedom during these centuries from the dark ages to the Reformation. The constant complaint that they wished to meddle in every question is a testimony to their restraining influence on the arbitrariness of king and prelate. In them alone some freedom of expression of opinion was preserved. The one class whose opposing views monarchs were bound to respect was the university students; even in the case of representatives from foreign and hostile people, such as often formed a part of the nations of a university, but rare instances of the violation of the privileges of students occurred.

But in regard to the intellectual life, restricted, formal, and meager as it was its greatest influence was exerted. Intellectual interests were now crystallized into a great institution, recognized as almost on a parity with Church, State, and nobility. While this interest and its resulting institutional organization were so reduced by the fourteenth or at least by the fifteenth century as to possess little but formal life, the university yet provided a retreat for the rare genius who kept alive the spark of real intellectual life and maintained a home for the new intellectual spirit when it did come.

However hostile it may have been during these centuries to innovation, to radicalism, and to rationalism, yet in preserving the spirit of speculation, the university kept alive the spirit of inquiry. And out of it came such men as Roger Bacon, Dante, Petrarch, Wycliffe, Huss, Copernicus, - the men who brought the modern spirit.

EDUCATION AT THE CLOSE OF THE MIDDLE AGES

The Renaissance of the Thirteenth Century

It will be seen from the discussion of the last two sections that the later Middle Ages were far from being "dark ages," and that the intellectual interests and educational activities of these centuries were very great. The later fifteenth century is usually taken as the transition period from medieval to modern times; but the idea which this section seeks to emphasize is that this transition educationally was for the most part in respect to spirit and content of the intellectual life. In these intervening centuries, the thirteenth to the fifteenth inclusive, there existed a place in social organization for an intellectual life, exerting profound influence, permitting much freedom having definite character, possessing peculiar merits, and developing an appropriate educational system.

Moreover with the thirteenth century, the intellectual interests and control passed from the monasteries to the schools; from under wholly ecclesiastical influences to one that while nominally ecclesiastical was in spirit chiefly secular. The leadership passed from Churchmen to doctors, who were prominently logicians, and hence inclined to rationalism. Intellectual interests which began by being wholly religious or theological in character ended by being almost wholly philosophical and logical. It is true, on the other hand, that the dominant conception of education remained the disciplinary one; that the function of schooling was to develop this peculiar intellectual power of logical character that would give one the ability to state, to interpret, to define, to argue, concerning abstract conceptions; and that in respect to its outcome, however deep or intense its influence might be, it was peculiarly narrow. Yet on the other hand intellectual interests received general recognition; schools of all grades became abundant; the science of the ancients within this limited field became well known; and the educational world but awaited the development of the new spirit, which came with the fifteenth and the sixteenth century, to become modern.

Even in our judgment of the education and the intellectual life of this period, we are apt to do it injustice because of its difference in spirit from our own; just as during the intervening centuries there has been a very general tendency to deny any merit whatever to the intellectual interests and ability of the entire period, and to hold that educationally it was to be judged and condemned along with the preceding "dark ages." Nevertheless, the education and the intellectual life of these three centuries possessed some merits a characteristic as the peculiar features of the age out of which these merit grow.

The chief of all these merits, though it carried with it certain demerits as well, was its unity. There was an internal unity possessed by the intellectual life itself; there was an external unity of the intellectual life in connection with the religious, the ecclesiastical, the artistic, the political, the economical, the social aspects of life. This unity was found in the dominant religious thought. The thirteenth century possessed a unity of life and of ideas beyond any other century in history.[5] It was the last century in which this peculiar unified life of the Middle Ages dominated. Realism - a monistic idealism - was not only the philosophy of the religion, it was the philosophy of the life of the Middle Ages. As the Gothic cathedrals, another great product of the thirteenth century, were expressions not merely of architectural art, but of the art of painting, sculptoring, glass staining, wood carving, mosaic designing, all unified in the one dominant expression of religious sentiment, so their education was harmonized with their religious life, their political activities their aesthetic aspirations, their moral sympathies, their mystical yearnings, their theological discussions, as well as with their intellectual development. This unifying element was embodied in the dominance of the idea, - of ideals as these express some form of authority. As the Church expressed the absolute authority of the religious life, the scholastic theology the same absolutism in religious belief; as the Holy Roman Empire expressed the same ideal politically, the feudal system socially, the guild system economically; so the universities on the institutional side and scholasticism on the intellectual side expressed in education the dominance of the same absolutism, the same authority.

As long as there is a widespread and general attempt to preserve this unity of life, - that is, during the fourteenth and fifteenth centuries, - the spirit of the Middle Ages persists. Nevertheles, there are continual eruptions of individualism and attempts to overthrow this absolutism, so that in these centuries the perfection and beauty of the system as seen in the thirteenth century no longer prevail. In the attempt to suppress these expressions of individuality, the harshness as well as the defects , the growing formalism and final lifelessness of the earlier period become apparent. It is not until the later fifteenth century that this effort to supplant the dominance of authority by the general sway of individual judgment, and the development of an educational system that possesses no such unity, take place in what is known, par excellence, as the Renaissance. Critical and destructive tendencies then come to demoniate as do the unifying tendencies during the thirteenth century.

Meanwhile there are a few aspects of education during these last mediaeval centuries, besides the universities, that demand brief notice.

THE FRIARS OR THE MENDICANT ORDERS came into general control of higher education by the middle of the thirteenth century. The Franciscans, or Gray Friars, were founded in 1212 and the Dominican, or Black Friars, in 1216. While the primary motive in the mendicant foundations was ascetic, they, especially the Dominicans, soon devoted themselves with their characteristic energy to philosophical study and to the control of educational institutions. The aim of the mendicants, differing from that of the earlier orders, was to save souls, to control people to build up the Church; and to do this they sought directly to control education. The great Schoolmen were mendicants. Alexander of Hales, Bonaventura, Duns Scotus, Roger Bacon, were Franciscans; Albertus Magnus and Thomas Aquinas were Dominicans. The prolonged antagonism between the Thomists and Scotists was but one aspect of the rivalry between these two orders. The fact that they disagreed concerning important theological doctrines and thus kept alive discussions and to a certain extent, the right of private judgment, was of great significance in the intellectual life of the times; the fact that each was at some time convicted of holding heretical doctrines somewhat mitigated the gravity of the offense for others not so powerfully connected, and postponed the day of absolute control of opinion.

The Dominicans, or preaching friars, especially sought to control leaders of thought and of the Church, and hence to establish themselves at the universities. They soon had a convent in every university town. Aiming first to "capture" bachelor or master, they soon sought to control the teaching. The dominance of Thomas Aquinas indicates a success of this ambition in regard to theology, at least. The Dominicans thus became the guardians of orthodoxy; while the Franciscans, with their work among the poor, their democratic sympathies and tendencies were rather the parents of new doctrines and new practical tendencies. The fact that these bodies were preeminently preaching orders, as previous orders had not been, called for a higher degree of intelligence and for more definite training. Hence these friars became educators, in a double sense; first, in that they gave a more general education to all their members than any previous monastic order; second, in that, as preachers, they were teachers of the people and preeminently preachers of doctrine.

INFLUENCE OF SARACEN LEARNING

The history of the learning and the educational activities of Mohammedan society would take long to narrate, but we are here interested in only one aspect of it, its influence upon the development of education in the West during the later Middle Ages. The study of Grecian philosophy on account of its heretical influences, especially in Gnosticism and in the Neoplatonic school, had been suppressed in the Eastern Church by the time of the sixth century and found a home among the Syrians and especially the Nestorian sect of the Christians in the region of western Asia. Here it came in contact with the Arabs and, after the Abbasid dynasty (750 A.D.), was fostered in the capitals of the East. Learned Nestorians were summoned to the Saracen courts; translations into Arabic from the Syriac or the original Greek were made; mathematics and the natural sciences more especially the medical sciences, were fostered. During the tenth century philosophical interests were similarly developed, especially under the leadership of Avicenna (980-1037). In other words, at the time when the Christian schools of both Eastern and Western Europe were falling into decay, the schools of Bagdad, Basra, Kufa, and other Saracen cities were growing into splendid activity and great renown. The character of this philosophical development, founded as it was upon Aristotle, was quite similar to the earlier movement in the Christian Church. It sought to substitute for the supernaturalism of the Mohammedan belief a rationalism or a mysticism similar to that of the Gnostics, and to develop a theology as well as a philosophy upon these later developments of the teachings of Plato and Aristotle. Meeting with the same opposition from orthodox Mohammedanism that it did from orthodox

Christianity, learning, both philosophical and scientific was expelled from the East by the less enlightened fanaticism of the orthodox masses and sought a home in the West among the Moslems of western Africa and of Spain where the caliphates, independent of that of Bagdad, had been established. It cannot be said that this philosophy and learning in general ever affected the massess of the population, or that there was any great creative genius inherent in the Arabic mind. But they were quick to assimilate and to learn, and skillful in elaborating and adapting Aristotelianism to their theology and their scientific knowledge.[5]

In Spain, especially, centering in the school of Cordova, from the tenth century on, this learning received development and many brilliant practical applications. Throughout their western caliphates the Saracens established libraries, higher schools similar to universities and, in connection with the mosques in many cities, schools for the instruction of the children. While Christian Europe was enforcing as a religious belief the idea that the world was flat, the Moors were teaching geography from globes. When the Christians finally conquered the Mohammedans, for want of the knowledge of any other use, they turned their astronomical observatories into belfries. From these Arabs came in the tenth or eleventh century the knowledge of Hindoo notation as a substitute for the cumbersome Roman method. Knowledge of algebra, as well as of advanced arithmetical processes, came from a similar source. In medicine, in surgery, in pharmacy, in astronomy, in physiology, they added much that is now considered elementary. They explained the refraction of light, gravity, capillary attraction, and twilight; they determined the height of the atmosphere the weight of air, the specific gravity of bodies; they constructed various astronomical tables, determined corrections for parallax and for refraction; they invented the pendulum clock; in commerce, in geographical explorations, in navigation, in improvements in all the arts of life, their culture was far ahead of that of the Europeans; they introduced the use of rice, sugar, and cotton, and the cultivation of silk; they made Europe familiar with the use of the compass of gunpowder, and of cannon. Thus in many way the Arab culture served as an educational agency to bring the civilization of the West to a higher level.

But it is in regard to the influence on the schools that we are more directly concerned. By the twelfth century all intellectual vitality had been crushed out in the East, while it was in its most flourishing condition in the West. In the middle of the twelfth century Raymund, archbishop of Toledo, commanded a Jewish scholar to translate the leading works on Arabic philosophy into Castilian; by monks it was translated thence into Latin. Shortly, after this the Emperor Frederick II had the commentaries of Averroes and other Aristotelian writings translated. Only a brief period intervened when, as a result of the Latin conquest of Constantinople, 1204, the Greek version of Aristotle became known and direct translations were made. By the thirteenth century rigid and narrow orthodoxy had triumphed in Saracen Spain, and Aristotelianism and Averroeism were driven out from their previously flourishing seats to find a new home among the Jewish philosophers and in the Christian universities.

Averroeism, at first identified with rationalistic free thought, became, as previously had Aristotelianism, reduced to orthodoxy. At least, this was true so far as it was a commentary upon Aristotle. With the renewal of nominalism in the fourteenth century, the master, upon being given the right to incept, took oath to teach no doctrines contrary to those of "Aristotle and his commentator Averroes". In this form, a well as in the study of medicine and astrology, Arabic learning continued to exert an influence throughout the Middle Ages, when every spark of intellectual vitality had long passsed from the Mohammedan population itself.

FEATURES OF STUDENT LIFE: THE WANDERING SCHOLAR

With the decline of the monastic school in the twelfth and thirteenth centuries, with the renewal of the influence of cathedral and Church school, and with the growth of the universities, student life, now much freer and no longer controlled by monastic rule, began to assume at least upon the Continent, a peculiar form. This feature, which at first affected only the university student, but soon became characteristic of the more elementary students as well, was the custom of migrating from school to school without remaining long in any one community. The friar organizations had conferred new dignity upon the customs of begging which for centuries had been considered a virtue in the clergy complementary to the virtue of giving in the laity, and had added new sanction also to the habit of wandering from place to place. The custom of religious pilgrimage and the Crusades had rendered this wandering life far more common and also more secure; so the wandering student added but one more element to the floating population made up of friars, pilgrims, merchants, craftsmen, knights, and wandering Churchmen.[8]

With the founding of the universities and the establishment of the nations in practically every university, it became quite customary for students to travel from university to university, finding in each a home in their appropriate nation. Many, however, willing to accept the privileges of the clergy and the students without undertaking their obligations, adopted this wandering life as a permanent one. Being a privileged order, they readily found a living or made it by begging. A monk of the early university period writes: "The scholars are accustomed to wander throughout the whole world and visit all the cities; and their many studies bring them understanding. For in Paris they seek a knowledge of the liberal arts; of the ancient writers at Orlean; of medicine at Salernum; of the black art at Toledo; and in no place decent manners."

Just as the resident students were organized into nations so these wandering students were organized into a guild, under the patronage of a titular magister or patron saint, - Golias. Hence they were called goliardi. The typical goliards, those who had accepted this life as a permanent calling, were riotous, unthrifty, unambitious students, who were hanger-on of the higher clergy or who wandered from place to place of ecclesiastical or lay lords. As such they appear in literature, contemporary and modern. They are responsible for a considerable literature of Latin songs similar in many respects to the song of modern college students.

But soon there appeared a new type of wandering student. As the many masters exceeded the demand for university instruction, wandering masters, seeking to attach themselves to chantry and parochial schools, became numerous; and to these were added the youth - the scholars vagantes- who sought to obtain a knowledge of the arts from these school, and at the same time an easy living. The attractions of the world were added to those of the arts for these wandering scholars, and soon the cities of the Continent, now since the thirteenth century numerous and prosperous, were thronged with such students. In the fourteenth and fifteenth century - the limits of the period cannot be assigned - the custom received a further extension. These wandering scholars added to their ranks smaller boys, often not over six or seven years of age, - ABC shooters they were called, - who accompanied them, ostensibly to acquire the rudiments of knowledge and to join the ranks of the older boys, but in reality to attend them as servants, to beg their food, to sing for money or food, in fact to make their living. Such wandering students became so numerous that they necessitated regulation by municipal ordinance. At Nuremberg, the center of German learning and Renaisance influence during the fifteenth century, a city ordinance required that such schools should end out only one begging student at a time, that his operations should be restricted to a given parish, and that he should be identified by the picture of the patron saint of the school, carried on the basket in which victuals were to be collected.

NEW TYPES OF SCHOOLS

The later Middle Ages were well supplied with schools, not all of which were dominated by the Church. For a century before the Reformation it is probable that schools were as numerous and that as wide an opportunity for study existed as for a century afterward, Monastic schools never recovered their importance after the Renaissance of the thirteenth century. Cathedral schools that grew into new prominence in the early university period were insufficient for the demand. Not only secondary but elementary education was provided in the fourteenth and fifteenth centuries in a much more general way than ever before.

An important and probably the most general class of these were the chantry school. Chantry foundations - the gift of property to support a priest in return for prayers for the soul of the benefactor and of his family, or for certain stipulated purposes—were the most common form of benefactions to the Church during the later Middle Ages. Thus it happened that foundations for priests existed beyond all demand for parochial service; as the religious services required by the foundations could occupy but a small portion of time, it became customary to stipulate that such priests should teach the children of the community. As a matter of course, the regulations of these foundations present the greatest variations. Some provide for a small number of children, some for all comers; some provide that instruction shall be gratis, some permit a fee; some indicate that the merest rudiments were taught, others stipulate that instruction shall be given in grammar and the higher branches. In the later towns, where chantry and similar foundations were numerous enough to support a body of priests under collegiate organization, and several priests could be designated as teachers, schools sometimes grew up that rivaled in size and in character of work the schools of the cathedral foundations. It no longer occurs that these schools are controlled by monastic teachers, for aside from the mendicant orders, the monks have largely ceased their general educational activities.

Another type of school, yet more free from ecclesiastical control, was the guild school. Very commonly did the merchant and craft guild support priests for the performance of all sorts of religious services for their members. Such priests saw the child of the guild member received into the world with proper religious rites and saw him decently out; he celebrated for him all the sacraments; frequently he kept school. Some guilds established schools of great repute, which have had long histories. The Merchant Taylors' School of London is probably the most notable. Ordinarily the school was but an elementary one, though often it was also a grammar school for the children of the guild members or for others. Such schools would ordinarily give instruction in other subjects than Latin, and frequently before the Renaissance came to give instruction in the vernacular.

With the coalescing of the guild organization and the early municipal government, these schools along with many of the parish school mentioned above, became in many communities the burgher schools. Such schools were largely controlled and supported by secular authorities, and in the content of their school work better represented the economic interests and demands of the citizen. They were often taught by priests, though lay teachers became more and more numerous. In a similar way private schools, usually of most elementary character, more responsive to new economic and social demands, sprang up. However irregular these private schools were, they yet contributed to the development of independent town schools. Clerical inspection was yet almost universal, and the Church through the scholaticus or some other episcopal officer or even through the parish priests, sought to extend its jurisdiction over both these types of schools.

The tendency toward the establishment of those schools was well marked in the Teutonic countries before the Reformation movement began. In Italy it is doubtful whether the municipal or at least secular private schools had ever ceased to exist. Certain it was that the early universities sprang from such schools where there had been some elementary study of Roman law previous to the foundation of Bologna. During these later medieval centuries such schools, not of a university grade yet free from ecclesiastical control and governed by secular interests, were quite numerous.

While this entire subject of secular schools previous to the Reformation is a question of controversy concerning the interpretation of historical material, it is evident that the preparation has been made before the Reformation for the secularization of education that was to follow.

THE NEW LITERATURES as well as new types of schools gave expression to the new intellectual interests and social demands, and indicated that neither the thought life nor the life of material interest could be restrained within the old channels. It is not to be understood that there were no vernacular literatures before these closing centuries of the Middle Ages. In German, Icelandic, and Anglo-Saxon among the Teutonic peoples, and in French, Irish, and Welsh among the Celts, not to mention other minor tongues, there was a literature covering in a general way the entire dark ages from the sixty to the eleventh century. Treating of the heroic deeds of their leaders, of the wonderful prowess and the petty intrigues of their pagan deities, of Biblical story or of the traditions of their race, such literature as that of the Anglo-Saxon and the old High German is for the most part either a preservation of the old Teutonic culture, now being committed to written record, that represents the continuation of the old in the face of the conquering and hostile Latin culture; or, less frequently, it represents the Latin culture of the Christian Church put into vernacular form.

With the twelfth century, fostered by chivalry and by the Crusade movement with its accompanying motives, there was developed in court and palace, by bard and minstrel, a wholly new literature that finds no parallel and no opportunity for expression in the dominant Latin and ecclesiastical culture. This literature, technically called the Middle English, the Middle German etc., was an outgrowth similar to that of the troubadours of southern and the trouveres of northern France. In amorous tale, knightly adventure, daring just or brilliant tournament, expressing alike the interest of the court and the laity's dislike and suspicion of motive and conduct of monk and priest, this literature is the beginning of modern literature in its expression of new interests and use of new forms, and at the same time a force making for the overthrow of the dominance of authority and a channel for the expression of heretical views.

One other type of literature that represents a protest against the dominant absolutism and bespeaks the coming individualism of the opening of the modern period in the fifteenth-century Renaissance was that created by the wandering scholars. As would be natural to those following the profession of scholarship, these wandering protestants against the fixed hierarchical despotism of established society used the Latin language; but in this they voiced their disgust for the hollow and hypocritical character of the established formalism, and expressed their frank enjoyment of natural interests and of forbidden pleasures and even of gross indulgence. Here, for the first time, is a clear and conscious return to the motives of the classical poets, and the themes and attitude of Horace and Ovid are now repeated in a Latin poetry very different in form from the old.

Both of these new type of literature are subjects, large in themselves, which thus relate to the new intellectual life of the people of the later Middle Ages. It is from the new vernacular literature that there is to develop the great influence, soon no longer connected with the class of chivalric nobility alone. In this respect a connection is made between the old chivalric education and the new education of the Renaissance period. But as yet, however much it may influence the general intellectual life, it has no influence upon school life and upon education in the narrower sense.

In a peculiar and intimate manner one of these works of the new literature, now of the fourteenth century, expresses this connection between the Middle Ages and modern times, and hence may be taken as the concrete connecting link between the two.

THE BANQUET OF DANTE (1263-1321)

It is not with Dante as the chief exponent of the spirit life of man, in which he is as modern as medieval, that we are here concerned; but with Dante as an exponent of mediaeval thought. In an attempt to explain his own writings and to sum up the learning of the times, Dante gives in *The Banquet* (II Convito) a characteristic exposition of the ideas, the intellectual life, and the meaning of education in the Middle Ages. Written probably about 1310, this treatise contains elements that are strikingly modern and others that are typically mediaeval. While in a way it aimed to be one of the encyclopedias of knowledge so characteristic of the Middle Ages, it did not seek to give a summary of facts and events, - the mere externalities of knowledge, - but sought rather to penetrate into the meaning of all this and to give an exposition of its spiritual significance. This desire to penetrate into the inner life, this interest in the subjective, this conception of philosophy and of learning as a means of personal development of culture, which is here approached though not fully set forth, is modern. Another element that is modern is the fact that a large portion of the work (Bk. I, Chs, V-VIII) is devoted to the justification of the use of the vernacular in this and in other of his works. As each one of the main reasons is amplified into a number of points in the most minute analytical manner, the form of the argument becomes a most striking example of the dominant Aristotelianism, although its spirit is a protest against it. The unbounded reverence paid to Aristotle, who is constantly referred to throughout the treatise as "the master," "the philosopher," or simply "he," the one who for Dante was preemininently the "master of those who know," together with this method of scholastic analysis borrowed from the master and the methods of fourfold interpretation (Bk. II, Ch. I), - the literal, the allegorical, the mystical, and the anagogical or moral, - all these are aspects of the mediaevalism of the great poet. In this respect The Banquet becomes a most striking exponent of the intellectual life of the Middle Ages.

In Dante's greatest work, the *Divine Comedy*, this fourfold interpretation is most readily seen. In a literal sense the Commedia is a presentation of the rewards and punishments, the destiny of man in the hereafter; allegorically, it is a presentation of the virtues and vices of the human soul as illustrated in concrete examples and in the details of the plan; morally, it has as its social, political, and ethical purposes, the making of worthier citizen, better neighbors, nobler men, mystically, it typifies the struggle of the human soul to become free, its growth through sin to holiness, its progress from the finite to the divine. In a similar way The Banquet is a fourfold interpretation of some stanzas, written in earlier life of Beatrice, - now identified with philosophy, - in which exposition the entire scheme of the thought-life and incidentally of the education of the Middle Ages is set.

The conception of the universe here presented (The Banquet, BKI. II, Chs. III-VI) gives the cosmology, the theology, the psychology, the educational theory, of the Middle Ages.

For the unintelligent the world was a flat disk, around which flowed the stream Oceanus, and over which was placed a crystal vault, in which were fixed, as in a ceiling, the sun, moon, and stars. Beyond this vault lived the gods and spirits, and thus the entire universe was composed. But in the minds of the intelligent there prevailed a system founded primarily on the idea of the Greek philosophers, and called the Ptolemaic. This universe as made entirely for man is thus described by Dante. With the earth as a center the heavens consist of nine huge spheres fitting one into the other, which turn one upon the other. To the first seven of these spheres are fixed in succession the moon, Mercury, Venus, the sun, Mars, Jupiter, and saturn. As the spheres move in one direction the "planets" move slowly in the opposite. Beyond the seventh heaven is that of the fixed stars; the ninth is the "crystalline heavens," or the Primum Mobile, moving with greatest rapidity and imparting its movements to all the rest. The tenth heaven is the Empyreum, or "luminous heaven," which alone as the abode of eternal rest, is without movement.

"And this is the reason that the Primum Mobile moves with immense velocity; because the fervent longing of all its parts to be united to those of this tenth and most divine and quiet heaven, makes it revolve with so much desire that its velocity is almost incomprehensible. And this quiet and peaceful heaven is the abode of that Supreme Deity who alone doth perfectly behold Himself. This is the abode of the beatified spirits, according to the holy church, who cannot lie, and Aristotle also seems to think so, if rightly understood, in the first of The Heavens and Earth. This is the supreme edifice of the universe, in which all the world is included, and beyond which is nothing; and it is not in space, but was formerly solely in the Primal Mind, which the Greek call Protoma. This is that magnificence of which the Psalmist spake, when he says to God, `Thy magnificence is exalted above the Heavens."

The entire explanation of Dante's (Bk. II, Ch. IV), in its

dependence upon authority, in its attempt to harmonize Greek philosopher and Hebrew psalmist, in its allegorical interpretation of texts, in its arrangement of argument, is typically mediaeval.

The hierarchy of heavenly spheres is paralleled by these successive hierarchies of spirits which preside over them. "The motive powers of the Heaven of the Moon are of the order of Angels; and those of Mercury of Archangels; and those of Venu are the Thrones, which informed of the love of the Holy spirit, perform their work, that is the movement of this heaven filled with love, according to the nature of that love." Vergil, Ovid, mediaeval astrology, and the Bible are unified in this interpretation. Then follow, corresponding to the appropriate spheres, dominions, virtues, principalities, powers, Cherubim, and Seraphim; finally the trilogy is completed with the dominance of the Trinity over the Empyreum. Thus again are the angels and spirits of the Bible, the ideas of Plato, the word of St. John, the gods of classic mythology, the mysticism and demonology of the Middle Ages unified and interpreted. Thus are explained the stages of development of the human soul; thus, in the impartation of movement from the crystalline to the other heavens, and the longing "of every particle of the crystalline heaven to be united with every particle of the most divine tranquil heaven," the pervading love and unifying tendency, the uplifting influence of the love of God.

But this unity and this interpretation includes not the spiritual and moral life alone; it dominates the intellectual, which is incorporated in the same general explanation. It is impossible in a restricted space to enter into all the intricacies of the reasons why, as he states, "he says heaven when he means science, and heavens when he means science," "To the first seven correspond the seven sciences of the Trivium and the Quadrivinum, that is, to Grammar, Dialectic, Rhetoric, Arithmetic, Music, Geometry, and Astrology. To the eighth sphere, that is, to the starry Heavens, correspond Natural

Science called Physics, and the first of sciences called Metaphysics; to the ninth sphere corresponds Moral Science; and to the Quiet Heaven corresponds Divine Science, which is called Theology." Hence throughout the treatise wherever he uses the term heavens or any particular heaven, he is referring to the appropriate science, and describing in an allegorical way its characteristics and influences.

The heaven of Venus is compared with rhetoric, because it is the most charming of all the sciences, as Venus is the brightest of the planets; and because as Venus is now a morning, now an evening star, so rhetoric now as oratory appears before the face of the speaker, now as literature, speaks from a distance. The sun is compared with arithmetic, because it illumines all the other sciences and because, as the eye cannot look upon the sun, so "the eye of the intellect cannot look upon it; because Number, considered in itself, is infinite, and that we cannot comprehend."

Though but three of the proposed fourteen books, or courses at this intellectual banquet were completed, and hence, though a most complete and authoritative summary of the learning of the Middle Ages by its greatest genius is denied us, yet in the fragment written the spirit of the intellectual life of the Middle Ages, the spirit that partakes both of scholasticism and mysticism, finds one of its clearest expressions. It illustrates perfectly this judgment of Federn; "There never was a time when so little, and at the same time so much was known a in the Middle Ages, for people really knew everything; they had a ready explanation for every phenomenon; very clever explanations they often were, but always untested; whatever was or seemed possible, whatever could be made plausible in words, was immediately accepted; people did not like to doubt, and even the impossible could be dealt with and accepted as a miracle."

REFERENCES

1. Books not dealing specially with education but of fundamental importance in acquiring an understanding of the period.

Adams, *Civilization during the Middle Ages.* (New York, 1899).

Draper, *The Intellectual Development of Europe.* (New York, 1876.)

Gibbon, *Decline and Fall of the Roman Empire,* esp. Chs. 16-20, and 37.

Hatch, *Influence of Greek Ideas and Usages on the Christian Church.* (London, 1895.)

Lecky, *History of European Morals from Augustus to Charlemagne,* (New York, 1870.)

MacCabe, *St. Augustine and his Age.* (New York, 1903.)

MacCabe, *Abelard.* (New York, 1901.)

Maitland, *The Dark Ages.* (London, 1890.)

Milman, *History of Early Christianity.* (London, 1883.)

Milman, *History of Latin Christianity.* (London, 1883.)

Montalembert, *The Monks of the West.* (New York, 1896.)

Poole, *Illustration of Mediaeval Thought.* (London, 1884.)

Sandys, *A History of Classifical Scholarship.*

Taylor, *Classical Heritage of the Middle Ages.* (New York, 1901.)

Townsend, *Great Schoolmen of the Middle Ages.* (London, 1881.)

II. Books relating directly to education.

Compayre, Abelard and the Origin and Early History of Universities (New York, 1897.)

Cornish, *Chivalry,* esp. Ch. III. (London, 1901.)

Drane, *Christian Schools and Scholars,* (London, 1881.)

Emerton, *Mediaeval Europe,* Ch. 13. (New York, 1894.)

Gaskoin, *Alcuin, his Life and his Works.* (London, 1904.)

Laurie, *Rise and Constitution of Universities,* (New York, 1887.)

Mill, *History of Chivalry,* Vol. I, Ch. II, (London, 1826.)

Monroe, *Thomas Platter and the Educational Renaissance of the Sixteenth Century.* (New York, 1994.)

Montalembert *The Monks of the West.* Bk. 18, Ch. iv.

Mullany, *Essay Educational,* I and 2. (Chicago, 1896.)

Mullinger, *The School of Charles the Great.* (London, 1877.)

Rashdall, *Univerities of Europe in the Middle Age,* 3 vol. (Oxford 1895.).

Robinson. *Readings in European History*. (Boston, 1904.)
West, *Alcuin and the Rise of Christian Schools*. (New York, 1892.)
Williams, *Education during the Middle Ages*. (Syracuse, 1903.)

Topics for Further Investigation

1. Compare the basis of the disciplinary conception of education in the Middle Ages with the basis of the modern conception of education as formal discipline.

2. What relation can you discover between the conception of the depravity of human nature held throughout the Middle Ages and the attitude toward interest in education?

3. What provisions for literary and intellectual education can you discover in the rules of the various monastic orders?

4. Work out the history of the educational influence of any one particular monastery, e.g. St. Gall, Fulda, Reichnau, Monte Cassino, etc.

5. Work out the educational influence of any one monastic order, especially of the mendicant orders in any one country; e.g. the Franciscans or Dominicans in England.

6. To what extent could the duty of copying manuscripts furnish education to the monks?

7. Trace the development of the conception of the Seven Liberal Arts.

8. What was the content of the Seven Liberal Arts as presented by any one writer? E.g. Alcuin, Rabanus Maurus, etc.

9. What similarity exists between the symbolism in education in mediaeval ages and that of modern time?

10. What connection do you find between the chivalric education and the conception of education of modern times, later discussed under the head of social realism?

11. What connection between these two and that modern view which holds that the chief function of college education is to produce the character of a "gentleman of leisure and of culture"?

12. Work out in detail the education of a page or of a squire.

13. What educational value can you discover in the study of dialectic as pursued by the Schoolmen?

14. Which of the two methods of scholastic study possessed the

greater educational value? Why? Which possessed the greater social value? Why?

15. Compare a day in the life of a university student in a mediaeval university with one in the life of a modern university student, with an attempt to discover the educational value of the activities of each.

16. Select some of the questions debated by the Schoolmen, and indicate the educational value to be derived from their study.

17. Study in detail the life of any one of the great Schoolmen, and from his teachings and writings indicate the educational significance.

18. Work out in detail the nature of the nations, the development of the faculty, the course of study of any one mediaeval university.

19. Describe the influence of the frairs on the life of any one mediaeval university.

20. Describe in greater detail the influence of Aristotle on the mediaeval university.

21. Trace the influence of the Saracens on any one subject of study during the later Middle Ages. (See the general hitorical material relating to the early histories of universities.)

22. Describe the life of the wandering scholar as given in the autobiography of Thomas Platter or of Johannes Butabach.

23. Describe the beginnings of the secular schools of any one country during these later mediaeval centuries.

Notes

1. What Professor McGiffert say of the institution as a whole, may quite a truthfully be applied to its educational importance: "Within monasticism's mighty bosom have urged the passions and the longings of multitudes of the noblest and of the meanest of the sons of earth. Hope, fear, love, hate, humility, pride, self effacing devotion, self-asserting ambition, world-renunciation, and world-conquest all the impulses of which the human heart is capable have flourished in monasticism's fruitful soil. The study of monasticism is the study not of a minor government or of a idea eddy within the Christian Church, but of Chritanity itself, for Christanity was for centuries monasticism. But the study of monaticism is study not of Christianity alone, but of life - for

monasticism was for centuries life at its noblest and its basest." (Harnack, Monasticism, Introduction.) In its educational relationship monasticism presents a similar diversity of types.

2. Furnival, *Education in Early England,* p. ii.

3. See Rashdall, Vol. I, pp. 518-525,

4. See Fredric Harrison, *The Meaning of History*, Ch. V, A Survey of the thirteenth century.

5. For a fuller convenient outline of Saracen learning, see Davidson, History of Education, pp. 138-149, and an article by Wallace in *Encyclopaedia Britannica* for it influence on philosophy, see Uberweg, *History of Philosophy*, Vol. I, pp. 402-428; for its relation to Christian theology, see Moeller, *History of the Christian Church during the Middle Ages*, pp. 422-435; for it influence on universities, see Rashdall, *University of Europe in the Middle Ages*, Vol. I, pp. 351-368; and for the general, scientific, and intellectual character of Saracen culture, see Draper, *Intellectual Development of Europe,* Vol. II, Ch. II.

6. See Chaucer' Canterbury Pilgrim for contempory description, Juscrand's English Wayfaring Life in the Middle Ages for modern description; also the author's Thomas Plattier and the Educational Renaissance of the Sixteenth Century.

2

The Larger Education of the Middle Ages

For more than three hundred years historians had represented the Middle Ages as almost completely benighted. Then came a reaction to this gross untruth which was often equally violent and tended to exaggerated praise. For a time the Middle Ages were a battlefield of biased writers. Latterly, under the lead of such accurate and scientific historian as Fustel de Coulanges, Denifle, Maitland, Poole, Langlois, Sandys, Paetow, Rand, and Haskins, a genuine history of the Middle Ages is being written. Cool and dispassionate consideration of the evidence at hand shows us the Middle Ages, from the eleventh century onward, as a period of great achievement in education, which deserves to stand out in history, both for its absolute excellences and by comparison with the educational development of mankind in other ages. The educational agents shaping the minds and characters of Europeans during those centuries which are the real Middle Ages were numerous and complicated.

The Crusades

First in time, and possibly in importance, are the Crusades. It cannot be too much stressed that these were more than mere military ventures; they were great social and religious movements. They affected, directly or indirectly, every man woman, and child in Europe. They profoundly influenced thought, feeling, and conduct. They were more significant, in their social effects, than the westward movement of peoples some seven or eight centuries before, which played a considerable part in what we think of as the 'fall of the Roman Empire'. There were four of these Crusades between 1096 and 1024. They began in an amazing enthusiasm, made up, in part of religious zeal, in part of sentimental and chivalrous romance, which gathered the isolated units of Western society into a united activity and a common purpose; the recapture for Christendom of the Holy Land. Although they failed in that purpose, they achieved something much greater for Europe.

Important, though not lasting, in their moral influence. The educational effect of such a gigantic unifying of thought and emotion can scarcely be exaggerated. Its moral results were, as is always the case, only temporary; but whilst they lasted, they were very great; in the sudden sweep of high purpose lifting a crude lot of men, for the moment at least, above the humdrum plodding selfishness of their individual lives. The enthusiasm flickered and very nearly died entirely; and when it was revived, it was revived by motives much more secular in character by greed for wealth, by mere vagabond love of adventure. The Firt Cruade was what the modern commercial mind considers a sublime insanity; but even that type of mind concedes that it was sublime. The Fourth Crusade culminated in the brutal sack of Constantinople; it fell to the level of a modern war. In 1095, the cry, "God wills it!" electrified Europe. In 1254, even so chivalrous a man as de Joinville is delicately balancing the call of the Crusade against his castle life in Champagane. In 1270, Rutebeuf's Descroizie bluntly argues for staying at home.

Even more important as means of social education. Yet, however much the moral influence of the Crusades diminished, their social effect was maintained and grew. They bound men together with new bonds, they stimulated communal effort, they brought about new industries, new intellectual efforts in organizing human relations, new activities of commerce. The growth of towns and cities is a direct result of the Crusades; the mediaeval guilds are at least an indirect result; and one would be very lacking indeed in historical sense who could not see how powerfully the momentum of closely organized town life influenced the education of Europe. Its effect upon the development of law has been studied. But much more important is its general social effect, upon manners, speech, customs, amusements, worships, industries, and arts.

The guilds

The most significant feature of that town life in the Middle Ages was the guild. There were four sorts of guilds: the strictly religious confraternity of lay folk; the frith (peace) guild, closely allied to the religious; the merchant guild; and the craft guild. Some of the religious and frith guilds date as far back as the early eleventh century, the oldest guild charter extant being that of Abbotsbury in Dorset, in the time of Canute. But the great period of the guilds is in the twelfth and thirteenth centuries. During the reign of Edward I, ninety-two of the one hundred and sixty towns represented in the English parliament had merchant guilds. It was the merchant guilds that formed the basis of the Hanseatic League, which was begun in the thirteenth century, reached the height of its influence in the fifteenth century, and held its last meeting in 1669. The craft guilds were still more important as part of the larger educational influences of the Middle Ages. They were the last type of guild to come into existence, and began to appear in the twelfth century. The merchant guilds promptly had come to be the real executive in most of the municipalities; but gradually the craft guilds supplanted them. By 1340 there were forty-eight craft guilds in London alone.

Informed with Catholic principles. All of these types of guild were permeated with Catholic principles. Each had its chaplain, its religious services, its masses for deceased members of the guild; each recognized and accepted the moral obligations of charity, care of orphans, justice amongst its members. Each was a relatively small company, a sort of overgrowth of the family, its members so closely bound together that a common spirit animated them. To compare them to modern labor unions is as absurd as to hope to revive them; for one thing, we should first have to revive the Catholic atmosphere of the Middle Ages. Particularly in the craft guilds was this spirit manifest. The members were divided into apprentices, journeymen (from journee, the day: as they were paid a daily wage), and masters. The guild demanded a proof of skill in its craft, the 'masterpiece', as a condition of admission to the grade of master; but it further demanded high moral qualifications before it allowed a master to take any youth as apprentice. The apprentice was bound to a fixed term of training, varying from two to ten years, according to the difficulties of each craft; he lived as a member of the master's household; and the master was bound to give him the best training with in his power. Wage disputes were settled within the guild. There were no class distinctions, no falsely opposed interests of employer and employed. Every master was simply an educated apprentice, and every apprentice a future master. Thus the whole industrial life of the towns was essentially a process of education, with carefully planned aims and methods, and with a balance of physical, intellectual, and moral elements which commands our admiration.

Mediaeval architecture and art. Detailed studies of the guilds are matters for the historical experts. But the guilds have left eloquent monuments throughout Europe which must impress even the dullest minds. These monuments are the cathedrals, town halls, and guild halls of the Middle Ages. The architecture and art of a people may always be taken as one of the soundest displays of its culture. They represent, not merely the technical skill of artists and artisans, but the mental and moral qualities of the whole society back of them. The Parthenon throws light upon the entire fabric of Attic civilization: so too does Chartres illumine the Middle Ages.

A spontaneous growth. Mediaeval architecture and art, which we now rather stupidly call 'Gothic,'[1] is most amazingly the lively and self-originated expression of the Middle Ages. Ralph Adams Cram says very significantly: "Normandy in the eleventh century was simply Cluny in action."[2] From Normandy the new art sprang, and when political turmoil checked its further development there, it leaped up like a flame in the Champagne and the Ile de France. The twelfth century saw the growth of architectural structure that still remains one of the great triumphs of human intelligence; the thirteenth century made beauty grow about that structure in exquisite sculpture, glass, and mural decoration. A very passion of church building swept over western Europe. "It was", says Rudolph of Cluny, in the midst of it, "as if the world, shaking itself, and casting aside old things, were putting on a white robe of churches."

And an unmatched educational movement. When a man of today looks at what remains of that 'white robe of churches', not great cathedrals alone, but parish churches in the smaller cities and towns and villages, he may not realize at first that whole peoples built them. They are not the work of an isolated genius, here and there, but the enthusiastic product of tens of thousands of craftsmen who seem to our modern minds almost incredibly inspired. There is abundant evidence to show that each locality furnished the skilled and devoted craftsmen who built the local church or town hall or guild hall. When we consider as Thorndike points out, that in our own time skilled workmen are too few even to build a copy of a mediaeval church.[3] we may get some concept of the nature and extent of mediaeval guild education.

Mediaeval drama. Another large factor in the education of a people is its drama, which mirrors as well as forms popular taste and ideals. It is most significant of the chaos of the 'Dark Ages' that they had no drama. The old Roman theatre had disappeared entirely, and nothing took its place until Europe was ready to produce a new drama of its own, expressing its own new spirit and its own new concept of art. The mediaeval drama owes nothing directly to antique Greek or Roman models; it is as fresh and vitally new as mediaeval architecture, and like that architecture it centers supremely in Catholic faith and worship.

Its development. Mediaeval drama took its origins from liturgical sources. It may be said to begin as far back as Carolingian times, in the dramatization of sequences in the Mass. Catholic churches were its first habitat, and continued exclusively to shelter it until the twelfth century, when it moved out, first into churchyards, then into town squares and marketplace. Its structure grew from a brief scene, with a few figures, into complete plays which would not appear at all strange to a Shakespeare. Its language was Latin in the beginning, but Latin was gradually supplanted by the developing vernacular. Thus in the 'mystery' of The Wise Virgins, about 1130 the chorus chaints in Latin, Christ and the VIRGINS speak a mixture of French and Latin, the angels speak French only. The Adam mystery is in French, but all the directions to the actors are in Latin.[4] The subject matter too changes. In the earlier plays the subject is strictly liturgical or scriptural; by the twelfth century, the `miracles' of saints become more prominent; and in the fourteenth century `renaissance' in France and England, the greater number of plays are `moralities,' concerned with a personification of vices and virtue.[5] The institution of the feast of Corpus Christi in 1264 gave a great impetus to mediaeval drama.

Its influence, Mediaeval drama was much more intimately a part of common life than is modern drama. It was produced not by a small group of professional actors, but by the people themselves. The plays quite simply grew up in the parishes and the guilds. They had the same local influence that mediaeval architecture had, since they drew their performers from the same town or village group which furnished the audience. There is a manifest educational character in this close conjunction of the drama with the people. It may not make for the highest dramatic art, but it does stimulate very widely the impuse to dramatic expression. After many generations, our 'little theatres' are trying to get back to it today. Further, as an important work of education, the mediaeval drama admirably Christianized one of the chief recreations of the people.

Mediaeval poetry. It is not too much to say that the huge masses of the mediaeval people had a finer appreciation of poetry than many even of our 'educated' people have today. It is hard to imagine an average college graduate of the present getting as much enjoyment out of poetry as did the simple common folk of the Middle Ages. Their poetry, like their drama, grew out of the Church. The Mediaeval hymns led the way into new forms of Latin verse,[6] into the development of vernacular verse. To the modern mind the mingling of sacred and profane subjects in mediaeval poetry is often shocking; but it was not shocking to a people for whom the most sacred elements of religion were part of their daily life. It is not without significance that the composition and popular spread of the *chansons de gestes* are bound up with religious pilgrimages, or that the wildest burlesques of the carmina burana are linked with Catholic worship. The road to Compostela or to Rome was, in the Middle Ages, also the road to Parnassus. The technical excellence of that poetry, both religious and secular, is very high.[7] For all its simplicity, it is vivid, intensely imaginative, melodious. And it went everywhere, was chanted in hovels as well as in castles. From mouth to mouth it travelled across western Europe, for books were scarce, and the people depended more upon hearing than upon reading. There was not a tavern in Europe that had not often rung to the splendor of epic song. The wandering minseral of the Middle Ages was a great educator.

The lessor schools. All these social, industrial, commercial, religious, and aesthetic activities are most vital agencies of popular education. The fact that they are not formally and consciously educational increases, rather than lessens, their influence upon the people. But to our modern minds, rooted in the mob conviction that formal schools are the most important means of education, it may be of comfort to know that the Middle Ages were also well supplied with schools. These were of several sorts; grammar schools attached to cathedral or collegiate churches, chantry schools,[8] parish schools, burgh or town schools, guild schools, 'venture' schools conducted privately.

The work of the Church. As is to be expected, the earlier elementary and grammar schools were always bound up with some church or monastery or hospital. Even in the twelfth century, most of these schools were actually conducted in a church or monastery;[9] and when they multiplied so as to need space beyond the church, they were still taught by priests and clerics. There was some jealousy of the growing schools. Bishops and abbots were loath to see them pass in any way from under their immediate control. The Third Lateran Council, in 1179 had to forbid local authorities to exact money from schoolmasters for license to teach,[10] and the Fourth Lateran, in 1215, had to renew the decree. But this only shows that the Church as opposed to some churchmen, was doing all it could to facilitate the spread of school. When the first new enthusiasm for schools for the people at large began to affect Europe, there were no religious orders dedicated to teaching; these were first instituted only in the fourteenth century, one of the earliest and most noted being the Brothers of the Common Life, founded at Deventer by Gerard Groot, about 1380. But in the meantime the Church fostered schools by every means which it found to hand.[11]

Increased steadily. It was naturally the demand for schools which caused the supply of them to grow. In the tax rolls of Philip the Fair, for the year 1292, Paris is shown to have, outside of the many church schools, eleven schoolmasters and one schoolmistress. Within sixty years the number had grown to forty-one masters and twenty two mistresses. Grant says that by the fifteenth century "schools were planted in every considerable town in Scotland."[12] Babeau asserts that schools were relatively more numerous in mediaeval France than in modern times.[13] Leach from a careful compilation of figures taken from contemporary records, estimates that in England in the fourteenth century, there was one grammar school to every 5,625 people, as contrasted with one to every 23,750 people in 1864.[14] This means a supply of schools in the fourteenth century about four times more abundant than in the nineteenth.

The character of the schools. In spite of natural diversities, the mediaeval elementary and grammar schools are of a distinct and common type. They were mostly small schools,[15] and mot frequently under single teacher. Although there was, of course, progression in studies, there was no distinction of grades, no grouping into classes, but each pupil was taught individually, just as had been done in Athenian schools of fifteen centuries earlier.[16] The discipline was rigorous; the bundle of rods was the school master's insignia.[17] Until the close of the Middle Ages, the first instruction was in Latin, the vernacular coming later.[18] The Catholic religion and Catholic practices, as is obvious, were interwoven with other instruction, since the whole Western world was still Catholic. After his ABC book (and even that contained Latin prayers), the child's first book was the collection of psalms and prayers for the Sunday Office.[19] Reading was more stressed than writing. Indeed, up to the fifteenth century, the general run of people were but little able to write. One reason for that is that writing was looked upon as a professional work, and since the schoolmaster was also frequently the village scribe, he jealously guarded his privilege, and was not eager to teach his art to others.[20] Arithmetic was mostly limited to little more than simple enumeration. Even though Leonardo Febonacci, a Pisan merchant published a book on arithmetic in 1202, in which he used what we now call the Arabic notation, and decimals, the primary schools did not study arithmetic during the Middle Ages. There is no mention of it in the schools upto 1541.[21]

Management of schools. In the management of such small schools, with so limited a curriculum, and with the comparatively simple methods of individual instruction, the chief problem of management was the supply of competent teachers.[22] It may seem curious to many persons that the procedure for the control of teachers should have changed so little from the Middle Ages to the present time. It consisted in the grant of a license to teach, issued by various corporate bodies: such as a cathedral chapter, or its official, a chancellor of a university or a diocese. In some cases, the license was granted "only to those who had already shown their capacity by actual teaching under supervision."[23] But so much care was not always taken. There were plenty of wandering schoolmasters, 'vagantes,' 'grammarians' such as Erasmus so bitterly describes in the Encomium Moriae.[24] In time, each town of any considerable size took over the control of licenses and of schools; and guild school and venture schools merged into burgh schools. It was naturally a gradual process, and although the resultant organization varied somewhat in different towns its general similarity throughout Europe was striking. The Middle Ages had a genius for uniformity, because of the spiritual and traditional bonds which linked one country with another. Such uniformity, however, could not, and did not, extend to the age at which children began to go to school; that age, and the number of years spent at school, obviously varied with varying conditions and circumstances. But roughly we may estimate three or four years of school as the average for the great mass of children. The school day was long, beginning at half-past seven in the summer and an hour later in winter.

Games. As in all ages, mediaeval children played various games of ball, the most popular being football and a form somewhat resembling hockey. In another game, two contestants, standing each on one leg, and putting the soles of their free feet one against the other, strove by pushing to topple each other over. They tilted at rings, in limitation of the jousts. They flew hawks. But the prime school-boy sport was cockfighting, or, where the boy were too poor to own fighting birds, the still more savage sport of chasing and killing a cock with sticks.[25]

Financial support of schools. Most of the earlier primary schools were endowed by pious founders, and made no charge for tuition. The guilds also maintained free schools in some places. When the towns took over existing schools or established new schools they usually made some provision for their support from communal funds. But as the number of pupils grew, these ancient foundations frequently became inadequate, and had to be supplemented by fees. In general, throughout the Middle Ages, the schoolmaster was both more respected and better paid than in classic antiquity; in many of the English schools, for instance, his salary amounted to three or four times the wages of a skilled craftsman.[26]

Town and country. Schools were by no means limited to the towns, yet in general town children fared better than country children in opportunities for school education, just as they do today. The children of burghers, merchants, craftsmen, had no legal disabilities in the way of their schooling, but the children of farm laborers had. It must be remembered that the common people of the country side were still in thrall under the feudal system, and were only gradually being freed from serfdom. In England, it was only as late as 1406, in the 'Statute of Apprentices,' that all restrictions regarding school were lifted from the farm laborers. Up to that time, the villein had to get leave of his feudal lord to send his child to school, and failure to get such leave was punishable by fine. It must be said, however, that in the thirteenth and fourteenth centuries such leave was generally granted. But the mere fact of having to ask for it militated to a great extent againt school education for children outside the towns.

Conclusion

It would be absurd to claim that these various agencies of education achieved anything approaching perfection in the development of the people of mediaeval Europe. But it would be unfair to deny that they did accomplish a great deal. They did develop in the people a broad grasp of great truths, a sound moral judgment, an appreciation of beauty, many social virtues, and a considerable capacaity for organization. They did not appreciably raise the level of material living, in comfort of housing sanitation, hygiene, and means of communication; and for that reason, we of today, who so highly esteem our progress in these matters, are likely to undervalue the great educational work of the Middle Ages, which was decidedly more in the spiritual than in the material order. It was very imperfect in that order too; but it lifted Europe to a balance between the temporal and eternal which it had never known before and seems never to have gained again since that time.

Topics for Discussion

1. The educational effect of the Children's Crusades.
2. The influence of the Crusades on hospitals and medical education.
3. The guild schools.
4. Comparison between mediaeval parish players and the modern "Little Theatre."
5. The relations between education and material progress in the Middle Ages.

6. The intimacy of mediaeval religion as shown in the miracle plays.

REFERENCES

1. The name 'Ghotic' is an honored one today, but it was first applied to mediaeval architecture and art as a term of derision. The fifteenth century 'renaissance' in Italy, enamored of all things Greek and Roman, affected to despise mediaeval art; and because that art had come to Italy through some German craftsmen, it was called 'Ghotic' as a synonym for 'barbaric.' Cram insists that it proper name is 'Catholic architecture and art.' But of course such a name would damn it a today as thoroughly as 'Gothic' damned it in the mouth of Giorgio Vasari.
2. *Catholic Encyclopedia*, Vol. 6, p. 667.
3. *History of Mediaeval Europe*, p. 418.
4. The oldest extant English play, *The Harrowing of Hell*, dates from the thirteenth century. There are one hundred and eight of the earlier mystery and miracle plays still in existence. The Towneley Mysteries, published by the Surtees Society, 1836, contains thirty three plays, which cover almost the complete historical outline of the Old and New Tetaments. The 1912 edition of Everyman (Everyman's Library, London and New York) contains eight miracle plays in modernized English, including *The Harrowing of Hell*; and has a useful introduction.
5. The 'miracle' plays of the fourteenth century are almost all about our Lady. Forty-two of them survive.
6. Mediaeval rhymed verse appears here and there even in the four thick volumes of Poetae Latini aevi Carolini. It reached its finest development in the twelfth century. Abelard wrote great poetry. The De Contemptu Mundi of Bernard of Morlaix, a Cluniac monk, is an astonishing work of verification in intricate triple rhyme. It contains nearly three thousand hexameter lines and was written about 1140 and dedicated to Peter the Venerable, Abbot of Cluny. It has been edited by Thomas Wright, *Master of the Rolls Series*, Vol. 59 (ii), 1872.
7. See the interesting technical discussion of mediaeval poetry in G. Kar, Thoughts on the Mediaeval Lyrics, Oxford, 1933; and for a handy collection of original texts (with English translation by H. Waddell), Mediaeval Latin Lyrics, London, 1929.
8. Endowed schools connected with some chapel or church, in which the priest was bound by terms of the endowment to chant

Mass for the repose of the souls of the founders, and to teach a certain number of children free of charge. It is estimated that there were over three thousand such chantries in England at the time of their suppression in the 'Reformation'; and though there is much uncertainty as to how many of them had schools attached, the most hostile reckoning concedes that there were some three hundred chantry schools.

9. See the story of Reginald of Durham, in Grant, *History of the Burgh and Parish Schools of Scotland*, p. 5.

10. Mansi, Conc. Ampl. Collectio, tom, xxi, col. 523, canon xviii Pope Alexander III made notable efforts to increase schools, and to make them readily accessible to the poor. Cf. Leach, Schools of Mediaeval England, pp. 132, 133.

11. There can be no manner of doubt that all the cathedral and collegiate churches kept schools, and that the schoolmaster was one of the most important of their officers and school teaching one of the most important of their functions." Leach, Schools of Mediaeval England, p. 115. "It may be stated with some confidence that at least in the later middle age, the smallest towns and even the larger villages possessed schools where a boy might learn to read and to acquire the first rudiments of ecclesiastical Latin, while except in very remote and thinly populated regions, he would never have to go far to find a regular grammar school." H. Rashdall, Universities of Europe in the Middle Ages, Vol. 2, p. 602.

12. History of the Burgh and Parish Schools of Scotland, p. 25.

13. Instruction Primairae dans les Campagnes avant 1789, p. 41.

14. The Schools of Medieval England, p. 331.

15. The number of pupils might be as small as twenty or thirty, and very rarely was more than a hundred and fifty. Leach, ibid., gives some definite figures, p. 330.

16. John of Salisbury (1110-1180) in Metalogicus, lib. ii, cap. x, gives a sketch of school occupations which impress us by their variety and which might come with a shock of surprise to modern opponents of the simultaneous method.

17. Though St. Anselm of Bec. had shrewdly argued against the rod (Cf. Drane, *Christian Schools and Scholars*, 2d ed., 1881, p. 314) yet Gulbert de Nogent, born a generation after him (c. 1053), tells us of getting such a severe beating in school that his mother in tears wished to forbid him to continue his studies. Monodiarum, lib. cap. 6 (Migne, P.L. 156:894).

18. The change to primary instruction in the vernacular was not completed in England until the sixteenth century. (Cf. Mulcaster Positions, p. 31.) St. Jean Baptiste de la Salle had a hard struggle to introduce the change in France in the seventeenth century. In the twelfth century the common language of western Europe was Latin ... Men prayed in Latin, sang in Latin, preached in Latin ... It was the language of learning and education everywhere... Latin remained a living language until it was killed by the revival of antique standards in the fifteenth century." C.H. Haskins, *The Renaissance of the Twelfth Century*, pp. 127-29.

19. "Beyond a doubt we must attribute to the study of the psalms made in schools the universal taste preserved by all classes of mediaeval society for the almost daily recital of the psalter." De Charmasse, Etat de Plnstruction Primaire dans PAncion Diocese Autun, Paris, 1878, p. 22. See also P.J. McCormick, *Education of the Laity in the Early Middle Ages*, Washington, 1915.

20. Cf. Rendu, De P Education populaire dans P Allemagne du Nord, p. 8.

21. Even in 1719, an arithmetic published at Litle, and called "Instruction nouvelle pour enselgner aux enfants le chiffre et a sommer."as looked upona novelty. Resbecq analyses it in his Histoire to Instruction Primaire dans le Department du Nord, Paris, 1878. pp. 84 - 85.

22. With all our complications of schools, that may be said to be still the chief problem of management. It is an open question whether or not we have made any nearer approach to a solution of it.

23. In the "Ancient Ordinances for Masters in Grammar" of the thirteenth century. Cf. Leach, Schools of Medieval England. pp. 174-175. The method of our normal schools is nearly as ancient as all else in school education; but their distinct organization dates only from St. Jean Baptiste de la Salle.

24. Pp. 34, 35 of ed. Florentlae, 1518. In translation by White Kennett of 1683, edited by H. Bridges. Chicago, 1925, pp. 108-12, See also H. Waddell, *The Wandering Scholars*, London, 1927.

25. Leach, Schools of Medieval England, p. 174. In many instances, the schoolmaster himself was bound to furnish the cook. Delisale cites a schoolmaster of Dieppe, in 1282, who was under obligation for four. Studies sur in Class Agricole en Norfmandie au Moyen Age, p. 185.

26. Leach gives some detailed statistics concerning fees and salaries, op. cit., pp. 171-75, 184, 196, 210, 211.

3

Mediaeval University Education

Moral equilibrium is always an unstable equilibrium; unfortunately, it even takes very little to upset it. Europe had reached, in the thirteenth century, a momentary moral equilibrium. In the fourteenth century, it toppled and crashed. That, in briefest outline, is the story of what many persons gloat over as the beginning of the Renaissance. The only possible justification for that gloating would be in the excellence of the education which, after some hundred years of confused struggle, took the place of the destroyed mediaeval education. In the present chapter we shall try to get some clear view of what happened in the break-up of mediaeval education.

In the eleventh, twelfth, and thirteenth centuries, there did occur in Europe a true renaissance, a true revival of civilization. It was moral, social, intellectual and artistic. It was, in the most complete sense, educational. That education was informed by the spirit of the Catholic religion. Its leaders were religious leaders: priests, monks, bishops, popes. For all its limitations and imperfections (and they were many) it was, in the judgment of competent and impartial historians, singularly successful. Its great monuments are scholastic philosophy and theology, the universities, the cathedrals, the developed social organization of Europe.

In the fourteenth century, the forward movement spent itself: in part, because of the strange inertia in all human activity; in part, through the gradual failure of its leaders; in part, because of the inevitable tendency to stasis and inflexibility in human institutions, a sort of social hardening of the arteries; in part, because of a terrible physical disaster, the Black Death, which destroyed within a few years nearly one half of the total population of Europe. The result was an approach to moral anarchy, beginning in the decay of the religious spirit of the various European peoples.

Churchmen largely to blame for it

Jesus Christ had promised that His Church would not fail; He had not promised that churchmen would not fall. Their failure in the fourteenth and fifteenth centuries was fraught with disaster to Europe. They had become increasingly immersed in secular politics, neglecting the care of their spiritual charges. They had become wealthy, and greedy for wealth and their wealth had led them to pompous pride and luxury. It seems to be a law of human endeavor that difficulties call forth finer efforts, and that ease atrophies out powers. Certainly it is an evident historical fact that the vitality of the Catholic Church in its members thrives under persecution and hardships, and decays in what the world looks upon as success. Catholic churchmen, being human did not well endure the accumulated prosperity of the thirteenth century. The popes were too much taken up with their temporal power, embroiled in endless and often in moral squabbles with the petty principalities of Italy, and through these with the developing nations of the rest of Europe. As one result of this, the papal residence was transferred to Avignon from 1305 to 1377, and the papacy became almost an appanage of the French crown. When Pope Gregory XI died, at Rome, in 1378, a struggle brokeout between the French, Italian, and Spanish powers for the control of the papacy, which led to the Great Western Schism, a chaotic condition of rival popes and partisan contentions, lasting forty years, and incredibly scaldalizing the masses of Catholic people. The bad example of the popes affected bishops and priests throughout Europe. An atmosphere of gross worldlines prevailed in the upper ranks of the Church. The people largely lost confidence in their religious leaders.

Sporadic and Misguided attempts at Reform

St. Bridget of Sweden and St. Catherine of Siena tried, but with feeble success, to influence the popes spiritually; the former persuaded Urban V, in 1367, to return from Avignon to Rome, where, however, he stayed less than three years; the latter had much to do with the final return of Gregory XI, ten years later, just before the Great Schism. John Wycline, and English secular priest, out of mixed motives of pique and zeal, set himself up as a reformer, during the papacy of Urban V. Lingard says of him: "Wycliffe, exemplary in his morals, declaimed against vice with the freedom and severity of an apostle ... but chiefly against the clergy." He organized bands of `poor priests,' barefoot, coarsely clad, who went about England, teaching the people the welcome doctrine that the laity might rightfully despoil sinful priests and monks. Anarchy was in the air. John Ball, another priest, was the associate of Wat Tyler in leading the peasant rebellion of 1381 in England. John Huss of Prague, influenced by the writings of Wycliffe, preached another politico-religious `reform,' was condemned by the Council of Constance in 1415, and was burned to death. The attempts at reform were violent, impassioned and therefore often unbalanced. They made the mistake, which Protestantism, a century later, was to make: of throwing out the baby with the bath, of condemning right uses as well as abuses of rejecting Christian truths as well as the distorted misapplications of those truths. There was no remedy in such `reforms'; but the people acclaimed them because they knew there was terrible need of some reform.

The Black Death

Such a gross and widespread failure of Church leadership might alone have disrupted the civilization of Europe, which was built upon the Catholic Faith. But there was added to it an appalling physical calamity, one of the most dreadful in the history of the human race, the Black Death. It seems to have been a particularly virulent form of bubonic plague, which, after raging in the East for three or four years, was carried to Europe by Italian trading ships in the autumn of 1347. During 1348 it swept through France, Spain, Switzerland, Bavaria, and by August 15th of that year had reached England, from which country it crossed to Flanders, Norway, Sweden, Poland, Hungary, the lower Rhine valley, in 1349. Within three years, from a third to a half of the population of Europe died of it. The mortality was all the more terrible because of the swiftness with which death struck, and the fact that it attacked chiefly the young and vigorous. There was a rather bad recurrence of the plague ten years later, in 1361, and other minor outbreaks occured during the rest of the century and well into the next century.

Effects on Survivors

One might possibly expect the enormous disaster to sober those who survived, to call forth a moral revival, to turn men's minds from this life-in-death to the hopes and aspirations of Christianity. As a painful matter of fact, it did just the opposite. Matteo Villani, contemporary historian, paints a picture of idleness, dissolute morals, frantic revelling.[1] "Priests and doctors flow in fear from those ill."[2] The laboring classes were inter chiefly on extorting higher wages.[3] The clergy too were engaged in profiteering, and the evil of plural benefice mutiplied.[4] Li Muisis has a shocking account of the churches of Tournay tolling the bells continuously for the sake of the fees, and of the town officials having to enact moral ordinances to meet the situation.[5] All contemporary accounts represent the moral apathy of the people as something more distressing to contemplate than the mortality itself.

And upon education

Schools and universities were obviously badly affected by this huge disaster, in the loss of both students and teachers. There is a manifest break in the development of architecture, and of stained glass; a change of style so marked as to help in dating many structures.[6] The arts in general begin to decay. Society becomes grosser in every way, more materialist, lacking in inspiration. Its educational leaders, already weakened in fiber of character and in equipment, suffer an enormous loss in both after the plague. Gasquet estimates that, for England, the loss in numbers of the clergy was about 25,000;[7] but their loss in quality was even more important. In the urgent need of the times, illiterate and untrained men were ordained priests; and these were, of course, the chief guides and educators of the people, in the churches, in the schools, in the homes. It is small wonder that mediaeval education went to pieces in the fourteenth and fifteenth centuries.

War

One human activity which the Black Death itself could not halt was the lust of fighting. The Hundred Years' War, between France and England began in 1346. Within seven years after the great plague, Edward of England and his son, the Black Prince, again invaded France, and at Poitierss defeated King John of France and captured him and his son Philip. It was in the midst of the Black Death that the populace of Rome drove out of the city Reinzi, whom seven months before they had acclaimed as their reforming leader. Whilst the plague was raging in the Germaniess, the new emperor, Charles IV, was fighting with Gunther of Schwartzburg and other princes. The *condottieri* in Italy fought each other amidst rotting corpses; and in Naples Louis of Hungary waged his war against Queen Joanna I, even whilst half of his army died of the disease. The Black Death brought peace only to its victims.

Scholasticism decadent

The great philosophical and theological system which was the intellectual core of the thirteenth century fell into feeble hand in the fourteenth. The number of students of philosophy multiplied, but they lacked thoroughness as well as originality. They lined up as partisan adherents of one of the three great schools, Ockhamists, Scotists, Thomists; and made up in contentiousness what they lacked in knowledge. Dialectic, which in the thirteenth century was only a preparatory discipline to real philosophical studies, became in the fourteenth the main subject of study, or rather of quarrel. Clearness and vigor of thought were lost in a fog of distinctions and sub-distinctions. Even the language of the schools suffered the terse, precise Latin of the thirteenth century giving way to a hodge-podge of barbarisms. Conceit took this place of intelligence; and skepticism, as always, was ready upon the heels of conceit. The English Franciscan, William of Ockham, who was born about 1300 and died in the Black Death at Munich, 1349, shook the foundations of Scholasticism and prepared the way for agnosticism. With him, scholasticism lost its place and force in the scheme of European education, and was ready for the gibes of the coming humanists.[8]

These Changes Reflected in the Universities

It must be repeated that schools do not lead social changes, but follow them. The school of life always dominates the school of formula. As the vitality of the twelfth and thirteenth centuries built the universities, so the decadence of the fourteenth century enfeebled them. Even in the earlier, vigorous ages, the universities suffered from the educational weakness of being too exclusively intellectual in their training; but it was, at any rate, a fine, clear, and noble intellectuality. Now it becomes petty, contentious, querulous, lost in insignificant details.[9] The faculty of theology is a hotbed of intrigue. True zeal for study disappears before the trivial ambitions of vanity or greedy campaigning for ecclesiastical preferment. Political jockeying, and even bribery by money, make easy the approach to the 'doctorate.' In the faculty of arts the years of study are shortened, and "beardless boys fill with infantile stammerings" the chairs of the masters.[10] The students are sputtering dialectic; and the 'form' of a syllogism has become more important than the truth it may contain. There are more and more monks and friars in the schools, but they are neither good students nor edifying religions.[11] Moreover, one of the glories of the mediaeval university, its cosmopolitanism, now vanishes, owing to the increasingly sharp demarcation between the developing nations of Europe. The fine solidarity of the Middle Ages is passing culture is becoming insular, provincial. New universities spring up, particularly in the German-speaking countries and they are all national, or even local , in character. Europe is splitting up; and European education is turning into French, English, Italian, Spanish, German education.[12]

And in the Lower Schools

Throughout the Middle Ages, the lot of the peasant was a hard one. The Black Death by making labor scarce, helped much to improve the material position of the laboring man; but it seems also to have stirred up in him an increased bitterness and resentment toward the higher classes, including, by all means the clergy. The social atmosphere was filled with conflict. The country schools became more and more lay schools in which, of course, fees were demanded for tuition. Mr. Simeon Luce indicates that the schoolmaster had considerable difficulty in collecting these fees.[13] Moreover, competent schoolmasters were increasingly scarce.[14] The town fared better. Commerce and industries were only temporarily halted by the plague. There was an actual increase in individual wealth, since there were suddenly fewer people to share possession of the total wealth. The burgher class solidified its social standing. One notable change in the lower schools was brought about by the growing spirit of nationalism; that was the increased use of the vernacular in school instruction.[15] We shall have to note a curious result of this when we consider the growth of humanism. And it must not be forgotten that the quality and intensiveness of religious instruction in these most important lower schools greatly fell off during the fourteenth and fifteenth centuries. The children trained in these schools had no little ground for discontent with their clerical teachers; the good-humored anti-clericalism of the thirteenth century becomes rather bitter in the fourteenth. Yet the Catholic religion had a more tenacious hold in these lower schools than in the higher; and throughout the troublous fourteenth century, the mass of the people everywhere retained the Faith, although it was gradually enfeebled through lack of adequate instruction. During this century and the next, diocesan and provincial synods repeatedly urged upon parish preists the duty of religious instruction of their people; a fact which testifies to the need of such urging.[16]

Conclusion

Even so cursory a sketch as this of educational conditions in the fourteenth century may make clear that Europe had pitifully gone back from the crest of mediaeval accomplishment. Nor can one hesitate a moment as to where to place the chief blame for that great failure. Just as the reform of Cluny had been the principal agency in bringing about the amazing improvement in education which ushered in the twelfth-century renaissance, so too the moral and religious decay of the bishops and clergy was now the greatest single factor in destroying the educational achievements of the Middle Ages. There were other destructive forces at work, just as there had been other up-building forces besides Cluny; but the failure of the Catholic leaders was the most powerful disintegrating agent, precisely as Cluny had been the most powerful constructive agent. The fourteenth and fifteenth centuries were the secular Spy Wednesday; the mystical body of Christ betrayed by some of His leading disciples, as His actual body had been betrayed by Judas.

One immediate result of this spiritual decay is to be found in the intellectual conceit of theologians. By the fourteenth century they had begun to take themselves very seriously as the guardians of Catholic truth; assuming an authority which was not from God; making the human science of theology the final test of the Faith. Theirs is a position singularly like that of the scribes at the time of Christ. Its effect upon the people was bad; it stirred a vague rebelliousness, which is never capable of distinguishing between assumed authority and true authority. It set up the councilliar idea, the subversive notion that a general council was superior to the spiritual authority of the people; and so prepared the way for future division of Christendom.

The Black Death was merely a hastening and intensifying incident in the general process of decay. It gave a violent thrust to a stumbling age; but the age would have fallen without it. It sprinkled corpses about what was already becoming the ruin of the Middle Ages; and mingled the effluvia of the dead with the stench of spiritual decadence. It made impressive in human bodies the greater horror that was happening in human souls. The fifteenth century Reniassance was to spring up in a physical and moral charnel house.

Topics for Discussion

1. The decay of the education of chivalry; how far affected by loss of religion? by growth of burgher class? by introduction of firearms?

2. Comparison between the German universities, sprung up in the fourteenth and fifteenth centuries, and the universities of France, England, Italy.

3. The educational influences, good and bad, of the mendicant religious orders during the fourteenth and fifteenth centuries.

4. The Brothers of the Common Life and elementary schools.

5. The effect upon education of the widening concept of geography during the fourteenth and fifteenth centuries.

6. The influence of Wycliffe and Huss upon the religious education of this period.

REFERENCES

1. Muratori, *Scriptores,* tom, XIV, coll, 11-15, Palataine ed., Milan.

2. *Idem,* tom, xvi, col. 286. Marcha di Marco Battagli da Rimin C. xxix, p. 54.

3. *Chronicle* of William Dene, a monk of Rochester, in MS. Br Mus. Faust. B, v. fol. 99.

4. Wharton, *Anglia Sacra,* 1, pp. 375, 376. Cf. also Wilkins, *Concilia,* pp. 735, 736.

5. De Smet, *Recueil,* Bruxelles, 1841, ii, pp. 279-81, 361-82.

6. Gasquet, *The Black Death,* 2d ed., London, 1908, p. 235.

7. *Idem,* pp. 237-39. He reckons that, prior to the plague, one in every fifty men in England belonged to the clergy. This goes far to explain why the common schools of England could be so well supplied with teachers, and why there were so many chantry priests and Morrow Mass priests to devote most of their time to the care of schools.

8. Maurice de Wulf, *History of Mediaeval Philosophy,* London, 1926, Vol. 2, pp. 159-69.

9. University work also began to be more a task of training than of educating, due to the fact that the doctorate was a necessary step on the way to teaching. The universities became trade schools of a sort, when even the logic-chopping was done chiefly as a preparation for teaching others to chop logic.

10. Richard de Bury, *Philobiblion*, c. ix, p. 87 (published 1344; reference to edition of 1888, London, by Ernest C. Thomas).

11. Denifile and Chatelain, *Chartularium Universities Parisinessis*, Paris, 1891, Vol. 2, p. 11. The entire introduction to Vol. 2 is concerned with the early fourteenth century conditions.

12. Cf. H.S. Denifle, *Die Universitaten des Mitelalter bis 1400*.

13. *History de Bertrand du Guesclin et son Europe (1320-1364) 15.* The incidents narrated are of the year 1377.

14. A.F. Leach, *The Schools of Medieval England*, London, 1911, pp. 210 sqq.

15. Up to the year of the Black Death, children in the schools of England construed their lessons in French. Shortly after 1350 schoolmaster named Cornwall introduced the use of English into the instruction of his pupils. His example was eagerly followed; with a single generation, the custom became nearly universal. About the same time, Chaucer was writing the Canterbury Tales, Cf. F.A. Gasquet, *The Black Death*, 2d ed., London, 1908, p. 234.

16. See monograph by F.A. Gasquet on "Religious Instructions in England during the Fourteenth and Fifteenth Centuries," *Historical Papers*, Vol. 3, Catholic Truth Society, London, 1908.

4

The Rise of the Universities

The municipal movement, the merchant guilds, the trade guilds, etc. which emerged during eleventh and twelfth centuries were doing for civil life what monasticism had earlier done for the religious life. They were collections of like-minded men, who united themselves into associations or guild for mutual benefit, protection, advancement, and self-government within the limits of their city, business, trade, or occupation. This tendency toward association, in the days when state government was weak or in its infancy, was one of the marked features of the transition time from the early period of the Middle Ages, when the Church was virtually the State, to the later period of the Middle Ages, when the authority of the Church in secular matter was beginning to weaken, modern nations were beginning to form, and an interest in worldly affairs was beginning to replace the previous inordinate interest in the world to come.

We also noted that certain cathedral and monastery schools, but especially the cathedral school,[1] stimulated by the new interest in Dialectic, were developing into much more than local teaching institutions designed to afford a supply of priests to some little education for the parishes of the bishopric. Once York and later Canterbury, in England, had teacher who attracted students from other bishoprics. Paris had for long been a famous center for the study of the Liberal

Art and of Theology. Saint Gall had become noted for its music. Theologians coming from Paris (1167-68) had given a new impetus to study among the monks at Oxford. A series of political events in northern Italy had given emphasis to the study of law in many cities, and the Moslems in Spain had stimulated the schools there and in southern France to a study of medicine and Aristotelian science. Rome was for long a noted center for study. Gradually these places came to be known as studia publica, or studia generalia, meaning by this a generally recognized place of study, where lectures were open to any one, to students of all countries and of all conditions.[2] Travelling students came to these places from a far to hear some noted teacher read and comment on the famous textbooks of the time.

From the first both teachers and students had been considered as members of the clergy, and hence had enjoyed the privileges and immunities extended to that class, but, now that the students were becoming so numerous and were travelling so far, some additional grant of protection was felt to be desirable. Accordingly the Emperor Frederick Barbarossa,[3] in 1158, issued a general proclamation of privileges and protection (R. IOI). In this he ordered that teachers and students travelling "to the places in which the studies are carried on" should be protected from unjust arrest, should be permitted to "dwell in security," and in case of suit should be tried "before their professors or the bishop of the city." This document marks the beginning of a long series of rights and privileges granted to the teachers and students of the universities now in process of evolution in western Europe.

University Evolution

The development of a university out of a cathedral or some other form of school represented, in the Middle Ages, a long local evolution. Universities were not founded then as they are today. A teacher of some reputation drew around him a constantly increaing body of students. Other teachers of ability, finding a student body already there, also "set up their chairs" and began to teach. Other teachers and more students came. In this way a studium was created. About these teachers in time collected other university servants - "pedells, librarians, lower officials, prepares of parchment, scribes, illuminators of parchment, and others who serve it," as Count Rupert enumerated them in the Charter of Foundation granted, in 1386, to Heidelberg. At Salerno, as we have already seen, medical instruction arose around the work of Constantine of Carthage and the medicinal springs found in the vicinity. Students journeyed there from many lands, and licenses to practice the medical art were granted there as early as 1137. At Bologna, we have also seen, the work of Irnerius and Gratian early made this a great center for the study of civil and canon law, and their pupils spread the taste for these new subjects throughout Europe. Paris for two centuries had been a center for the study of the Arts and of Theology, and a succession of famous teachers - William of Champeaux, Abelard, Peter the Lombard - had taught there. So important was the theological teaching there that Paris has been termed "the Sinai of instruction" of the Middle Ages.

By the beginning of the thirteenth century both students and teachers had become so numerous, at a number of places in western Europe, that they began to adopt the favourite mediaeval practice and organized themselves into associations, or guilds, for further protection from extortion and oppression and for greater freedom from regulation by the Church. They now sought and obtained additional privileges for themselves, and, in particular, the great mediaeval document—a charter of rights and privileges.[4] As both teachers and students were for long regarded as clerici the charters were usually sought from the Pope, but in some cases they were obtained from the king.[5] These associations of scholars, or teachers, or both, "born of the need of companionship which men who cultivate their intelligence feel," sought to perform the same function for those who studied and taught that the merchant and craft guild were performing for their member. The ruling idea was association for protection, and to secure freedom for discussion and study; the obtaining of corporate rights and responsibilities; and the organization of a system of apprenticeship, based on study and developing through journeyman into mastership,[6], as attested by an examination and the license to teach. In the rise of these teacher and student guilds[7] we have the beginning of the universities of western Europe, and their organization into chartered teaching groups (R. 100) was simply another phase of that great movement toward the association of like-minded men for worldly purposes which began to sweep over the rising cities in the eleventh and twelfth centuries.[8]

The term universities, or university, which came in time to be applied to these associations of masters and apprentices in study, was a general Roman legal term, practically equivalent to our modern word corporation. At first it was applied to any association; and when used with reference to teachers and scholars was so stated. Thus, in addressing the masters and students at Paris, Pope Innocent, in 1205, writes: "Universis magistris et schoolaribus Parisionsibus"; that is, "to the corporation of masters and scholars at Paris." Later the term university became restricted to the meaning which we give it today.

The University Mothers

Though this movement for association and the development of advanced study had manifested itself in a number of places by the close of the twelfth century, two places in particular led all the others and became types which were followed in charters and in new creations. These were Bologna and Paris.[9] After one or the other of these two nearly all the universities of western Europe were modeled. Bologna or Paris, or one of their immediate children, served as a pattern. Thus Bologna was the university mother for almost all the Italian universities; for Montpellier and Grenoble in southern France; for some of the Spanish universities; and for Glasgow, Upsala, Cracow, and for the Law Faculty at Oxford. Paris was the university mother for Oxford, and through her Cambridge; for most of the northern French universities; for the university of Toulouse, which in turn became the mother for other southern French and northern Spanish universities; for Lisbon and Coimbra in Portugal; for the early German universities at Prague, Vienna, Cologne, and Heidelberg; and through Cologne for Copenhagen. Through one of the colleges at Cambridge - Emmanuel—she became indirectly, the mother of a new Cambridge in America-Harvard-founded in 1636. It shows the location of the chief universities founded before 1600. Viewed from the standpoint of instruction, Paris was followed almost entirely in Theology, and Bologna in Law, while the three centres which most influenced the development of instruction in medicine were Salerno, Montpellier, and Salamanca.

While the earlier universities gradually arose as the result of a long local evolution, it in time became common for others to be founded by a migration of professors from an older university to some cathedral city having a developing studium. In the days when a university consisted chiefly of master and students, when lectures could be held in any kind of a building or collection of buildings, and when there were no libraries, laboratories, campus, or other university property to tie down an institution, it was easy to migrate. Thus, in 1209, the school at Cambridge was created a university by a secession of masters from Oxford, much as bees swarm from a hive. Sienna, Padua, Reggio, Vicenza, Arezzo resulted from "swarmings" from Bologna; and Vercelli from Vicenza. In 1228, after a student riot at Paris which provoked reprisals from the city, many of the masters and students went to the studium towns of Angers, Orleans, and Rheims, and universities were established at the first two. Migrations from Prague helped etablish many of the German universities. In this way the university organization was spread over Europe.

In 1200 there were but six studia generalia which can be considered as having evolved into universities—Salerno, Bologna, and Reggio, in Italy; Paris and Montpellier, in France; and Oxford, in England. By 1300 eight more had evolved in Italy, three more in France, Cambridge in England, and five in Spain and Portugal. By 1400 twenty-two additional universities had developed, five of which were in German lands, and by 1500 thirty-five more had been founded, making a total of eighty. By 1600 the total had been raised to one hundred and eight. Some of these (approximately thirty) afterwards died, while in the following centuries additional ones were created.[10]

Privileges and Immunities Granted

The grant of privileges to physicians and teachers made by the Emperor Constantine, in 333 A.D. and the privilege and immunities granted to the clergy (clerici) by the early Christian Roman Emperors, doubtless formed a basis for the many grants of special privileges made to the professors and students in the early universities. The document promulgated by Frederick Barbarossa, in 1158 (R. 101), began the granting of privileges to the studia generalia, and this was followed by numerous other grants. The grant to students of freedom from trial by the city authorities, and the obligation of every citizen of Paris to seize any one seen striking a student granted by Philip Augustus, in 1200, is another example, widely followed, of the bestowal of large privileges. Count Rupert I, in founding the University of Heidelberg, in 1386, granted many privileges, exempted the students from "any duty, levy, imposts, tolls, excises, or other exactions whatever" while coming to, studying at, or returning home from the university. The exemption from taxation became a matter of form, and was afterwards followed in the chartering of American colleges. Exemption from military service also was granted.

So valuable an asset was a university to a city, and so easy was it for a university to move almost overnight, that cities often, and at times even nations, encouraged not only the founding of universities, but also the migration of both faculties and students. An interesting case of a city bidding for the presence of a university is that of Vercelli, which made a binding agreement, as a part of the city charter, whereby the city agreed with a body of masters and students "swarming" from Padua to loan the students money at lower than the regular rates, to see that there was plenty of food in the markets at no increase in price, and to protect the students from injustice. An instance of bidding by a State is the case of Cambridge, which obtained quite an addition by the coming of striking Paris masters and students in 1229, in response to the pledge of King Henry III, who "humbly sympathized with them for their sufferings at Paris," and promised them that if they would come "to our kingdom of England and remain there to study" he would assign to them "cities, boroughs, towns, whatsoever you may wish to select and in every fitting way will cause you to rejoice in a state of liberty and tranquillity."

One of the most important privileges which the universities early obtained, and a rather singular one at that, was the right of cessatio, which meant the right to stop lectures and go on a strike as a means of enforcing a grievances against either town or church authority. This right was for long jealously guarded by the university, and frequently used to defend itself from the smallest encroachments on its freedom to teach, study, and discipline the members of its guild as it saw fit, and often the right not to discipline them at all. Often the cessatio was invoked on very trivial grounds, as in the case of the Oxford cessatio of 1209, the Paris cessatio of 1220, and the numerous other cessationes which for two centuries[11] repeatedly disturbed the continuity of instruction at Paris.

Degrees in the Guild

The most important of the university rights, however,

was the right to examine and license its own teachers, and to grant the license to teach. Founded as the universities were after the guild model, they were primarily places for the taking of apprentices in the Arts, developing them into journeymen and masters and certifying to their proficiency in the teaching craft.[12] Their purpose at first was to prepare teachers, and the giving of instruction to students for cultural ends, or a professional training for practical use aside from teaching the subject, was a later development.

Accordingly it came about in time that, after a number of years of study in the Arts under some master, a student was permitted to present himself for a test as to his ability to define words, determine the meaning of phrases, and real the ordinary Latin texts in Grammar, Rhetoric, and Logic (the Trivium), to the satisfaction of other masters than his own. In England this test came to be known by the term determine. Its passage was equivalent to advancing from apprenticeship to the ranks of a journeyman, and the successful candidate might now be permitted to assist the master, or even give some elementary instruction himself while continuing his studies. He now became an assistant or companion, and by the fourteenth century was known as a baccalaureus, a term used in the Church, in chivalry, and in the guilds, and which meant a beginner. There was at first, though, no thought of establishing an examination and a new degree for the completion of this first step in studies. The bachelor's degree was a later development, sought at first by those not intending to teach, and eventually erected into a separate degree.

When the student had finally heard a sufficient number of courses, as required by the statutes of his guild, he might present himself for examination for the teaching license. This was a public trial, and took the form of a public disputation on some stated thesis, in the presence of the masters, and against all comers. It was the student's "masterpiece", analogous to the masterpiece of any other guild, and he submitted it to a jury of the masters of his craft.[13] Upon his masterpiece being adjudged satisfactory, he also became a master in his craft, was now able to define the dispute, was formally admitted to the highest rank in the teaching guild, might have a seal, and was variously known as master, doctor, or professor, all of which were once synonymous terms.[14] If he wished to prepare himself for teaching one of the professional subjects he studied still further, usually for a number of years, in one of the professional faculties, and in time he was declared to be a Doctor of Law, or Medicine, or of Theology.

The Teaching Faculties

The students for a long time grouped themselves for better protection (and aggression) according to the nation from which they came,[15] and each "nation" elected a councilor to look after the interests of its members. Between the different nations there were constant quarrels, insults were passed back and forth, and much bad blood engendered.[16] On the side of the masters the organization was by teaching subjects, and into what came to be known as faculties.[17] Thus there came to be four faculties in a fully organized mediaeval university, representing the four great divisions of knowledge which had been evolved-Arts, Law, Medicine, and Theology. Each faculty elected a dean, and the deans and councilors elected a rector, who was the head or president of the university. The chancellor, the successor of the cathedral school scholasticus, was usually appointed by the Pope and represented the Church, and a long struggle ensued between the rector and the chancellor to see who should be the chief authority in the university. The rector was ultimately victorious and the position of chancellor became largely an honorary position of no real importance.

The Arts Faculty was the successor of the old cathedral-school instruction in the Seven Liberal Arts, and was found in practically all the universities. The Law Faculty embraced civil and canon law, as worked out at Bologna. The Medical Faculty taught the knowledge of the medical art, as worked out at Salerno and Montpellier. The Theological Faculty, the most important of the four, prepared learned men for the service of the Church and was for some two centuries controlled by the scholastics. The Arts Faculty was preparatory to the other three. As Latin was the language of the classroom, and all the texts were Latin texts, a reading and speaking knowledge of Latin was necessary before coming to the University to study. This was obtained from a study of the first of the Seven Arts-Grammar-in some monatery, cathedral, or other type of school. Thus a knowledge of Latin formed practically the sole requirement for admission to the mediaeval university, and continued to be the chief admission requirement in our universities up to the nineteenth century. In Europe it is still of great importance as a preparatory subject, but in South American countries it is not required at all.

Very few of the universities, in the beginning, had all four of these faculties. The very nature of the evolution of the earlier ones precluded this. Thus Bologna had developed into a studium generale from its prominence in law, and was virtually constituted a university in 1158, but it did not add Medicine until 1316, or Theology until 1360. Paris began sometime before 1200 as an arts school, Theology some instruction in Canon Law was added by 1208, a Law Faculty in 1274, and a Medical Faculty in 1274. Montpellier began as a medical school sometime in the twelfth century. Law followed a little later, a teacher from Bologna "setting up his chair" there. Arts was organized by 1242. A sort of theological school began in 1263, but it was not chartered as a faculty until 1421. So it was with many of the early universities. These four traditional faculties were well established by the fourteenth century, and continued as the typical form of university organization until modern times. With the great university development and the great multiplication of subjects of study which characterized the nineteenth century, many new faculties and schools and colleges have had to be created particularly in the United States, in response to new modern demands.[18]

Nature of the Instruction

The teaching material in each faculty was much as we have already indicated. After the recovery of the works of Aristotle he came to dominate the instruction in the Faculty of Arts.[19] The Statutes of Paris, in 1254, giving the books to be read for the A.B. and the A.M. degrees, show how fully Aristotle had been adopted there as the basis for instruction in Logic, Ethics, and Natural Philosophy by that time. The books required for these two degrees at Leipzig, in 1410, show a much better-balanced course of instruction, though the time requirements given for each subject show how largely Aristotle predominated there also. Oxford kept up better the traditions of the earlier Seven Liberal Arts in its requirements, and classified the new works of Aristotle in three additional "philosophies"-natural, moral and metaphysical. From four to seven years were required to complete the arts course, though the tendency was to reduce the length of the art course as secondary schools below the university were evolved.[20]

In the Law Faculty, after Theology the largest and most important of all the faculties in the mediaeval university, the Corpus Juris Civilis of Justinian and the Decrelum of Gratian were the textbooks read, with perhaps a little more practical work in discussion than in Arts and Medicine. The Oxford course of study in both Civil and Canon Law gives a good idea as to what was required for degrees in one of the best of the early law faculties.

In the Medical Faculty a variety of books - translations of Hippocrates, Galen, Avicenna and the works of certain writers at Salerno and Jewish and Moslem writers in Spain -

were read and lectured on. The list of medical books used at Montpellier,[21] in 1340, which at that time was the foremost place for medical instruction in western Europe, shows the book-nature and the extent of the instruction given at the leading school of medicine of the time. It was, moreover, customary at Montpellier for the senior students to spend a summer in visiting the sick and doing practical work. We have here the merest beginnings of clinical instruction and hospital service, and at this stage medical instruction remained until quite modern time. The medical courses at Paris and Oxford were less satisfactory, only book instruction being required. Both Law and Medicine were so dominated by the scholastic ideal and methods that neither accomplished what might have been possible in a freer atmosphere.

In the Theological Faculty the Sentences of Peter Lombard and the Summa Theologia of Thomas Aquina were the text books used. The Bible was at first also used somewhat, but later came to be largely overshadowed by the other books and by philosophical discussions and debates on all kinds of hair-splitting questions, kept carefully within the limit prescribed by the Church. The requirements at Oxford give the course of instruction in one of the best of the theological faculties of the time. The teachers were scholastics, and scholastic methods and ideal everywhere prevailed. Roger Bacon's (1214-1294) criticism of this type of theological study, which he calls "horse loads, not at all [in consonance] with the most holy text of God," and "philosophical, both in substance and method," gives an idea of the kind of instruction which came to prevail in the theological faculties under the dominance of the scholastic philosophers.

Years of study were required in each of these three professional faculties, as is shown by the statement of requirements as given for Montpellier, Paris and Oxford.

Methods of Instruction

A very important reason why so long a period of study

was required in each of the professional faculties as well as in the Faculty of Arts, is to be found in the lack of textbooks and the methods of instruction followed. While the standard textbooks were becoming much more common, due to much copying and the long-continued use of the same texts, they were still expensive and not owned by many.[22] To provide a loan collection of theological books for poor students we find, in 1271, a gift by will to the University of Paris of a private library, containing twenty-seven books. Even if the students possesed books, the master "read"[23] and commented from his "gloss" at great length on the texts being studied. Besides the mere text each teacher had a "gloss" or commentary for it-that is, a mass of explanatory notes, summaries, cross-references, opinions by others, and objections to the statements of the text. The "gloss" was a book in itself, often larger than the text, and these standard glosses,[24] or commentaries were used in the university instruction for centuries. In Theology and Canon Law they were particularly extensive.

All instruction, too, was in Latin. The professor read from the Latin text and gloss, repeating as necessary, and to this the student listened. Sometimes he read so slowly that the text could be copied, but in 1355 this method was prohibited at Paris and students who tried to force the masters to flow it "by shouting or whistling or raising a din, or by throwing stones," were to be suspended for a year. The first step in the instruction was a minute and subtle analysis of the text itself, in which each line was dissected, analyzed, and paraphrased, and the comments on the text by various authors were set forth. Next all passages capable of two interpretations were thrown into the form of a question; pro and contra, after the manner of Abelard. The arguments on each side were advanced, and the lecturer's conclusion set forth and defended. The text was thus worked over day after day in minute detail. Having as yet but little to teach, the masters made the most of what they had. A good example of the mediaeval plan of university instruction is found in the announcement of Odofredus, a distinguished teacher of Law at Bologna, about the middle of the thirteenth century, which Rahdall thinks is equally applicable to methods in other subjects. Odofredus says:

First, I shall give you summaries of each title before I proceed to the text; secondly, I shall give you as clear and explicit a statement as I can of the purport of each Law (included in the title); thirdly, I shall read the text with a view to correcting it; fourthly, I shall briefly repeat the contents of the Law; fifthly, I shall solve apparent contradictions, adding any general principles of Law (to be extracted from the passage), and any distinctions and subtle and useful problems arising out of the Law with their solutions, as far as the Divine Providence shall enable me. And if any Law shall seem deserving, by reason of its celebrity or difficulty, of a Repetition, I shall reserve it for an evening Repetition.

It will be seen that both students and professors were bound to the text, as were the teachers of the Seven Liberal Arts in the cathedral schools before them. There was no appeal to the imagination, still less to observation, experiment, or experience. Each generation taught what it had learned, except that from time to time some thinker made a new organization, or some new body of knowledge was unearthed and added.

Another method much used was the debate, or disputation, and participation in a number of these was required for degrees. These disputations were logical contests, not unlike a modern debate in which the students took sides, cited authorities, and summarized arguments, all in Latin. Sometimes a student gave an exhibition in which he debated both sides of a question, and summarized the argument, after the manner of the professors. As a corrective to the memorization of lectures and texts, these disputations served a useful purpose in awakening intellectual vigor and logical keenness. They were very popular until into the sixteenth century, when new subject-matter and new ways of thinking offered new opportunities for the exercise of the intellect.

In teaching equipment there was almost nothing at first, and but little for centuries to come. Laboratories, workshops, gymnasia, good buildings and classrooms—all alike were equally unknown. Time schedules of lectures came in but slowly, in such matters each professor being a free lance. Nor were there any libraries at first, though in time these developed. For a long time books were both expensive and scarce. After the invention of printing (first book printed in 1456), university libraries increased rapidly and soon became the chief feature of the university equipment.

Value of the Training Given

Measured in terms of modern standards the instruction was undoubtedly poor, unnecessarily drawn out, and the educational value low. We could now teach as much information, and in a better manner, in but a fraction of the time then required. Viewed also by the standards of instruction in the higher schools of Greece and Rome the conditions were almost equally bad. Viewed, though, from the standpoint of what had prevailed in western Europe during the dark period of the early Middle Ages, it represented a marked advance in method and content - except in pure literature, where there was an undoubted decline due to the absorbing interest in Dialectic - and it particularly marked a new spirit, as nearly critical as the times would allow. Despite the heterogeneous and but partially civilized student body, youthful and but poorly prepared for study, the drunkenness and fighting, the lack of books and equipment, the large classes and the poor teaching methods, and the small amount of knowledge which formed the grist for their mills and which they ground exceeding small, these new universities held within themselves, almost in embryo form, the largest promise for the intellectual future of western Europe which had appeared since the days of the old universities of the Hellenic world. In these new institutions knowledge was not only preserved and transmitted, but was in time to be tremendously advanced and extended. They were the first organizations to break the monopoly of the Church in learning and teaching; they were the centers to which all new knowledge gravitated; under their shadow thousands of young men found intellectual companionship and in their classrooms intellectual stimulation; and in encouraging "laborious subtlety, heroic industry, and intense application," even though on very limited subject matter, and in training "men to think and work rather than to enjoy", they were preparing for the time when western Europe should awaken to the riches of Greece and Rome and to a new type of intellectual life of its own. From these beginnings the university organization has persisted and grown and expanded, and to-day stands, the Catholic Church alone excepted, as the oldest organized institution of human society.

The manifest tendency of the universities toward speculation, though for long within limits approved by the Church, was ultimately to awaken inquiry, investigation, rational thinking, and to bring forth the modern spirit. The preservation and transmission of knowledge was by the university organization transferred from the monastery to the school, from monks to doctors, and from the Church to a body of logically trained men, only nominally members of the clerici. Their successors would in time entirely break away from connections with either Church or State and stand forth as the independent thinkers and scholars in the arts, sciences, professions, and even in Theology. University graduates in Medicine would in time wage a long struggle against bigotry to lay the foundations of modern medicine. Graduates in Law would contend with kings and feudal lords for larger privileges for the as yet lowly common man, and would help to usher in a period of greater political equality. The university schools of Theology were in time to send forth the keenest critics of the practices of the Church. Out of the university cloisters were to come the men-Dante, Petrarch, Wycliffe, Huss, Luther, Calvin, Copernicus, Galileo, Newton-who were to usher in the modern spirit.

The Universities as a Public Force

Almost from the first the universities availed themselves of their privileges and proclaimed a bold independence. The freedom from arrest and trial by the civil authorities for petty offenses, or even for murder, and the right to go on a strike if in any way interfered with, were but beginnings in independence in an age when such independence seemed important. These rights were in time given up,[26] and in their place the much more important rights of liberty to study as truth seemed to lead, freedom in teaching as the master saw the truth, and the right to express themselves as an institution on public questions which seemed to concern them, were slowly but definitely taken on in place of the earlier privileges. Virtually a new type of members of society-a new Estate-was evolved, ranking with Church, State and nobility, and this new Estate soon began to express itself in no uncertain tones on matters which concerned both Church and State. The universities were democratic in organization and became democratic in spirit, representing a heretofore unknown and unexpressed public opinion in western Europe. They did not wait to be asked; they gave their opinions unsolicited. "The authority of the University of Paris," writes one contemporary, "has risen to such a height that it is necessary to satisfy it, no matter on what conditions." The university "wanted to meddle with the government of the Pope, the King, and everything else," writes another. We find Paris intervening repeatedly in both church and state affairs, and representing French nationality before it had come into being, as the so-called Holy Roman Empire represented the Germans, and the

Papacy represented the Italians. In Montpellier, professors of Law were considered as knights, and after twenty years of practice they became counts. In Bologna we find the professors of Law one of the three assemblies of the city. Oxford, Cambraidge, Paris, and the Scottish universities were given representation`in Parliament. The German universities were from the first prominent in political affairs, and in the reformation struggle of the early sixteenth century they were the battle-grounds.

In an age of oppression these university organizations stood for freedom. In an age of force they began the substitution of reason. In the centuries from the end of the Dark Ages to the Reformation they were the homes of free thought. They early assumed national character and proclaimed a bold independence. Questions of State and Church they discussed with a freedom before unknown. They presented their grievances to both kings and popes, from both they obtained new privileges, to both they freely offered their advice, and sometimes both were forced to do their bidding. At times important questions of State, such as the divorce of Philip of France and that of Henry VIII of England, were submitted to them for decision. They were not infrequently called upon to pass upon questions of doctrine or heresy. "Kings and princes," says Rashdall, in an excellent summry as to the value and influence of the mediaeval university instruction, "found their statesmen and men of business in the universities, most often, no doubt, among those trained in the practical science of Law." Talleyrand is said to have asserted that "their theologians made the best diplomats." For the first time since the downfall of Rome the administration of human affairs was now placed once more in the hands of educated men. By the interchange of students from all lands and their hospitality, such as it was, to the stranger, the universities tended to break down barriers and to prepare Europe for larger intercourse and for more of a common life.

On the masses of the people, of course, they had little or no influence, and could not have for centuries to come. Their greatest work, as has been the case with universities ever since their foundation, was that of drawing to their classrooms the brightest minds of the times, the most capable and the most industrious, and out of this young raw material training the leaders of the future in Church and State. Educationally, one of their most important services was in creating a surplus of teachers in the Arts who had to find a market for their abilities in the rising secondary schools. These developed rapidly after 1200, and to these we owe a somewhat more general diffusion of the little learning and the intellectual training of the time. In preparing future leaders for State and Church in law, theology, and teaching the universities, though sometimes opposed and their opinions ignored, nevertheless contributed materially to the making and moulding of national history. The first great result of their work in training leaders we see in the Renaissance movement of the fourteenth and fifteenth centuries, to which we next turn. In this movement for a revival of the ancient learning, and the subsequent movements for a purer and a better religious life, the men trained by the universities were the leaders.

Question for Discussion

1. Why should the studia publica tend to attract a different type of scholar than those in the monasteries, and gradually to supersede them in importance?

2. Show how the medieval university was a gradual and natural evolution, as distinct from a founded university of to-day.

3. Show that the university charter was a first step towards independence from church and state control.

4. Show the relation between the system of apprenticeship developed for student and teacher in a mediaeval

university, and the stages of student and teacher in a university of to-day.

5. Show how the chartered university of the Middle Ages was an "association of like-minded men for worldly purposes."
6. To what university mother does Harvard go back, ultimately?
7. Show how the English and the German universities are extreme evolutions from the mediaeval type, and our American universities a combination of the two extremes.
8. Do university professors today have privileges akin to those granted professors in a mediaeval university.
9. What has caused the old Arts Faculty to break up into so many groups, whereas Law, Medicine, and Theology have stayed united?
10. Do universities, when founded to-day, usually start with all four of the medieaval faculties represented?
11. Which of the professional faculties has changed most in the nature and character of its instruction? Why was this been so?
12. Enumerate a number of different things which have enabled the modern university greatly to shorten the period of instruction?
13. Aside from differences in teachers, why are some university subjects today taught much more compactly and economically than other subjects?
14. After admitting all the defects of the medieaval university, why did the university nevertheless represent so important a development for the future of western civilization?

15. What does the long continuance, without great changes in character, of the university as an institution indicate as to its usefulness to society?

16. Does the university of to-day play as important a part in the progress of society as it did in the mediaeval times? Why?

17. Is the chief university force to-day exerted directly or indirectly? Illustrate.

18. What is probably the greatest work of any university, in any age?

19. Compare the influence of the mediaeval university, and the Greek universities of the ancient world.

20. Explain the evolution of the English college system as an effort to improve discipline, morals, and thinking. Has it being successful in this?

21. Show how the mediaeval university put books in the place of things, whereas the modern university tries to reverse this?

22. Show how the rise of the universities gave an educated ruling class to Europe, even though the nobility may not have attended them.

23. Show how, in an age of lawlessness, the universities symbolized the supermacy of mind over brute force.

24. Show how the mediaeval universities aided civilization by breaking down, somewhat, barriers of nationality and ignorance among peoples.

25 . Show how the university stood, as the crowning effort of its time, in the slow upward struggle to rebuild civilization on the ruins of what had once been.

Questions on the Readings

1. What does a glance at the page giving the university foundations before 1600 (I00) show as to the rate and direction of the university movement?

2. How do you account for the very large privileges granted university students in the early grants (I0I, I02) and charters (I03)? Should a university student to-day have any privileges not given to all citizens? Why?

3. Do universities, when founded to-day, secure a charter? If so, from whom, and what terms are included? Do normal schools? What form of a charter, if any, has your university or normal school?

4. Compare the freedom from taxation granted to masters and students at Paris (I04) with the grant to professors at Brown University (I87b). Was the Brown University grant exceptional, or common in other American foundations?

5. Do any American cities to-day maintain colleges or universities, as did the Italian cities (J05)? Normal schools? Are somewhat similar ends served?

6. What does the cessatio, as exercised by the mediaeval university (I07, I08), indicate as to standards of conduct on the part of teachers and students?

7. Why is the licensing of university professors to teach not followed in our American universities? What has taken the place of the license? What did the mediaeval license (II0, III, II2) really signify?

8. Compare the license to teach (II2) with a modern doctor's diploma.

9. Compare the requirements for the Arts degree II3, II4, II5) with the requirements for the Baccalaureate degree at a modern university.

10. Compare the additional length of time for professional degrees (II6,II7).

11. How do you account for the American practice of admitting students to the professional course without the Arts course? What is the best American practice in this matter to-day, and what tendencies are observable?

12. Characterize the medical course at Paris (II7) from a modern point of view.

13. Compare the instruction in medicine at Paris (II7) and Toulouse (I22). How do you account for the superiority shown by one? Which one?

14. What does the extract from Roger Bacon (II8) indicate as to the character of the teaching of Theology?

15. What was the nature and extent of the library of Master Stephen (II9)? Compare such a library with that of a scholar of to-day.

16. Show how the Paris statute as to lecturing (I2I) was an attempt at an improvement of the methods of instruction and individual thinking.

17. What do the two time-tables reproduced (I22, I23) reveal as to the nature of a university day, and the instruction given?

18. Show how Rashdall's statement (I24) that lawyers have been a civilizing agent is true.

REFERENCES

1. By the twelfth century the cathedral schools had passed the monastic schools in importance, and had obtained a lead which they were ever after to retain.

2. As contrasted with the monasteries, which were under a "Rule." The opportunities offered by such open institutions in the Middle Ages can hardly be over-estimated.

3. Frederick I, of the mediaeval Holy Roman Empire of Germany and Italy.

4. No individual during the Middle Ages was secure in his rights, even of life or property, certainly not in the enjoyment of ordinary freedom, unless protected by specific guarantees secured from organization. Politically, one must owe allegance to some feudal lord from whom protection was received; economically, one must secure his rights through merchant or craft guild; intellectual interests and educational activities were secured and controlled by the Church." (Monroe, P. *Text Book in the History of Education*, p. 317.)

5. At first the older institutions organized themselves without charter, securing this later, while the institutions founded after 1300 usually began with a charter from page or king, and sometimes from both.

6. The degree of master was originally the license to practice the teaching trade, and analogous to a master shoemaker, goldsmith, or other master craftsmen.

7. "The universities, then, at their origins, were merely academic associations, analogue, as societies of mutual guaranty, to the corporations of working men, the commercial leagues, the trade-guilds which were playing so great a part at the same epoch; analogous also, by the privileges granted to them, to the municipal associations and political communities that date from the same time." (Compare, G., *Abelord and the Rise of the Universities*. p. 33).

8. "M. Bimbenet, in his *History of the University of Orieans* (Paris, 1853) reproduces several articles from the statues of the guilds, the provisions of which are identical with those contained in the statues of the universities." (*ibid.*, p. 35).

9. Bologna and Paris were the great "master" universities of the thirteenth century, while those founded on a model of either were more in the nature of "journeymen" institutions.

10. Between 1000 and 1700, although most of the cities capable of supporting universities were provided with them, twenty one more were created, chiefly in Germany and Holland. The first American university (Harvard) was established in 1636 and the second (Vale) in 1702. In the eighteenth and nineteenth centuries, without counting the United States or any western-hemisphere country, forty more were created. Among the important nineteenth-century creations were Berlin, 1810; Christiana, 1811; St. Petersburg, 1819 Brussels, 1834; London, 1836; and Athens, 1836.

11. See Compayre, G., *Abelard*, pp. 87-90 for list of these "strikes."

12. "It is impossible to fix the period at which the system of degrees began to be organized. Things were done slowly. At the outset, and until towards the end of the twelfth century, there existed nothing resembling a real conferring of degrees in the rising universities. In order to teach it was necessary to have a respondent, a master authorized by age and knowledge.

    The license to teach, neertheless, became by slow degrees, as master and pupils multiplied, a preliminary condition of teaching, a sort of diploma more and more requisite, and of which the bishops (or their representatives, the chancellors) were the dispensers. Up to the fourteenth century there was hardly any other clearly defined university title." (Compare, G., Abelord, pp. 142-43).

13. It is manifest that the universities borrowed from the industrial corporations their companionships, their 'masterships,' and even their banquets; a great repast being the ordinary sequel of the reception of the baccalaureate or doctorate." Compayre G., Abelora.

14. The term professor has become general in its significance, and is used in all countries. In England, the term master was retained for the higher degree, while in Germany the term doctor was retained, and the doctorate made their one degree. American followed the English plan in the establishment of the early colleges, and the degree of A.B. and A.M. were provided for. Later, when the German university influence became prominent in the United States, the doctor's degree was superimposed on the English plan.

15. At Paris, for example, there were four nations - France, Picardy, Normandy, and England. These were again divided into tribes, as for example, there were five tribes of the French - Paris, Sens, Rheims, Tours, and Bourges. Orleans had ten nations - France, Germany, Lorraine, Burgundy, Champagne, Picardy, Normandy, Touraine, Guyenne, and Scotland. In those days, these represented separate nationalities, who little understood one another, and carried their constant quarrels up to the very lecture benches of the professors.

16. A contemporary writer, Jacobus de Vitraico, has left us an account of student life at Paris, in which he says:

    "The students at Paris wrangled and disputed not merely about the various sects or about some discussions; but the differenes between the countries also caused dissensions, hatreds and virulent animosities among them, and they impudently uttered all kinds of affronts and insults against one another.

"There affirmed that the English were drunkards and had tails; the sons of France proud, effeminate and carefully adorned like women. They said that the Germans were furious and obscene at their feasts; the Normans vain and boastful; the Poitevins traitors and always adventurers. The Burgundians they considered vulgar and stupid. The Bretons were reputed to be fickle and changeable, and were often reproached for the death of Arthur. The Lombards were called avaricious, vicious and cowardlly; the Romans, seditious, turbulent and slanderous; the Sicilians, tyrannical and cruel; the inhabitants of Brabani, men of blood, incendiaries, brigands and ravishers; the flemish, fickle, prodigal, gluttonous, yielding as butter, and slothful. After such insults from words they often came to blows." (Pa. Trans. and Repts. from Sources, vol. II, no. 3, pp. 19-20).

17. In an American university the term *college or school* has largely replaced the term *faculty*; is still used. Thus we say College of Liberal Arts, or School of Law, instead of Faculty of Arts, etc.

18. For example, one of our modern state universities is organized into the following faculties, schools, and colleges; (1) college of liberal arts; (2) school of medicine; (3) school of law; (4) school of fine arts; (5) school of pure science; (6) college of engineering; (7) college of agriculture; (8) school of history, economics, and social sciences; (9) school of business administration; (10) college of education; (11) school of household arts; (12) school of pharmacy; (13) school of veterinary medicine; (14) school of library science; (15) school of forestry; (16) school of sanitary engineering; (17) the graduate school; and (18) the university-extension division.

19. "He was called `The Philosopher'; and so fully were scholars convinced that it had pleased God to permit Aristotle to say the last word upon each and every branch of knowledge that they humbly accepted him, along with the Bible, the church fathers, and the canon and Roman law as one of the unquestioned authorities which together formed a complete guide for humanity in conduct and in every branch of science." (Robinson, J.H, *History of Western Europe*, p. 272).

20. This tendency increased with time, due both to the development of secondary schools which could give part of the preparation, and to the increasing number of students who came to the university for cultural or professional ends and without intending to pass the tests for the mastership and the license to teach. Finally the arts course was reduced to three or four years (the usual

college course), and the master's degree to one, and for the latter even residence was waived during the middle of the nineteenth century. The A.M. degree has recently been rehabiliated and now usually signifies a year of hard study in English and American universities, though a few eastern American institutions still play with it or even grant it as an honorary degree. In Germany the arts course disappeared, being given to the secondary schools entirely in the late eighteenth century, and the universities now confer only the degree of doctor.

21. For a list of the books used in the faculty of medicine at Montpellier, in 1340, see Rashdall, H., *Universities of Europe in the Middle Ages*, vol. II, pt. I, p. 123; pt. II, p. 780.

22. After the latter part of the thirteenth century the book-writing and selling trade was organized as a guild industry, and the copying of texts for sale became common. Then arose the practice of erasing as much of the writing from old books as could be done, and writing the new book crosswise of the page. In this way the expense for parchment was reduced and in the process many valueless and a few valuable books were destroyed. Still, the cost for books during the days of parchment must have been high. Walsh estimates that "an ordinary folio volume probably cost from 400 to 500 francs in our (1914), that is, between $80 and $100."

23. In Germany the old mediaeval expression has been retained, and the announcements of instruction there still state that the professor will "read" on such and such subjects instead of "offer courses," as we say in the United States.

24. Norton, in his *Readings in the History of Education; Mediaeval Universities*, pp. 59-75, gives an extract from a text (G. atian) and "gloss" by various writers, on the question - "Shall Priests be Acquainted with Profane Literature, or No?" which see for a good example of mediaeval university instruction and the manner in which a small amount of knowledge was spun out by means of a gloss.

25. Not many early library catalogues have been preserved, but those which have all show small libraries before the days of printing. At Oxford, where the university was broken up into college, each of which had its own library, the following college libraries are known to have existed. Peterhouse College (1418), 304 volumes; King College (1453), 174 volumes: Queens College (1472), 100 volumes; University Library (1473),, 339 volumes. The last two were just before the introduction of printing.

The Peterhouse library (1418) was classified as follows:

Subject	Chained	Leanable
Theology	61	63
Natural Philosophy	26	
Moral Philosophy	5	19
Metaphysics	3	
Logic	5	15
Grammar	6	
Poetry	4	13
Medicine	15	3
Civil Law	9	20
Canon Law	18	19
Totals	152	152

(Clarke, J.W., *The Care of Books*, pp. 145, 147.)

26. Survivals of these old privileges still exist in the German universities which exercise police jurisdiction over their students and have a university jail, and in the American college student's feeling of having the right to create a disturbance in the own and break minor police regulations without being arrested and fined.

5

From Charlemagne to the Rise of the Universities: Ninth to Twelfth Centuries

To be obsessed with the idea that education and schools are synonymous is a handicap in studying any period of the history of education; but it makes simply impossible an intelligent evaluation of education in the 'Dark Ages.' It is that obsession which has misled many historians to exaggerate the value of Charlemagne's influence upon the education of the period, and even to trace a connection between his efforts on behalf of schools and the marked intellectual revival which took place in Europe in the twelfth and thirteenth centuries, three or four hundred years after the death of Charlemagne. There is a manifest huge gap to be bridged between these two ages; and it is not bridged by schools.[1] This chapter will try to show how the barbarian Europe of the ninth century came to be the civilized Europe of the thirteenth century; the process is essentially one of education.

The 'Dark Ages' continue after Charlemagne

It is no injustice to Charlemagne's fine efforts to say that they had little to do with bringing light to the 'Dark Ages.' If the vigorous government of Charlemagne had been maintained with equal vigour by his successors, and if these successors had shown the same wise interest in education which was one of the chief glories of Charlemagne, a scant hundred years might have put an end to the 'Dark Ages.' But the statement is painfully like the old saying in the army, "If we had some ham, we could have ham and eggs, if we only had some eggs." Charlemagne's efforts on behalf of schools practically died with him. His successors were, for the most part, incompetent to further them. More than that, important as those efforts were, they were limited even in his own time. They had not a wide enough influence to affect the general state of education in Europe. The Germanies were scarcely touched by them. Spain was almost wholly in the power of the Saracens. The Christian East, struggling desperately against the Moslems, was in disorder; it was only in 860, half a century after the death of Charlemagne, that Michael III was able to refound the University of Constantinople; and the restoration was not very vigorous even then.[2] In Charlemagne's own domain, the schools he set up would have needed generations to make an impression upon the feudal anarchy of the times.

Early Feudalism Anarchic

We must not let the military successes and glory of Charlemagne blind us to the fact that Europe was still seething in barbarian ferment. The civilization of the Middle Ages was still in its feeble infancy. The most important organization of society was in local efforts to climb out of anarchy. Small freeholders banded together for mutual aid, their immediate aim being merely security of life and property. It was an organization primarily for war, not for the development of civilization. It was a most necessary organization; but its very necessity is a terrible revelation of the bad conditions which prevailed. Out of it some fine things were to grow; but they were not envisaged in the early organization itself. It affected but very little the wretched slavery which the various peoples of Europe had inherited from the Romans or had brought from their own vague antiquity. Feudalism of itself did nothing to improve the lot of the slaves and serfs; it merely included them in the compacts which their masters made. Later, as we shall see, it tended indirectly to give to the serf a slightly better status, by attaching him to the land. He was no longer to be a mere chattel; he had some roots in the soil. But the whole of society, despite its elaborate organization in detail, was so loosely knit together as scarcely to merit the name of a society. This exaggerated local independence was a great hindrance to the spread of any general scheme of education, such as Charlemagne had hoped and striven for. Even in 885, seventy years after the death of Charlemagne, a like attempt of Alfred in England came to practically nothing, and for precisely the same reasons.[3]

The Church involved in Feudalism

It is to be noted that all of Charlemagne's zeal for schools found its practical expression through the clergy and the monks. Not even the most hostile writer disputes the fact that these churchmen were in almost exclusive possession of what educational tools the age could look to.[4] Charlemagne had no choice but to use the clergy and the monks. And it must be frankly admitted that most of them were poor instruments. One Alcuin does not make a learned and pious clergy, any more than one swallow makes a summer. The bishops and the abbots had become feudal lords; no doubt, by sheer necessity. But the fact involved them, and through them the priests and monks, in the turbulent anarchy of the time, in the riot of individualism, which, sifting all elements, we find at the bottom of barbarism. For all practical purposes each bishopric, each abbey, stood by itself; concerned chiefly, if not only, with its relations to its feudal suzerains and feudal subjects. Bishops and abbots were more interested in caring for their feudal rights than in raising the tone of civilization, either morally or intellectually.

Conditions made worse by Further Barbarian Raids

Baronius is perhaps the first to give to the ninth and tenth centuries the name of the 'Iron Age.' It was an age marked not merely by constant feudal quarrels, but by savage and destructive inroads from the still less civilized outer world. There are three of these invasions to be specially noted. The first is the Norman raids, which occupied the greater part of the ninth century, and ended only in the shameless bribe by which Charles the Simple, in 911, turned over to the pirate Rollo the splendid Duchy of Normandy. Then, beginning in 831, the Saracens ravaged northern Italy and southern France, pushing up the valley of the Rhone. More terrible still, huge armies of Huns devastated central Europe during most of the tenth century. In 926 their savage waves had come up to the very frontiers of Lorraine; and they continued in a succession of invasions until the death of their leader Tatsong in 972.

With particularly disastrous results to clergy and monks

Such events alone would demoralize even a well-established civilization; they were incredibly injurious to the difficult beginnings of mediaeval civilization. All the elements of society suffered through the confusion and insecurity brought about by these invasions, but perhaps the clergy and the monks suffered most of all. Their material losses were great. The Norman pirate, Hastings, in 851, burned the monasteries of Fontanelles, St. Ouen, and Jumieges. Within a few years, Marmoutier was pillaged, St. Martin of Tours was burned, Malmedy, Corbie, Liege, and scores of others, were destroyed. In the course of the ninth century, the abbey of Nonantula in Italy was plundered seven times, ending with the last savage onslaught of the Huns, who in 899 killed all the monks together with their abbot, Gregory. It has been said that by the beginning of the tenth century scarcely one of the great French abbeys was left standing. Many of these monasteries had possessed considerable libraries. Fontanelles had a famous one. The chronicles of Novalesa in Italy record that when the Saracen invaders came, in 906, the fleeing monks carried away with them to Turin more than six thousand volumes. Most of these were later burned by the Sarcens in the sack of Turin. Beyond a doubt the monastery libraries suffered great losses in all these raids and invasions. But more grievous to mediaeval society was the demoralization of the monks and clergy, caused by their dispersion and the inevitable breakdown of what religious discipline the rude times had been able to boast. Wars always tend to breed license.[5]

The darkest part of the 'Dark Ages'

Shephards and sailors and other watchers of the night have made us believe that the darkest hours come before the dawn. Certainly, the latter part of the 'Dark Ages' grows steadily more gloomy. Rulers were incompetent; and what energies they had were almost entirely dovoted to war. There was no cohesion in the social order, little or no intercommunication of ideas. Roads had pretty nearly ceased to exist.[6] All life was narrowed to the small circle of feudal domains; and even that life was made sullen and savage by its insecurity. The Catholic Church, the one great hope of civilization in these turbulent times, found only pitifully feeble instruments to its hand, in a dispersed and demoralized huddle of monks, in its swaggering, incontinent, and ignorant bishops and priests.[7] Perhaps in no part of Europe were conditions worse than in Rome itself, during most of this time torn by factions which made the papacy the sport of their ambitions.

Optimistic writers try to see an area of light amidst all this darkness, in the Germany of the Ottos. But the exception there is more apparent than real. In the tenth century, the descendants of Henry the Fowler, and notably Otto the Great, who ruled as king from 936 to 973, and was crowned emperor of the West by the Pope at Rome in 962, established a strongly autocratic government in Germany, and made a vigorous stand against the Hun invaders. But far from curbing the turbulence of the age, they added to it by engaging in the fractional wars of Italy. Otto the Great appointed his brother, St. Bruno, and his cousins, Poppo and Henry, to episcopal sees.

These were three good men, who tried earnestly to stir up some enthusiasm for learning and piety amongst their clergy. But the little good they did was more than offset by the vicious policy which gave them their appointment as bishops, and which led to such grave abuses in the Church. And they no more succeeded in making a home for learning in Germany, or in effecting any widespread reform in the German clergy or people, than had Charlemagne in France or Alfred in England.

Needed Revival

What the age needed was, not a scattering of learned men, not an occasional pious bishop here and there, not even a wise sovereign who would encourage schools. If the education of men was to develop in any way befitting human beings, society needed two things. The first was a definite stabilizing, on some sound and healthy basis, suited in a practical way to what the men of the time were capable of appreciating. And the second was a moral reform, some return to Christian principles of conduct. These two processes would constitute the real education of Europe, and upon them alone could be built any further development of civilization. The instruments of these two processes were at hand; in the tradition of Roman law and the civil organization, which, though obscured, had never been wholly lost to Europe; and in the Catholic Faith, which smouldered with a divine vitality under all the ashes of violence, simony, ignorance, superstition, and immorality. But that Europe of the ninth and tenth centuries should be so revivified would seem to be a greater moral miracle than even the survival of the Church during the first three centuries of persecution.

Brought about through Cluny

It is no exaggeration to say that the foundation of Cluny marks the turning point in the history of education in the Middle Ages. Cluny was a Benedictine abbey, about four miles from Macon, founded in 910 by Berno, on a grant of land from William, the Duke of Aquitaine. There had been Benedictine monasteries continiously for nearly four hundred years. In their early history, as we have seen, the Benedictine monks were a most important factor in the civilizing of the barbarians. But although all the monasteries had a common 'rule,' or way of life, each monastery was an isolated unit. That fact involved them in the feudal organization which grew up round about them. Further, it exposed them to the great weakness of being unable to resist or oppose the bad conditions which might prevail in their particular locality; they had no common fund of spiritual vigor upon which to draw in their need. Hence they inevitably suffered decay in the social anarchy of the ninth century. Berno saw the need of closer organization, for the mutual support of the monasteries. During the seventeen years of his government of the new abbey of Cluny, he succeeded in getting five other monasteries to revive the spirit of the old Benedictine rule,[8] and to place themselves under the central jurisdiction of Cluny. His successor, St. Odo, abbot from 927 to 942, added seventeen more abbeys to the organization. Both Odo and Maieul, who was abbot from 948 to 975, carried the new spirit into Italy, which had perhaps suffered more greviously from the distress of the times than any other country. Bishop Gennadius of Astorga, in Spain, restored a number of abbeys destroyed by the Saracens, and placed them under the rule of Cluny.[9] And so the organization grew, until, in the twelfth century, three hundred and fourteen Benedictine houses were included in the Cluny system.[10] It was this growing system which changed the character of feudalism, and therefore of all mediaeval society. The change was an amazing work of education. We shall have to consider it a little in detail, though as briefly as possible.

Which brought back the Roman concept of organization

As has been said, early feudal society needed stabilizing.

All its elements were in flux. A great man like Charlemagne could hold them together momentarily with his strong hand; but when his grasp was relaxed, they scattered again. Yet the memory of the great Roman organization was never wholly lost, even during the wildest times of anarchy in Europe. Indeed, from the time of Charlemagne on, there were repeated efforts to revive the Roman Empire itself. For the most part the revivals were in name only. When they approached any reality, it was always by a mere forced imposition of physical power: a necessarily unstable condition. Now the reform of Cluny was modeled on the Roman idea of a central organization; but it did not impose that central government; it got men to accept it voluntarily.[11] It is true, Cluny was concerned with organizing a comparatively small number of men, in the distintive (and what some would stupidly call 'unsocial') monastic life. But those monks were an influential part of mediaeval society, and their monasteries were intricately involved in the feudal system. The drawing together of the monks could not but affect the complicated feudal world in which they lived. A new idea of union was actively at work in that world, and its value appealed to many, who had no notion whatever that it was a very old idea brought again into practice.[12] It would be out of proportion, and beyond our purpose, to follow the development of that idea in the feudal system. Every honest history of the Middle Ages shows it. But we should not forget that it takes its beginning at Cluny.

And revived the Christian spirit

More important even than the civil reform of feudalism, was the revival of Christian principles of living; without which, indeed, the civil reform itself would have been impossible. It must not be forgotten that by the tenth century most of western Europe had accepted Christianity in theory at least; but it is always a harder task to get people to reduce a theory to practice than to get them to accept the theory. Even those who may not admit that moral and religious education is more important than intellectual education,[13] must confess that it is more difficult. Cluny set about the moral education of Europe both by example and by precept. Within fifty years of its foundation, the holy lives of its own monks had made the name of Cluny famous throughtout the Western world, had impressed the imagination of peasants and nobles alike, and had begun to leave the mass of Europe.

Immediately by its influence on the Clergy and Monks

The Popes John XI and Leo VII welcomed and furthered this revival. By their charters they exempted Cluny from all jurisdiction save their own. They made of the Cluniacs a rock in the swirling waters of feudalism. Bishops turned to Cluny for aid in reforming various monasteries; often to find the peaceful Cluniacs ending by reforming the bishop himself. It is impossible to reckon accurately the number of restorations and new foundations of monasteries in the tenth century, but in the lifetime of Odo alone we have record of more than fifty in France, Italy, and the Germanies. The Christian fervor of the monks was contagious. Often, as in Upper Lorraine, laymen and the lower clergy besieged the bishops with clamors for reform; this was very notable in Toul, Verdun, and Metz. Corruptio optimi pessima: a bad bishop is harder to Christianize than a prostitute; but at times even a bad bishop gave way to popular demand, as Adalbero did at Metz in 933.[14] It is not implied that suddenly all the clergy and monks became saints; but unquestionably the moral and religious tone of the clergy and monks was raised, the scandal of dissolute clerical lives was lessened, the teachings of Christ were more earnestly preached to the people at large. There are three particular effects of this educational movement to be noted.

By introducing the truce of God

First, and perhaps most important, was the repression of feudal violence. In 989, at the Council of Charroux,[15] was decreed the Pax Dei; by which the sentence of excommunication was uttered against all who should attack unarmed travellers, steal from a church, or steal from the poor. It was declared again at Narbonne and at Le Puy, in 990; more solemnly at Poitiers, in 999.[16] Twenty like councils repeated the decree between 1000 and 1038. This was a significant stand against the anarchic violence of feudalism; and it is to be observed that it is distinctly based on religious belief and backed by religious sanction. But it was to go further. At the Council of Elne, in 1027, the 'truce of God' was first proposed: an agreement by which the knights bound themselves not to fight "from the ninth hour on Saturday to the first hour of Monday."[17] Within fifteen years the movement had grown so that Odilo, the fifth abbot of Cluny, backed by Reginald, the Archbishop of Arles, Benedict, the Bishop of Avignon, and Nithard, the Bishop of Nice, could appeal to the clergy of Italy to receive and keep the Treva Dei, "which we have accepted and firmly hold."[18] This developed truce of God was to extent from sunset on Wednesday to sunrise on Monday. The days of peace between Wednesday and Monday were to be kept sacred to the memory of the Christian mysteries; the motive of peace was the Christian religion. For a homicide committed on a day of the Truce, the penalty was exile from the province and pilgrimage to Jerusalem; for other offenses against the peace, reparation under the civil law, and a double canonical penance. It is astounding to know that the truce of God was accepted; even though it was not perfectly kept, its acceptance marked a great educational advance; and it was kept in sufficient measure to lift Europe out of anarchy.[19]

By Christianizing the institution of chivalry

Chivalry at first meant only cavalry, soldiers on horseback. Later it meant the order of feudal nobility, based upon the military and social distinction of knighthood. In theory, knighthood was not hereditary. It was to be conferred as a recognition of valor and worthiness. It was to be a democratic institution, open to every one who could earn entry into it. In reality, of course, it was practically hereditary; with rare exceptions, only the sons of knights became knights. For centuries the distinction of knighthood was nothing more than a distinction of physical prowess; and if to our modern minds the very name is filled with the fine moral flavor of loyalty, devoted courage, courtesy, if today chivalrous means considerate, unselfish, and morally noble, we must recall that the change in meaning came from that Cluny which introduced the truce of God. The Chansons de Geste read back into the earlier chivalry a spirit which it did not have until the influence of the Cluniac monks made Christian principles an essential part of chivalry. Without ceasing to be military, chivalry became religious.[20] Its ceremonies of initation were acts of worship of God. The oath of knighthood was an oath to defend religion, to practice justice and charity and mercy.[21] The penalties for violation of the oath were religious penances. The knight was a man dedicated. It was this fusion of the martial and the religious which prepared the way for the Crusades, the epic adventures of the Middle Ages. When Pope Urban II, once a Cluniac monk, proclaimed the First Crusade at Clermont, in 1095, the chief inducement he offered to the Christian knights for taking part in the Crusade was an indulgence.[22]

And by improving the lot of the serfs

It is not within the purpose of this chapter to go into the history of serfdom. But a reform which opened the way for serfs to develop themselves is a very important event in the history of education, and its importance is stressed by the fact that in the tenth and eleventh centuries the serfs constituted by far the largest part of the population of Europe. Old Roman Laws[23] had forbidden rural slaves to be removed from the land of their origin. The barbarians, besides adding greatly to the number of slaves, suppressed these laws. The Church revived them for her own serfs, and gradually, both by the influence of her example and by the persuasions of Cluniac monks in the various regional councils, got the feudal lords to accept them.[24] Seebohm points out that serfdom was a transitional stage between slavery and freedom.[25] And it was the application of Christian principles to feudal society by and through Cluny which furthered that transition. Peter the Venerable, Abbot of Cluny, replying to the Apologia of St. Bernard in 1125, says: "We look upon our serfs, not as slaves and handmaids, but as brothers and sisters."[26] The way to freedom opened through Christian charity and the Christian sense of spiritual equality. In the twelfth century Walter Mapes could say that the villeins were educating their ignoble offspring in the liberal arts.[27] In France and Italy serfs increasingly gained their freedom during the eleventh and twelfth centuries, and serfdom had practically disappeared by the end of the fourteenth century. There were, obviously, many causes at work in this change;[28] but a notable impetus comes from Cluny.[29]

A restored society ready for intellectual development

It is unwise to forget that all educational development is not merely slow (and not always in a forward direction), but that it is continuous, linking a constant succession of causes and effects. A mere handful of intelligent and energetic men may speed up the process, but only when the mass of men are ready to follow their leadership. It is this fact which at times tempts the historian of education to despair; he can never catch and put upon paper adequately that most elusive yet most important element of development, the temper and spirit of the people. Now it was that temper of the age which Cluny had changed, in every part of society, from the highest nobles to the lowest of the peasants. It is perhaps significant that schools begin to multiply in the eleventh century; but it is more significant that there is a growth of interest in things of the mind. Yet it appalls one to find modern historians sneering at the fact that great part of that interest should concern itself with revealed truths. The Christian ideal was finding a home again in the family, that basis of all society. The home life of

Guibert de Nogent, appealingly described in his autobiography,[30] was typical of an increasingly large number of homes. Family life began to take precedence over the business of war. It is a sort of symbol of the age that within little more than a long lifetime, the pirate Normans became builders, founding between 1050 and 1125 a new and admirable style of architecture. Christendom was beginning again to indulge in the luxury of thinking.

Material for intellectual revival supplied in part by Saracens

Left to itself, Europe would have revived the arts and sciences. The peoples who created Gothic architectures and sculpture, who made the glass of the marvelous windows of Saint-Denis and Charters, who determined the diatonic scale in music, who invented the mariner's compass, and who wove the tapestry of Bayeux, were not intellectually or aesthetically helpless, to say the least. Gerbert, born about 950, who became a monk in the Benedictine abbey of St. Geraldus at Aurillac in Auvergne, might seem to sum up in his one person the learning of the time; and a study of his extant writings, and the life by his disciple Richer, make clear that that learning was not inconsiderable. [31] The ferment of thought in Europe was vigorous.[32] But it moved more swiftly for the help it got from a strange source, the once threatening Saracens or Moors of Spain.

The contribution of the Saracens should not be undervalued. It consisted chiefly in reintroducing to Europe the learning of the Greeks, particularly their writings in philosophy and medicine, and in bringing to Western civilization the great gift of the Hindu numerals and some of their mathematics.[33] But two facts should be remembered, in this connection. The first is that the new acquaintance with foreign learning would have been useless unless the peoples of Europe were actively ready to profit by it. Mere exposure to learning is not education (though many schools are conducted on the supposition that it is). It was what Europeans of the eleventh and twelfth centuries brought to the new learning that determined its value to them.[34] The second fact is that, at the very time that Europe was entering upon the astonishing intellectual development of the thirteenth century, the Saracens were slipping back into stagnation and decay.

The strange history of learning amongst the Saracens

Lack of space forbids going into any study of the education of the Saracens; but it is important to our history to consider their learning. Mohammed, an illiterate man, founded his religion about 621 A.D. It was not an intellectual movement, but one of militant fanaticism; the Koran, committed to writing only after the death of Mohammed, is a jumble of disconnected sentences. The new religion spread rapidly. Before the close of the seventh century it came into contact with the cultured people of Syria. Some Nestorian monks had made a Syriac versions of the writings of Aristotle and the neo-Platonists and some of the Greek authorities on medicine; these they again translated into Arabic. When, about 750, the Khalifate was moved to Baghdad, some of the influential Moslems favored the new learning. Harun-al-Raschid, Khalif from 786 to 809, urged the establishment of schools. His son, Al-Mamum, who ruled from 813 to 833, founded a great school, with a library and observatory, at Baghdad.[35] A small number of Moslems developed enthusiasm for study. They borrowed a good deal in mathematics from the Hindus, including, of course, their convenient system of numerals; which we today commonly call Arabic. But the enthusiasm never spread widely. The mass of the people looked upon it with suspicion and aversion. Nevertheless it persisted for centuries, based chiefly upon two noble interests: an interest in medicine, and a desire to rationalize the fanatic vagaries of Mohammedanism. Both these pursuits reached their best development, in the East, in Avicenna (Ibn Sina) a Persian physician, who was born in 980 and died in 1037. However, the popular opposition to learning had been growing, and was driving the scholars out of the East into the new Khalifate of Spain. In the East the movement dwindled into the writing of silly chronicles and lascivious romances. In its new home in Spain it thrived mightly. It became the fashion for men of wealth to collect manuscripts[36] and to act as patrons to scholars. Most of the learning was centered in the study of medicine, based upon the writings of Galen and later of Hippocrates and Aristotle. But the medical studies involved chemistry and even astrology: in the search for the elixir of life and the philosopher's stone and a control of the influence of the stars. These researches often carried keen minds into real philosophy and real discoveries in the sciences. Geber discovered nitric acid, and Rhazes sulphuric acid. Back in the time of Al-Mamum, Ptolemy's geography and astronomy had been translated into Arabic as the Almagest; and in 1196 Geber had built an observatory in Seville and made real developments in astronomy. Very many of the so-called 'Arabian physicians' were not Arabs, but jews; and it was a group of Jewish scholars who founded the famous school of medicine Montpellier, about 1090. The Moors of Spain were proud of their scholars as physicians, but began to look askance at them when they went into the study of philosophy. The greatest of their philosophers, Averroes (Ibn Roshd) was driven into exile before his death in 1198. The Jews received him and befriended him. After his death, the orthodox opposition to philosophical study triumphed; and in fact all zeal for learning began to die out amongst the Moors of Spain, as it had already died in the East.

How the Saracen learning came into Europe

From the tenth to the close of the twelfth centuries, the peoples of western Europe had many contacts with the Saracenic learning developed in Spain. Perhaps the first to be noted is that which came through the Moorish physicians, who were welcomed throughout Europe. Although their primary concern was with medicine, many of them had picked up no small smattering of other sciences. They impressed the awakening intellects of Europe, and were able to give them, both in speech and in writing, a great deal of information. Next, there are indications, in part historical, in part legendary, that Europeans went into Moorish Spain to study. Such a seeker after knowledge was the Englishman, Aethelhard of Bath, often called the greatest English scientist before Roger Bacon. He lived in the time of Williams Rufus, and probably went into Spain about 1090. Such were the English Robert de Tetines and the Dalmatian Herman, whom Peter of Cluny found studying astrology at Evora when he went there himself to enquire more exactly into Moslem doctrines. Peter persuaded the two to translate the Koran into Latin, in 1143. But the most important of all the media of communication between Europe and the Saracen learning were the Christian Spaniards themselves, who, in the course of the heroic reconquest of their country from the Moors, took over also the intellectual importations which the Moors had made from the Greeks and the Hindus.

The story of the reconquista has no place here. Unfortunately, though it is one of the great epic stories of the world, it has very little place in any modern writing of history. From the Battle of Covadonga, in 718, in which king Pelayo defeated the invading and conquering Saracens, and saved the little foothold of the Asturias, to the Battle of Las Navas de Toledo in 1212, covers the most inspiring part of the great struggle, which in its entirety lasted nearly eight hundred years. During the reign of Alfonso VI (1065-1109), Rodrigo Diaz, Count of Vivar, the hero whom the Spaniards call El Cid Campeador, stirred the soul of a whole people. With the capture of Toledo in 1085, the way began to open for a mastering of the Saracen learning. Christian Spain partook of the intellectual revival of all Europe, and she found at hand a considerable store of the ancient lore of the East as material to work with. Most of the men who came from various parts of Europe to profit by the Saracen learning did not actually go to Moorish teachers, but studied in Christian schools attached to monastery or cathedral. So Gerbert had studied, at the Abbey of Cusan in Catalonia, before the close of the tenth century. At the end of the eleventh and beginning of the twelfth centuries, the monastic and cathedral schools of Spain were flourishing; and by 1150, Raymond, the Archbishop of Toledo, had gathered a group of fifty scholars, from nearly all the countries of Europe, to make a huge translation into Latin of all the learning that the Moors had compiled.[37]

Conclusion

This whole chapter is a summary. But to compact it still more, we may say that for a hundred years after the death of Charlemagne Europe was thrust farther back into barbarism by internal conflicts and foreign invasions; that it was raised from this bad state by the renewal of the Christian spirit and the revival of Roman principles of social organization, brought about largely through the Cluniac reform; that, with the restoration of some social and moral stability, the intellectual life of Europe began to function once more; and that it providentially found a rich mental provender awaiting it in the antique learning which the Saracens had so strangely carried out of the East. The twelfth century marks the definite passing of the Dark Ages, and the coming of a new civilization, as sharply characterized as has been that of the Greeks and the Romans.

Topics for Discussion

1. The training of a knight.
2. The place of women in the education of chivalry.
3. The educational function of the Jongleurs.
4. Schools in the Cluniac monasteries.
5. Gerbert and his disciples.

6. The schools of Rheims and Chartres.
7. The libraries of this period.

REFERENCES

1. Cf. Laurie, Rise and Constitution of Universities, Lect. III. See especially S. R. Maitland, The Dark Ages, Rivington, London, 1844.
2. Cf. Finlay, Byzantine Empire, Bk. I, p. 265.
3. The educational influence of Alfred has been as much exaggerated by some writers as has been that of Charlemagne. Historical perspective would seem to be rare. It is almost amusing to note that, school,' Alfred, when he in turn wished to establish a 'palace school,' had to send to the continent for masters: Grimbald, of St. Omer, and John, a monk of Corbie. Learning had no real foothold anywhere in that age, which needed first to be civilized before it could be interested in such things as books and schools. Alfred's 'revival' failed even more signally that Charlemagne's.
4. In the matter of schools, this was true until after the year 1000. Indeed, the fact is constantly made the basis of a malevolent charge that the Catholic Church in the Middle Ages held a monopoly in education. Of any monopoly by design, there is simply no evidence: beyond the essential monopoly conferred on it by its Founder, when He commissioned it to 'teach all nations,' and gave His revelation into its keeping. The monopoly in fact (i.e., that there were no other schools) is patently explained by the equally evident facts that no other organization made any attempt to establish schools.
5. Cf. Acta Conc. Metz, 909, Mansi, Vol.18. pp. 270 sqq. Odo, the second abbot of Cluny (927-42), expressly attributes the corruption of the monks to the dispersion caused by the invasions. Cf. Vita Odonis a Joanne, 3:2, Migne, P. L., 133:96.
6. Cf. H. Belloc, The Road, New York, 1925, pp. 147 sqq.
7. Cf. Collationes Odonis, Migne, P.L., 133:518 sqq.
8. Benedict of Aniane, who died in 821, had, with the aid and encouragement of Louis the Mild, reformed the monks of a number of Benedictine abbeys; but his work died with him. The changes he introduced into the Benedictine 'rule' were adopted by Berno, and made the base of his new reform. They may be read in Migne, P. L., 103:701-1380.
9. A. K. Porter, Romanesque Sculpture on the Pilgrimage Roads, 10

vols., Boston, 1923, recounts in detail how the influence of Cluny spread first to Burgundy, then to England, northern Spain, the Germanies, southern Italy; and most strikingly how it passed along the great highway which led to the shrine of St. James at Compostella.

10. Under Huge, abbot from 1049 to 1109, the total number of Cluniac monks was reckoned at some ten thousand. At the general chapter of 1132, summoned by the abbot, Peter the Venerable, more than two hundred priors attended.

11. It is significant that, although Odo definitely aimed at a general reform of monasticism, and was empowered by Pope John XI in 931 (Migne, P.L., 132:1057) to receive "any monk from any monastery who should wish to pass over to your manner of living," he reformed twice as many monasteries as those which he added to the Cluny system; and although he had the backing of civil lords, he used no force, but relied upon persuasion. (See the reform of Fleury: Migne, P.L., 133:81. Vita Odonis a Joanne, 3:8.)

12. The Cluniac monasteries were placed directly under papal jurisdiction. This fact and its political consequences, in establishing an influenctial organization within the various feudal states which was free of control by those states, are of enormous importance in the social and political history of Europe. Whether men managed that new central political power well or ill in the succeeding centuries, there is no denying that in the eleventh and twelfth centuries the papal power was the great source of social unity in Europe and a most potent influence in bringing Europe out of barbarism.

13. It is stupid, furthermore, to ignore the obvious fact that moral and religious education involves a very energetic use of the intellect in grasping and applying great truths.

14. Bollandists, *Acta SS.*, 27 Febr., p. 697.

15. Mansi, *Conscilta*, Vol. 19, 89-90. It is worth remark that at this council, as also at the councils of Hery (1024) and Eine (1027) women took part. Cf. Mansi, Vol. 19, 483.

16. Mansi, Vol. 19, 267.

17. Mansi, Vol. 19, 483.

18. Mansi, Vol. 19, 593.

19. It may help us to realize the educational significance of the truce of God. If we compare the effort which brought it into existence

with the efforts expended, since the World War of 1914-18, upon a covenant of peace: (1) in the conditions under which the two have been made (a semibarbaric feudalism and a supposedly high civilization); (2) in the means employed (the universal Catholic religion, and congresses of diplomats); and (3) in the relative success of the two attempts.

20. Cf. L. Reynaud, *Les origines de Pinfluence francaise en Allemagne*, Paris, 1913, pp. 43, 339. Kenelm Digby, *The Broadstone of Honour*.

21. The distinctive education of a knight is well known. In its later development, it included an elementary training in letters and in moral conduct, then a training in the use of arms and the military art and finally training in elaborate courtesy and such graces of life as the age knew; the whole strongly pervaded by the spirit of religion. Although it was concerned with only a small percentage of the population, its influence was considerable, because that small part of society constituted the social leaders.

22. Can. 2: Quicunque pro sola devotione, non pro honoris vel pecuniae adeptione, ad liberandam ecclesiam Del Jerusalem profectus fuerit, iter illud pro omni penitentia reputetur. Mansi, *Concilia*, Vol. 20, 816.

23. Constantine in 332, Valentinian I in 377. Cf. Cod. Justin., XI, xivii, 2.

24. St. Ives of Chartres in his Decretum, collects many of the ancient canons which imposed upon churches the duty of defending the liberty of freed slaves. See particularly pars xvi, cap. 46-54 (Migna P.L., 161:915 sqq.). There is an interesting letter of Pope Geiasius (492-496) to Bishop Bonifacius, which implies that churches had even gone much further than this, and given sanctuary to rum away slaves (Migne, *P.L.*, 59:152). In the laws of St. Stephen King of Hungary (who died in 1038) there is clear evidence that the manumission of slaves was a frequent act, done out of the motive of Christian charity (Ch. xvii; Migne, *P.L.*, 151:1248). The 66th chapter of the laws of William the Conqueror, granting liberty to any serf who dwelt for a year and a day in one of the King's cities of camps, or in a walled town, is an outgrowth of the Christian practice of monasteries and churches (Cf. Migne, P.L., 149:1320). The freeing of the serfs was necessarily, and wisely a slow and gradual affair: but it would never have had its beginning except in the spirit of Christian charity. The influence of the great St. Hugh Abbot of Clunny from 1049 to 1109, in furthering the growth of this spirit both by precept and by example, may be gathered from various details in his life, as recounted in the *Bibliotheca Cluniacensis*, pp. 413-35: 447-62; 557-60. Stubbs, in *Select*

Charters, says that serfs might not become clerics or monks and quotes the Assize of Clarendon, under Henry II, of 1166. But that decision merely repeats the law of Cap. xvi. Constitution of Clarendon, 1164, which does not forbid the eradination of serfs, but only cautions that before a serf be accepted as monk or cleric due inquiry be made to safeguard the rights of his feudal lord. The text is: "Prohibet dominus rex ne monachi canonici vel aliqua domus religionum recipiat aliquem de popul minuto in monachum vel canonicum vel fratrem, donec sciatur of Quali testimonio ipse fuerit, nist ipse fuerit infirmus ad mortem". which latter case, of course, the rights of the serf's lord were on the verge of eternal cancellation.

25. *The English Vilage Community*, London, 1833, Vol. 8, pp. 252-316. He is in agreement with Fustel de Coulanges, *Histoire des Institutions Politiques de P Ancienne France*, Paris, 1901.

26. Epist., 28: Migne, *P.L.*, 189:146.

27. Nicholas Breakspear, who, as Adrian IV, was the only English pope, had been a serf. He was pope from 1154 to 1159. See his Life by Cardinal Boso, in Migne, *P.L.*, 188:1351-60.

28. Many writers have exaggerated the influence exerted through all the developments of the tenth century by the superstitious fear that the year 1000 was to see the end of the world. Contemporary records make clear that, though this fear was widespread amongst the peasants and the more ignorant of the nobility and clergy, it had little hold or influence upon the men who wre shaping the course of events, and its influence upon the common people was neither profound nor lasting. See for instance, the quarrel between Arnulph and Gerbert (five years later to be the first French Pope, under the title of Sylvester II) over the see of Rheims, and the decision against Gerbert by Pope Gregory V in 996 (Mansi, *Concilia*, Vol. 19, 103 sqq. and 173 sqq.). See also the Life and Letters of Sylvester II, Popefrom 999 to 1003, in Mansi, Vol. 19, 240 sqq.; especially Sylvester's letter of 999, proposing to arm Christendom in a crusade to deliver the holy sepulchre from the hands of the Moslems, in Muratori, Script. Vol. 3, p. 400, and Recueil des historiens des Gaules, etc.,Plame, Paris, 1874, Vol. 10, p. 426. In the same way, the English monastic and educational reforms of Sts. Dunstan, Ethelwold, and Oswald, and the famous Abbot of Fleury, during the last quarter of the tenth century, are the work of forward-looking men, not of men paralyzed by fear of an impending end of the world. In the eighteen years he was Archbishop of Canterbury (he died in 978), St. Dunstan founded or restored more than forty abbeys, reformed large numbers of

the clergy, and to some extent revived the system of parish elementary schools which had been destroyed in the Danish invasions. See also the Annales of Thietmar of Meres burg, for the Germanies, referring to the year 1000; in Pertz, Mos Germ. Hist., Vol. 5; and the life of Bornward, Bishop of Hildeshelm from 992 to 1021, by his teacher Thangmar, in Migne, *P.L.*, Vol. 140. *The Chronicon Vanetum* of John the Deacon, in Migne, *P.L.* 139:871, covers the period to 1008. The only man of note who seems to have been affected by the popular fear was the boy-Emperor, Otho III, crowned in 996, poisoned in 1002 by his mistress, Stephania, whose husband he had ordered beheaded in 997 for a conspiracy against Pope Gregory V. But Otho's age (he was only sixteen when he became emperor) may help to account for the exception.

29. There is pitiful irony in the fact that later on Cluny fell into decay, through wealth and the inertia of overgrown numbers and power. Its place was taken by the new reform of Citeaux, under the great St. Bernard. But the incomparable work of Cluny in the education of western Europe was well done before Cluny itself went the way of all human institutions.

30. *De Vita Sua sive Monodiarum;* Migne, *P.L.*, Vol. 156. It has been rather clumsily translated into English by C.C. Swinton Bland, Dution and Co., New York, 1926. See also B. Monod, *Le Moine Guibert et Son Temps*, Paris, Hachette, 1905. Gulbert was born at Clermonten Beauvaisls in 1053, died Abbot of Notre Dame de Nogent in 1124.

31. Richerus, *Historiarum Libri IV*, Migne, *P.L.*, 138:17 sqq. See especially lib. iii. Cr. also Picavet, *Gerbert, un Pape Philosophe*, Lerous, Paris, 1897.

32. Evidences of the intellectual awakening of Europe in the eleventh century are found also in the growth of scholarship outside the monastic and cathedral schools. For the first time in centuries lay teachers begin to appear and soon become rather numerous. Possibly the elevation to the papacy of Gerbert, the brilliant school teacher of Rheims, stimulated the ambition of men, and pointed to the fact that books might be as useful as the sword in achieving success. Cf. Rodulfus Glaber, *Historiarum Libri*, Migne, *P.L.*, 142:611-93. Berengar, of unhappy fame, was one of these teachers. He was born about the year 1000. Cf. Ep. Adelman., Migne, P.L., 143:1261 sqq.

33. Von Humboldt (Cosmos, II, p. 226, note to p. 358) considers it more than probable... that the Christians in the west were familiar with Indian numerals even earlier than the Arabs," and bases his

acceptance of the statement on the work of the mathematician Charles. Aperqu historique des Methodes en Geometric 1837, pp. 464-72. The question is discussed in the Comptes renderde I'Accededmte des Sciences, Vol. 8 (1839), p. 78; Vol. 9 (1839), p. 449; Vol. 16 (1843), pp. 156-73, 218-46; and Vol. 17 (1843), pp. 143-54.

34. Even in the latter half of the tenth century there are evidence of intellectual enthusiasm in the reformed monastic and cathedral schools. See, for instance, Richer's Life of Gerbert, in Pertz, Monkmenta Germaniae Historica, Vol. 3, and Richeri, Hist., Lib. iii, 47-53 in Migne, 138:102-05, where Gerbert is said to have taught rhetoric from the classic Latin poets, dramatists and satirists, and astronomy with the aid of globes, showing a knowledge of the sphericity of the earth, the elliptical planes, and the movements of the stars. Gerbert's pupil. Fulbert, Bishop of Chartres from 1006 to 1028, and a friend of Odilo of Cluny, founded a great school, or rather re-established as old school, at Chartres, which was deservedly famous. Cf. Les. Ecoles de Chartres au Moyen Age, by the Abbe Clerval (Memoires de li Societe archeologique d'Eure-et-Loir, Vol. 11, 1895).

35. By way of comparison, it may be pointed out that Al-Mamum's astronomers never attained to an accuracy in determining the solar year equal to the work of the Etruscans (Cf. Niebuhr. *Hist. of Rome*, Vol. 1, 274) or the even better work of the Mayas in America (Cf. Humboldt, *Vues des Cordilires et Monuments des Peuples indigenes de L'Amerique*, p. 125).

36. The Khalif Al-Hakem II (961-76) is said to have gathered together in his library at Cordoya 600,000 books and manuscripts. Though this is a manifest exaggeration, the legend testifies to the prestige attaching to the possession of a great library.

37. It must not be forgotten that, during the twelfth century, the Crusades brought western Europe into direct touch with the Greeks and other peoples of the East, and were the occasion of at least some slight infiltration of learning into the West. But that, at best, was a thin stream. More came by way of Northern Africa and Sicilly. But Spain was the chief channel. Roger Bacon (Opus Majus, pars I, Cap. xiii) credits the introduction of Aristotle to the version by Michael Scot which appeared in 1230. However, the greatest of the translators was jGerard of Cremona, who was born in 1114 and died at Toledo in 1187, and who turned into Latin more than eighty Arabic works; three on logic a half dozen on mathematics, a score or more on astronomy and other sciences, and a long list of medical treatises.

6

Scholasticism and the Rise of the Universities

Return of school education to Europe

The work of education, as has been seen, was carried on for several centuries without much assistance from schools; and that lack was, as we know, a great handicap in the work. It must be insisted upon once more that schools are by no means essential instruments of education; but they are, or can be, very useful. Schools are short-cuts to experience, systematized attempts to convey to a new generation, in condensed formulas, the experiences and acquisitions of preceding generations. They are limited in their effectiveness (a) by the skill or want of skill of those who formulate these past experiences; (b) by the immaturity of the students; (c) by the essentially imperfect process implied in attempts to reduce living knowledge to a theoretical formula. Within these limits they can be of real and great value in education; as supplementary to the students' actual experience of living, and to the more vital influences of their homes and surroundings. Now, once again, the peoples of Europe had reached a stage and condition of social life which made schools in any number possible; and the schools began to appear and multiply.

Cycles of school education

It may be of service here to take a broad preliminary

survey of this school education which, from the twelfth century to our own time, is to play so large a part in the history of education. A very interesting fact to note is that school education moves in curious cycles; of which there have been three, clearly marked, in the past eight hundred years; and a fourth is, apparently now well begun. The beginning of these cycles is often called a 'renaissance' or rebirth; which is rather an absurd name, springing from the perennial vanity which leads each generation of men to see in its efforts a splendid improvement upon the efforts of preceding generations.[1] Each of these 'renaissances' has been characterized by a strikingly similar cycles of progress: (1) an intense, and fairly widespread, enthusiasm for some particular line of studies is the first stage; (2) then comes a period of more careful organization in the studies; (3) then a fixed method, a formula of procedure, tending to become more and more rigid and dwarfing in importance the actual subjects studied; (4) then boredom, discontent, reaction, ending in (5) a final turning away from the now discredited line of study, and the eager acceptance of a new line. Thus the cycle begins over, and repeats itself with exquisite precision. In a large view, the process is both amusing and pathetic. To add to the humor, we may note that the close of each cycle sees the recurrent use of a wildly exagagerated appeal to the theory of 'formal discipline' for a justification of the waning system. We shall have to consider that theory in its place.

Dominant subjects in each cycle

The subjects that claimed enthusiastic attention in the schools of the first 'renaissance,' from the twelfth to the middle of the fifteenth centuries, were predominantly logic and metaphysics; during the second 'renaissance,' from the middle of the fifteenth to the end of the eighteenth centuries/Latin and Greek 'classic' literature; during the third 'renaissance,' from the eighteenth to the latter part of the nineteenth centuries, the positive sciences. At present we are developing in our schools an enthusiasm for the application of these positive sciences to industry, communication, and comfort of living.

These cycles closely bound up with social changes

In order to keep our view clear upon education in general, it must be recalled that these cycles in school education have been associated with great social, religious, and political changes, which are, in many ways, much more important in education than the changes in the school, and which have even conditioned the school changes, since the schools by their very nature must follow the social environment. Thus, for example, the school change from metaphysics to a borrowed antique literature came upon the heels of an increase in wealth and material comfort of living, and was accompanied by a change from the principles of Christianity to an outworn, but ever appealing, pagan delight in the world of the senses. The changes from 'classic' literature to positive science was influenced, not merely by the striking scientific discoveries of a handful of geniuses in the seventeenth century, but also, and profoundly, by the breaking away of a large part of Christendom from Catholic unity and the consequent growing skepticism in the separate fragmants.[2] With it came an increase of individualism in society, and of so-called democratic forms of government.[3]

And each still affected by its predecessors

The whole process is enormously complicated, as all living activities are. For one thing, each cycle is not so sharply set apart as might be indicated in this brief summary; but instead, carries over a confused heritage, from one generation to another, from one cycle to another, of educational methods largely discredited yet still curiously persisting. Schools, like men in general, drag a lengthening chain of memories. One may be tempted to sympathize, at least momentarily, with Rousseau in his desire to sever the chain and leave it behind him. But of course the thing cannot be done. Then too the swirling cross currents of social changes strongly affect life in the family as well as procedure in the schools; sometimes with consequences which set the home and the school in conflict. It is easy for the historian to ignore that great fact, and to look upon schools as isolated instruments of education. To make matters still worse, these eight hundred years are a period of quarrel between upholders of diverse educational procedures; a fact which adds to the difficulty of being even honest and unbiased in trying to outline their history. A great many histories of education blow up about the year 1100.

It will be a natural division of the later history of Western education to consider each of the cycles of school education; attempting, at the same time, to keep in mind the very important forces, other than the schools, which shape the development of each new generation of men.

The first cycle: Logic and Metaphysics

Interest in sharp, hard, clear thinking was no new thing to men; but it offered considerable novelty to the tumultuous peoples coming out of the semibarbarism of the 'Dark Ages.' Metaphysical speculation, that last fine luxury of the mind, had fascinated ages long since dead. It began again to fascinate the peoples settling down, after their centuries of turmoil, into a shaped and coherent mediaeval civilization. The Catholic Church, with her divine mission of spreading certain exact, definite, though often incomprehensible, truths, had done most of the shaping of that civilization. Its truths offered a field for organized, systematic thought. Its mysteries provoked speculation. When leisure came to Europe, the challenge was accepted. It was often riotously, exuberantly accepted; and led to heresy, to an implicit or explicit rejection of the truths themselves. Then, and only then, did the raw metaphysician find himself in opposition to the supernaturally endowed guardian of the truth. For the rest, churchmen encouraged the new intellectual interest, indeed took a foremost part in it; and it thrived mightily.

The genesis of Scholasticism

There had been great minds exercised in this same organization of thought and in metaphysical speculation, long before intellectual darkness had crept out of the forests of Europe with the barbarians. Their writings were at hand, voluminous, weighty: Tertullian, Cyprian, Jerome, Ambrose, and greatest of all, Augustine. Cassiodorus at the Vivarium in Italy, Isidore in Seville, had made redactions of these: clumsy enough, without the personality and charm of the original writers; but reduced to the tabloid form perhaps best suited to a people beginning to take the first tottering steps out of their intellectual infancy.[5] Aristotle supplied to the method, the cold, hard method of formal logic. Formal logic is not a glory of the human mind, but a sign of its weakness. The syllogism is a mental crutch. A finer intelligence than ours would not move upon truth by slow and laborious inference; it would apprehend. But for halting human beings the syllogism is a pitiful necessity. Armed with it, the mediaeval peoples set out in the footsteps of the great thinkers of the fourth and fifth centuries. That was the real genesis of Scholasticism.[6]

Scholasticism not a conscious, planned development

Few, if any, of the great movements in society are consciously and definitely planned.[7] Like Topsy, they 'just grow'. A countless multitude of minor changes in agriculture, commerce, manufacturing, housing, social relations, religious practices, ideas of civic government, accumulate through several generations, give to society a certain momentum in a more or less well-defined direction. The men and women who are both the causes and the subjects of these changes scarcely notice them, so gradual are they. But in time they acquire a cumulative power; each one small, the mass of them is great; and they produce a geat change, a real revolution in society. As a rule, only the long perspective of history makes clear how great the final change is. It was in this gradual way that Scholasticism developed from a multitude of causes, operating through a long period of time.

Its character traceable through three preceding centuries

Interest in the logical systematization of knowledge and thought had shown itself for a generation or two in the Carolingian times. Rabanus Maurus had insisted on the value of logical training,[8] had applied an exact logical procedure in his theological dispute with Gottschalk over the knotty problem of predestination, and had made a systematic redaction of patristic commentaraies on Scripture.[9] His contemporary, the neo-Platonist John Scotus Erigena, had ventured, on the crutch of logic, into the trackless lands of divine mystery. His exploration not unnaturally led him into heresy; for which, of course, the moderns praise him.[10] Walafrid Straboa, a disciple of Rabanus, polished up his master's Commentaries and brought them into more exact systemic form; so that his Glossa Ordinaria[11] became a sort of standard and model of system for centuries to follow. The dialectic method of Paschasius Radbertus,[12] Abbot of Corble, and of Ratramnus,[13] a monk of Corbie, in their controversial works on the Eucharist, are not remote in manner from the theological treatises of three and four centuries later. Thus, although the troublous tenth century, following upon these efforts, made intellectual expansion practically impossible, the lines of future development were already well indicated. When the schools revived, they had a subject matter and a method ready to hand.[14]

Its cradle at Bec

In the very nature of this new enthusiasm for schools, it is rash to assign to any one particular place the honor of having given the first impetus to the movement. Yet this may be ventured; that, as Cluny was the starting point of the important moral and social education of the tenth and eleventh centuries, so the monastery of Bec in Normandy may be looked upon as the radiating center of the interest in intellectual education which was growing into Scholasticism. Bec was founded in 1039 by Herluin, a Norman knight, who became its first abbot; its monks were few in number, poor, and illiterate. But three years after its foundation, there came to it an Italian noble, Lanfranc of Pavia, learned in letters and the law. He was then thirty-seven years old, and had already been engaged in teaching, at Avranches and other places. He had gained a certain notoriety by his disputations with the heretic Berengarius. When he opened his school at Bec, men, lay and clerical, noble and baseborn, came in numbers to hear him. He taught there for some twenty years, and reckoned amongst his pupils Ives of Chartres, Anselm of Bagio (who later became Pope Alexander II), and the more renowned Anselm of Aosta,[15] who was to succeed Lanfranc, both at Bec and in the archbishopric of Canterbury. From a time shortly after its beginning. Lanfranc's school never numbered less than a hundred students; and a hundred students made a large school in those days. Many of those students went forth, in their turn, to found other schools, and to carry through Europe the new enthusiasm for studies.

The trivium and quadrivium

The basis of these studies was the long-established system of the seven liberal arts, divided into the trivium and the quadrivium and formulated as long before as the time of Cassiodorus. The trivium consisted of grammar, rhetoric, and dialectic or logic; the quadrivium, of arithmetic, geometry, astronomy, and music. Medicine was a later supplement to the quadrivium; and all the liberal arts were looked upon as the handmaids to theology, the 'queen of sciences,'[16] In spite of the work of Gerbert, Hermann Contractus,[17] Adelard of Bath, and of the many Jewish and Moorish scholars who influenced European thought, the mediaeval schools in general paid little attention to the physical sciences. The simple fact is, of course, that many of these sciences did not even exist in the Middle Ages. It is scarcely fair, therefore, to crap at the mediaeval schools for neglecting them.

Particular branches of the trivium and quadrivium were emphasized in various schools. Grammar, in the broad sense of a study of the Latin language, was everywhere a fundamental school subject; but the earlier emphasis on rhetoric more and more gave way to the new enthusiasm for dialectic, and this enthusiasm tended even to swamp the quadrivium altogether. The trend of study became more severely and narrowly logical, hard, sharp-edged. However, the ancient scheme of the seven liberal arts, with something in it still reminiscent of Greek balance and grace, was never entirely abandoned throughout the Middle Ages, even when the chief studies had become logic, metaphysics, and scholastic theology.[18] Logic was studied largely in Boethius' translation of the Categories and de Interpretatione of Aristotle, with Porphyry's Introduction. There is evidence of acquaintance with the Timaeus of Plato, in a Latin version.[19] Of course, in grammar Donatus continued to be the textbook for beginners; Priscian, and the Etymologiae of Isidore, for those more advanced.

The studia generalia

The twelfth-century enthusiasm for school education was bound to bring about great changes in the character and organization of the schools themselves. For over five centuries, it will be recalled, the types of schools throughout Europe were almost exclusively the monastic and caathedral schools; uniformly small in the number of their students, and closely allied to religious purposes. These were to give place to new types; foremost amongst them those which we now call 'universities, but which in their earlier stages were known as studia generalia.[20] There were also, as we shall see, lesser schools, burgher, guild, chantry.

The rise of the studia generalia is closely bound up with another very interesting fact, the growth of towns and cities. The Dark Ages had seen the decay of city life, especially outside Italy. For centuries, the monastery and the feudal castle were the chief centers of civilization. The great mass of the people lived rather isolated lives, travelled little, had few occasions for wide social relations. But the Crusades, beginning in 1095, stirred men out of their isolation, set them in motion huge masses, gave them new contacts, not only with their fellows of the West, but with the men of the old Eastern civilization. The result was new ideas, new tastes, new standards of living. Industries began to develop on a larger scale, men banded together for manufacture and commerce, villages grew into towns.[21]

As might be expected, the seething ferment of intellectual life was more marked in the towns than in the sparsely settled countryside. The monastery was no longer the most important center of ideas. Bec gave way to Chartres and Paris. The monastery school had seen the beginning of the twelfth-century renaissance, but it was the cathedral school which carried it on; in a city.

Their origins obscure

Various circumstances, not always clear to us now, determined which of the growing cities should become seats of the new and great schools. Some medicinal springs near Salerno brought the ailing to the place; and therefore brought physicians. A school of medicine was almost inevitable. Great teachers, like Irnerius (who codified civil law) and Gratian (who redacted Church law) drew students to Bologna, or, in the case of William of Champeaux, Hugo of St. Victor, and Abelard, gathered them to be the making of a university at Paris.

Owing to the gradual character of the change from a cathedral school to a studium generale, it is rash to set any very definite dates for the beginnings of the various universities, more especially the earlier ones. Bologna came into recognizable existence some time between 1100 and 1150. The organization of the university was largely in the hands of the students themselves, who elected the rectors of the various nationes, paid the professors their salaries, determined the time and manner of lectures. The University of Paris, a more direct growth from the cathedral school of Notre Dame, which William of Champeaux had made famous, became a studium generale about 1150, and a recognized university about 1210. In it the corporation of masters, originally licensed to conduct schools by the Chancellor of Notre Dame, was the governing body Bologna furnished the type of organization for many, if not most, of the universities of the South, and Paris the type for the North. Occasionally, a migration of students from one university led to the founding of another; such as that of the law students from Bologna to Arezzo in 1215 and to Padua in 1222; or that of the Paris students who, according to Rashdall, flocked from Paris in 1167 to swell a small school at Oxford into a university. In one way or another, between 1100 and 1250 some fourteen or fifteen universities came into existence, in France, Italy, Spain, and England.[22] The Germanies developed universities considerably later. At the time of the Reformation the number of universities in Europe is variously estimated at from seventy-seven to eighty-one.

General structure of universities

It is to be noted that, primarily, a studium generale or university was a corporation of students with their masters, rather than an impersonal institution, and that it had for its purpose the training of students to be masters in their turn; pretty much like an apprenticeship in one of the craft guilds. It began quite simply in that essential relation of pupil to teacher, though in time it developed a complex social code too elaborate for discussion here. The term of years of study seems to have been generally seven, but with an increasing tendency to shorten that period. Students might enter as young as twelve or thirteen years of age; twenty or twenty-one was the common age for reaching the mastership. After some four years the student became baccalaureus, rather equivalent to a journeyman in the craft guild. The ceremony of his admission into this stage was called 'determination.' After three years more came his 'inception' or 'commencement' as a master. Rashdall notes that at least one half of the students did not go on even so far as the baccalaureatus.

Student life

The students were by no means drawn entirely from the locality of the school. As a cosmopolitan body, they grouped themselves according to the regions of their origins into nationes, which to a greater or less extent they determined and regulated by a sort of home rule. Some of them banded together and lived in a rented hall, under the management of one of their own number whom they elected as principal.[23] Some lodged with the townsfolk. They had, from very early times, their own legal privileges, and were exempt from much of the ordinary civic control. They were frequently turbulent. The often quoted account of their disorderly lives, by Cardinal Jacques de Vitry,[24] who was a student at Paris shortly after the rise of the studium generale, may be representative of the rude beginnings; but it is too drastic to be true of university life in general.[25] After the coming of the friars (the Dominicans settled at Paris in 1217, at Oxford in 1221; the Franciscans at Paris in 1230, and at Oxford in 1224), colleges were founded for the poorer students, and discipline was much improved.[26] But youth, then as now, was ebullent and rough. Quarrels between 'town and gown' were frequent and violent. The boisterous manners of the age possibly accentuated all this. But we must not let it make us forget that these students worked hard. Their hours of lecture and disputation were long. Poverty forced many of them to wearisome copying out of textbooks. From that poverty also came the custom, distasteful of course, but not at all looked upon as dishonorable, of spending their vacations in begging tours to gather funds for their maintenance at the schools.

Methods

The mediaeval universities aimed chiefly at intellectual education.[27] The method centered about books, and consisted of lectures on the texts by the masters, and disputations carried on by the students under the supervision of the masters. The plan of lecture was analytic; explanation and definition of terms used in the statement of a truth to be discussed; a detailed division and sub-division of the subject matter under consideration, followed by a summary recapituation; the presentation of problems suggested by the text; and the solving of objections to the doctrine taught. At certain of the lectures, the students were encouraged to ask questions, or to express their doubts, or their opinions on the meaning of the texts. The disputations were of two kinds; the ordinary, which took place every week, and lasted from early morning to noon, or often to evening; and the extraordinary, or disputation de quodibet, which was held once a year, covered a wide range of subjects, and lasted from two or three days to even a fortnight. Discussion was carried on in strict syllogistic 'form.' Objections were cast in a syllogism or series of syllogisms, and were answered in the rigorously analytic method of dialectic. The method makes for clearness, of a narrow analytic sort, but is cold, rather inhuman, and utterly lacking in persuasion. Out of these lectures and disputations the written works of the doctors were developed. The whole method, with all its good and bad points, survives to this day; and in many Catholic universities and particularly in ecclesiastical seminaries, survives quite unchanged.

Numbers and influence

Estimates of the number of students in the various universities differ to an almost grotesque extent. Richard Fitz

Ralph, who died in 1360, says that Oxford at one time had 30,000 students, and 6,000 in his own time. Wycliffe, who died in 1384, set down 60,000 as the ancient attendance at Oxford, but claimed only 3,000 for his own day. Paris has been credited with as high as 40,000 students at one time. Odofredus gives Bologna 10,000 in the year 1200. All these numbers are exaggerated. Modern estimates allow Paris a maximum of 6,000 or 7,000 Bologna rather less, Oxford between 1,500 and 3,000. The later German universities were still smaller in number of students, ranging from the one hundred or so at Freiburg in 1460 to about one thousand at Prague in 1380.

The total number of students at any time in the Middle Ages was small in proportion to the entire population: though possibly by the fourteenth century it was relatively larger than it is now. But their influence upon the culture of the time was pronounced. They were not numerically strong enough to raise the whole intellectual quality of mediaeval civilization to such a level, say, as that of Greece in the time of Percicles. But they did form a core of accurate and clear-cut thinking which made definite intellectual principles a common possession, in fact a rather amazingly common possession, throughout all Europe; and for one great century they tended to stabilize the civilization of Europe upon a plane of thought more lofty than it had ever before known as a whole. The complete and perfect stability of civilization upon that plane was, of course, not reached; one may reasonably doubt that it ever will be.

The great weakness of the mediaeval universities was that they were almost exclusively intellectual in their character and their influence; an inhuman and dangerous thing. And though something of that danger was lessened by the atmosphere of living faith, of supernatural religion, which clothed the great age of the universities, the blight of intellectualism was to spread more and more over the schools as time went on, and ultimately to render them dry and sterile.

The Middle Ages learned the lesson which we today are learning over again; that to unbalance education is to destroy it. The mediaeval universities were concerned with Christian truths, but rather as subject matter for analysis and discussion than as a guide to living.[28] And if the thirteenth century can lay claim to have approached more nearly than any earlier century to a successful combination of training for this life and training for the next, the basis of the claim is not to be found exclusively, or even chiefly, in the work of the universities. There were education of another sort shaping the people. We shall consider it in the next chapter.

Topics for Discussion

1. The development of scholastic method, from the Sic et Non of Abaclard to the Sentences of Peter Lombard and the Summae of St. Thomas Aquinas.
2. The mystical and rational schools in Scholasticism.
3. The function of colleges in the mediaeval universities.
4. Peter of Biois on the relation between metaphysics and the liberal arts.
5. The subjects studied in mediaeval universities.
6. The method of Bernard of Chartres in teaching.
7. Guibert de Nogent on the discipline of students.
8. Mediaeval libraries.
9. The Friars at the universities.

REFERENCES

1. The only 'renaissance' that in some way really deserves such a name is the one that took place in the eleventh and twelfth centuries. So far as schools are concerned, that was a genuine 're-birth,' inasmuch as schools had so nearly ceased to exist in the preceding centuries. But it must be noted that the term 'renaissance' has a wider range than this application to schools. In that wider

meaning, in which it embraces the whole culture of a people or of a world, it is much more tragic than conceited; since it is an implicit confession that the culture of the time is decaying. Indeed, there is even much humility of mind in each of the great 'renaissances,' in so far as the men who bring them about turn to an earlier generation for light on the problems of living. So, when Roman culture failed, there was a 'revival' of a dead Greek culture. When that earlier Greek civilization failed, there was in Greece a 'revival' of a dead Eastern culture. There are manifest strong agencies at work today toward a 'revival' of mediaeval culture. We can never entirely get away from our roots in the past; that past which repeatedly revenges itself on our scorn of it by becoming again a present.

2. History shows that the inevitable tendency of non-Catholic opinion is to sporadic division and individualism. Sir Samual Dill, Merovingians, p. 93. The late Sir Samuel Dill was not a Catholic.

3. Perhaps it is scarcely necessary to note that changes in school curriculm lag a long way behind those in general interests. for instance, a marked general interest in the positive sciences existed for fully a century before it affected the schools.

4. The twelfth and thirteenth centuries were rich in heresies; and these are often hailed today as evidences of superior rational development amongst men. Yet it is a plain fact, and one not astonishing to the thoughtful mind, that these heresies are singularly lacking in originality. Nothing in the history of man seems so painfully stereotyped as his intellectual and emotional revolts. the Bogomill, apparently the first of the significant mediaeval heretics came out of the East, from the borderland between Christianity and Islam. Intellectually, they date back to the Persian Manes, and the fourth century Manichaeans. The many European sects of the 'Cathari' (the Pure) derive from the Bogomill. Some modern Protestants like to think that they derive from the Cathari. Many of them still raise a cry against the Catholic Church, because it strove to protect its truths against these revolts; and accuse it of obscurantism, because it is refused to admit novelties in its doctrines. But whether one likes the Catholic Church or not, it is intelligent to recognize that granted its concept (which alone marked it as a Church), it was bound to reject opposing doctrines, and to guard against the corruption of what it held to be truth. Thus, even the new enthusiasm for Aristotle underwent an ecclesiastical scrutiny during the first half of the thirteenth century. In 1215, the Papal Legate at Paris forbade teachers to lecture on Aristotle. In 1231, Pope Gregory IX

appointed a commission to expurgate his works before they might be used to the schools. Yet thirty years later, we find Aristotle accepted freely everywhere, with all ecclesiastical suspicion quite allayed. There is an excellent brief discussion of intellectual liberty in the Middle Ages in Haskins,' *The Renaissance of the Twelfth Century*, pp. 360-65.

5. And whilst our historians are sneering at the compends of Isidore, they might also think for a moment of the almost incredible popularity today of "Outlines of History." "Outlines of Science," "Outlines of Philosophy," and the like. There is food for thought in the comparison.

6. The name is derived from the title of "Scholasticus," the head of a cathedral school.

7. Some maintain that the revolutionary movement, evident in Western history since the early 18th century, and still functioning very vigorously, is a planned social movement; and that the three "Internationales" are connected in a direct and purposive line of descentg. Cf. World Revolution by Nesta Webster, Boston, 1921.

8. De Cleric. Inst., iii. 20; in Migne, P.L. 107:397.

9. Migne, P.L., Vol. 108. He wrote also, somewhat after the model of Isidore of Seville, an encyclopedia, De Universo Libri XXII, Migne P.L. 111:9-614.

10. Some of his writings are given in Migne, P.L., Vol. 122.

11. It takes up two volumes in Migne's collection: P.L., Vols. 113-114.

12. De Corpore et Sanguine Domini in Migne, P.L., 120:1267-1350.

13. Migne, P.L., 121:125-70.

14. It is interesting to note that the revival took place so rapidly that Gulbert de Nogent (died 1124) can complain of a distressing scarcity of teachers in his boyhood, although within his lifetime good teachers and become abundant. (Monodiarum, Bk, I, c. IV; Migne, P.I., 156:844.)

15. Born in 1033, died in 1109. His life is excellently written by his companion Eadmer (Migne, P.L., 158:50 sqq.). His works are in Migne, P.L., Vols. 158, 159. His famous argument, proving the existence of God from the very concept of God, is in the Proslogion, cap. 2 (Migne, P.L., 158:227).

16. The theological side of Scholasticism was unquestionably its most

important work. Although it was much concerned with purely philosophical and metaphysical speculation, its great accomplishment was that it dogmatized Christian truths, set them in moulds of rigorous definition, in a scientific system. It is much derided for having done that. But is not that a human tendency with all knowledge? Why should we exclude it when there is question of knowledge given us through divine revelation? When Bateson says, "No one can survey the work of recent years without perceiving that evolutionary orthodoxy developed too fast, and that a great deal has yet to come down..." (Darwin and Modern Science, Cambridge Press, 1909, p. 101) he admits that evolutionists too are dogmatising, gathering fragments of fact, opinion, theory, into a system. All he asks is that they go slowly. The Scholastics had eleven centuries of Christian teaching back of them before they began a scientific synthesis.

17. Writings in Migne, P.L., Vol. 143.

18. Hugo of St. Victor has an interesting discussion of the subject matter of studies in Didascalion, iii. 4 (Migne, P.L., 176:768-69). See also Henri d'Andeli, Bataille des septs arts, in Histoire litteraire de la France, t. xxiii, p. 225, in which allegorically, Logic, at Paris, Vanquishes Grammar, in its stronghold at Orieans. This was written at Rouen, about 1259.

19. Even this translation, done by Chalcidius in the fourth century is incomplete, comprising only the first fifty-three chapters. Aristipus of Catania furnished Latin versions of the Meno and Phaedo about 1156, but they seem to have made little impression on the students at the time.

20. "Universitas" was originally a legal term, signifying any corporation or group of persons organized for commerce, industry, or like purpose. It was not applied to the great schools until long after their origin.

21. By the year 1200 there were over two hundred city-republics in Italy alone. In passing, we may refer to one detail of mediaeval life which has been much misrepresented: cleanliness. For a good account of bathing in mediaeval Times, see T.E. Bridgett, Blunders and Forgeries, 2d ed., London, 1891, pp. 20-51.

22. There is dispute over Salerno. Rashdall denies that there was ever a university there.

23. Brother Azarias, Essays Educational, pp. 111, 113, 123-24.

24. Historia Occidentalis, lib, ii, c. vii. He was born 1160, died 1240. In the edition of Historia Occidentalis, Douai, 1597, the passage

occurs on p. 278. Rashdall quotes it. Universities of Europe in the Middle Ages, Vol. 2, p. 690. It is commented on and interpreted by Denifle, Universitaten Mittelalters, Vol. 1, p. 672.

25. Possibly the strictures on student conduct are to some extent based on a comparison with the discipline students were subjected to in monasteries. Chapter 21 of the Decreta pro Ordine S. Benedicti of Lanfranc, when he was archbishop, lays down disciplinary regulations for the monastery students which are appallingly stringent; the strictrest surveillance, an attitude of suspicion and mistrust worthy of a prison. (Migne, P.L. 150:506-07.) On the other hand, the daily order of students, as outlined by Marbodus (1035-1128) in Carmina XXX, XXXI (Migne, P.L., 171:1724) indicates great industry on the part of the students, a routine of hard work as the normal thing: four hours of study before dinner; a short period for rest or play after dinner; then meditation, writing, study until supper; after which, another brief period for play: and then to bed. for an excellent short study, see "Life of Medieval Students," by C.H. Haskins, in Vol. 3, Amer, *Hist. Review*, pp. 203 sqq. Rashdall, Universities, Vol. 1, p. 218, has a good account of a day's work at Bologna in the thirteenth century.

26. The first college was founded at Paris, in 1248, by Pope Innocent IV for the study of oriental languages, and was followed in 1257, by the Theological College of Robert de Sorbonne. These furnished the model for most of the succeeding colleges. The first English university college was founded at Salisbury, in 1262, by Bishop Giles of Bridport, "for two chaplains, and twenty poor, honest, and teachable scholars" (A.F. Leach, *Schools of Medieval England*, p. 165). Walter de Merton's college at Oxford, founded the same year, was for future secular priests (Maxwell-Lyte. *History of Oxford University*, pp. 73 sqq.). Colleges were at first looked upon with suspicion, as nurseries for friars. It was not until 1550 that they became dominant in the universities (Marxwell-Lyte, *op. cit.*, p. 69; Brother Azarias Essays Educational, p. 122).

27. See the treatise De Magistro of St. Thomas Aquinas; English translation, pp. 39-86 of M.H. Mayer. *The Philosophy of Teaching of St. Thomas Aquinas*, Milwaukee, 1929.

28. H. Rashdall, *Universities of Europe in Middle Ages*, Vol. 2, pt. 2, p. 687.

7

The Education of the Classic Renaissance

Before attempting a sketch of education in the Classic Renaissance, it seems advisable to consider briefly a few important facts about that Renaissance itself. First to be noted is that the vast, slow, tortuous upheaval of European civilization which is generally known as the renaissance stretched over a period of about two hundred years: considerably longer than from the American War of Independence to our present day. Its limits may be roughly set as between 1350 and 1550: between the enthusiasms of Petrarch and the cold formalism of Sturm and Jesuits. The second great fact is that the character of that social upheaval varied in different lands, in different stages of its progress, under the varying local conditions of life. It is a fatal mistake to think of the renaissance as a compact, coherent, and unified movement of Europe as a whole. Indeed, diversity, division, even separatism essentially marked the movement. Europe was not merely changing; it was breaking up. A third, and very important, fact to be kept in mind is that the period of the Renaissance was largely a period of negations. This may the more readily be seen when one compares it with the twelfth-century renaissance, which built up European institutions. The Classic Renaissance found much of its enthusiasm in hatred and destruction of the immediate past;

and all warmth tended to leave it when that function was fulfilled. Except in the one great art of painting, it had no creative force; even its panegyrists make that clear. In none of its efforts did it have any of the joyousness and ease of the twelfth century. It was restless, turbulent; the whole period was one of turmoil and bitterness. These facts have much to do with the difficulty of estimating the Classic Renaissance aright; and they complicate any study of its educational efforts. In attempting that study, we must first draw a distinction between Renaissance education outside the schools and within the schools; and of these the former is by all means the more important.

I. EDUCATION OUTSIDE THE SCHOOLS

General character

This new education affected the minds and characters of grown men and women; it sprang from the social and intellectual tendencies of the age, and in turn strongly shaped those tendencies; it was intensely vital. It began in Italy, which had always been the closest Western link with the long-dead past; but in a chaotic Italy, torn by dissensions, insecure in principles, groping amidst ruins. It began in a revolt with the immediate past, which men were inclined to blame for their present social ill-ease: in a revolt against an intellectual system which undeniably had become hard, dry, sterile; against a moral system which had become insincere through the almost complete divorce of practice from precept. It turned men's minds in a great hope to a culture, a philosophy of life, which had been brought to its highest development more than a thousand years before. It saw in the revival of that ancient culture the cure for the moral and intellectual dry-rot which was everywhere manifest in the decadent mediaeval civilization. There was not lacking nobility of purpose in the leaders of the movement; there was fine enthusiasm, which spread with amazing rapidity amongst the leisured classes;

and there was tremendous industry. Every trace of the old Graeco-Roman culture was eagerly ferreted out, and acclaimed as a treasure. The first new welcome to the antique was not at all pedantic; it thrilled with life, it was looking for a solution of living problems; and it thought to find that solution in the many sided interests of a civilization more elaborate than the mediaeval civilization.

Shaped by individuals

Such a turning-back of the clock is in itself remarkable; but more remarkable still is the way in which it was done. It was done, not by the slow evolution of a whole people, but by the energetic action of a few gifted individuals. Even when we recall that, in the very midst of the Italian renaissance, the invention of printing came to increase the power of the individual over the masses, this power is amazing. From that time onward, names begin to count more and more in European history; single individuals more and more shape the principles and conduct of multitudes of men.[1] It is significant that, in the past, great men came most often at the tail of an educational movement, not at the head. Socrates, Plato Aristotle appear just before Greece decays; St. Augustine stands at the edge of the Dark Ages; St. Thomas Aquinas is only a long lifetime away from the break-up of mediaeval education; and Dante died in 1321, just twenty-six years before the Black Death. The great man more naturally marks the completion of a stage in the up-and-down progress of humanity. He is debtor to the lesser dead for what made him capable of high development. He follows, even more than he leads. And if he comes when the wheel of human achievement is on the down-swing, he is powerless to swing it upward, or even to keep it level. But with the Classic Renaissance the procedure seemed to change. Men who disclaimed all allegiance to the immediate past, who scorned its offered helps, who broke with it in complete condemnation, took the lead in a new movement; and the people followed them.

Toward an appealing objective

One explanation of this new power of the individual is that the old, established leadership had lost its hold upon men, and that a leader less people welcomed new guides. But a more important explanation lies in the fact that the goal of the new leaders was so obvious, so immediately appealing. They pointed to no remote, supernatural standard of excellence; they imposed no rigorous discipline, called for no difficult faith. There, on the near horizon, was a rich culture, purely human, easily attainable, outwardly alluring. It promised nobility without restraint, excellence without more than moderate effort. By contrast with the otherworldly ideals of mediaeval civilization, it appeared joyous, warm, glowingly colored; it appealed to the senses, to the emotions; it was rich in promises of immediate delight, with no grim portals of death standing in the way. No wonder that men who had so largely lost the vision of the Faith, turned at the first shout of the new leaders, to follow this new ideal of achievement! Petrarch and Boccaccio, for all that they were still Catholics, set back the ill-disciplined peoples of Italy at a point where Augustine had stood as a young man; and equivalently told them to take up the path that Augustine was abandoning. The modern world has ever since been divided in its opinion as to whether or not the choice urged by the Renaissance leaders was a disastrous choice; and that division of opinion is, beyond question, the most important division separating men today.

But at once divides into two

As a matter of fact, not all of Italy (nor later, all of Europe) accepted the lead of the Renaissance into a break with Christianity. For the moment, the Italians of influence were in three very unequal groups; the first group frankly pagan, positively hostile to Christianity; the second, largely made up of monks frairs, clergy, and tehological faculties of universities, violently Catholic (at least in speech), fanatically opposed to the revival of the ancient civilization in any form; the third, composed of laymen and ecclesiastics alike, eager to seek a compromise, some blending of Graeco-Roman culture with Christian beliefs and practices, such as had been sought a thousand years earlier bý Christians of the age of Ambrose and Jerome and Augustine. In the course of time, the second group was absorbed into the first and third, and there remained but two: the pagan humanists and the Catholic humanists. As representatives of the former, may be mentioned Giovanni Boccaccio (1313-1375). Braccolini Poggio (1380-1459), Francesco Filelfo (1398-1481), Nicolo Machiavelli (1469-1527); as representative of the latter, Francesco Petrarca (1304-1374), Pier Pao Vergerio (1349-1420), Gasparino Barzizza (1370-1431) Lionardo Bruni, Aretino (1369-1444), Battista Guarin (1434-1513). There is no denying that, owing in great measure to the wretched condition of the Church at the time, the paganizing group was by far the more influential and that the temper of the Renaissance in Italy was pre-dominantly pagan. Nicolo Machiavelli, writing when the Italian Renaissance was at its highest point of development, says bluntly: "We Italians are irreligious and corrupt beyond all others."

Aims of the pagan education: fame and pleasure

The first principle of the paganizing education of the Italian Renaissance was insistence upon education for this world. Its leaders, by speech and writing, emphasized the world ideal of 'success,' an ideal which we should have no difficulty in understanding today, and which, on their lips on ours, meant chiefly two things, fame and pleasure:[3] the gratification of our human craving for personal glory, and the satisfaction of appetitle and emotional desire. The only immortality worth while for them was the immortality conferred by poets and biographers: to live in the memory of succeeding generations.[4] In many cases, mere notoriety was considered a sufficient goal of endeavor; even some of the most detestable crimes of the period are frankly attributed to the ambition to attract attention, to be remembered, if only as a moral monster.[5] Lorenzo Valla, about 1430, wrote a book on pleasure, which represents the views of many leaders of the Renaissance. He takes the outspoken position that enjoyment alone is the aim of life, and praises the ancients who raised voluptuousness to a cult.[6] Naturally such an ideal implies very active hostility toward Christian aspirations; nor did the pagan Renaissance writers leave any doubt about their attitude toward Christianity. They attacked it constantly, with open scorn, with ridicule and parody: in poems such as Luigi Pulci's "Morgante Maggiore," Boccaccio's "Three Rings"; in plays such as Machiavell's comedies, Mandragpla and Clizia.[7]

Exaggerated individualism

In line with this emphasis upon fame as one of the great goals of living, the pagan Renaissance developed an exaggerated individualism. It was an era of boastfulness, of vigorous assertion of one's personality, of resentment toward authority. Everyone insisted upon his right to criticize, and, if he had the power to do so, to repress all criticism on the part of others. A touchy sort of pride prevailed everywhere, yet without any high principles of conduct or very keen sense of responsibility. A decidedly empty 'honor' took the place of religion as the basis of moral conduct.[8] The effective result of all this was a pretentious sophistication, which seems curiously modern, a cynicism at once arrogant and childish. "An easy-going contempt of everything and everybody was probably the prevailing tone of society."[9] The pagan Renaissance, in casting away divine faith, seemed also to have lost human faith; and for all the current prating about honor, few ages have ever been so horribly and so persistently stained by treachery as this was.

Yet it is a strange fact that, with rare exceptions, these Italian Renaissance pagans, when death gave them any warning of its approach, turned to the religion they had travestied and scorned, and tried to die as Catholics. Even Machiavelli, and Sigismond Malatesta who seemed to revel in crime for its own sake, called for a priest at the end made confession of their sins, and received the Viaticum with devotion.[10]

The Christian Education

These deathbed repentances for one thing, testify to the latent vitality of the Christian spirit. It never died out in Italy, even in the worst stages of the Renaissance. In spite of adverse conditions, of failure of spiritual leaders, of multiplied temptations, thousands of the people continued sincerely and steadily in their Catholic belief and Catholic lives. For them, the changing enthusiasms of the time, the new flair for the long-deal antique culture, were simply a new circumstance which they must adapt to the unchanging faith. Petrarch himself made some efforts toward this adaptation; but it was not until the Classic Renaissance was well under way, the succeeding generation, that Catholic efforts became vigorous and well organized.

Pier Paolo Vergerio (1349-1420) wrote an admirable treatise, De ingenuis Moribus et Studiis Liberalibus, in 1392. His educational aims are the recognized Catholic aims, with which he combines the new feeling for style, for classic excellence, for a larger and more rounded culture.[11] Gasparino Barzizza (1370-1431), who taught rhetoric and Latin literature at the University of Padua, and who was prominent in classic scholarship, was completely Catholic in his character and influence. One of his pupils was Vittorino da Feltre, a man recognized as worthy of a place amongst the little handful of the world's great teachers. Contemporary with Barzizza was Lionardo Bruni (1369-1444), often called Aretino from his birthplace, Arezzo. He too wrote an excellent, and thoroughly Catholic, treatise, De Studiis et Literis. Two pupils of the paganizing Filelfo became popes: Tommaso Parentucelli, as Nicholas V, who founded the Vatican Library about 1450; and Aeneas Silvius Piccolomini, as Pius II; and, what is more, they were good popes. The period draws to a close in Italy with the really remarkable treatise of the younger Guarino (Battista, 1434-1513), De Ordine Docendi et Studendi.

Extent of its Influence

These men represent large numbers back of them. But it is hard to make any exact estimate of the relative influence of the Catholic spirit in Renaissance education. It certainly failed in its efforts to keep the drama Christian, in spite of the impressively large number of religious plays produced,[12] and the momentary success of such dramatic organizations as that of the Dominicans at Pistoja.[13]

On the other hand, in the one new art of the Renaissance, painting,[14] the Christian spirit is strikingly manifest. Muntz, in a careful listing, estimates that the Italian Quattrocento pictures present twenty religious subjects for one classical subject.[15] The guilds kept alive the Catholic spirit that had always animated them.[16] Pious confraternities flourished, most of them dedicated to works of charity; some of them an inheritance from mediaeval times; some of them new, such as the famous Misericordia of Florence,[17] founded in 1488 or the many confraternities established at Rome under Alexander VI and Leo X.[18] At the time, no other country had such splendid hospitals and charitable foundations as Italy.[19] Nor was there lacking abundant influence from the greatest sources of Christian education, religious instruction, prayer, and the Sacraments. The effect of this is shown in the admirable family life to be found so widely existing amongst the middle classes, in the earnest, even if sporadic, attempts at social reform, above all in the large number of men and women whose lives displayed heroic virtue.[20] But there was a certain unsteadiness about this essential religious education amongst the people at large; it had a tendency to extreme fluctuations, to flare up violently at one time, and die down to a fainta spark at another. It must further be admitted that, although there were many zealous preachers and priests of exemplary lives, especially amongst the new Benedictine congregations,[21] too many of the clergy were swamped in greed and licentiousness, too many of the preachers were conceited and bombastic, parading their smattering of heathen mythyology in the pulpit, indulging in exaggerated accounts of the abuses of the day, aiming more at fame, or at least notoriety, for themselves than at real religious influence over their hearers; so that the direct power of religious education was much impaired by the gross lack of Christianity in the educators.[22] The general impression produced by a careful study of the period is that Christian education was less effective upon Renaissance society than was the pagan education. Unfortunately, this is most true as regards the clergy, high and low.[23]

Effects of the Renaissance on language

One of the aims of the Classic Renaissance was to replace the mediaeval forms of the Latin language by the literary forms of Latin in the stage of its highest academic development. The leaders of the movement either did not know, or else simply ignored, the important fact that such literary Latin was never the popular speech of the Roman people, that classic Latin, at the very time it was produced, was remote from the popular forms. All literature, it is true, is remote from common speech; but Latin classic literature peculiarly so. It was an exotic.

Early in the fifteenth century, English ecclesiastics, coming into contact with the humanist secretaries of the Papal Curia, brought back to England vivid impressions of the new learning. Poggio himself visited England in 1419. William Gray, of Balliol College, Oxford, studied under Guarino at

Ferrara, and returned to Oxford in 1449 with a valuable collection of Latin manuscripts, which are still treasured in Balliol library. At the close of the Wars of the Roses, in 1485, Italian teachers came to Oxford, seeking pupils. In the same year, Linacre went to study in Italy. Grocyn, after a like period of study in Italy, taught Greek in Oxford in 1491; and Colet, with the same background of Italian training, began to lecture in theology at Oxford from the Greek text of St. Paul's letters, in 1496. But the true center of humanism in England was the house of Saint Thomas More in Chelsea. It was from his association there, from 1505 onward, with More, Erasmus, Linacre, Warham, Colet, Fisher, and Grocyn, that Sir Thomas Elyot gathered the ideas which he embodied in his famous The Boke named the Governor, published in 1531, the first book written in English to present the humanist ideal in education. A few years later, out of fear of Henry VIII, Elyot repudiated his religion, as well as his friendship for More and Fisher. It is to be noted that, with this one exception, the leaders of the Classic Renaissance in England were Catholics, and most of them priests or bishops.

In the Germanies

The two earliest importers of the Classic Renaissance into the Germanies (in which are included here the Low Countries) were Rudolph Agricola (1443-1485) and Alexander Hegius (1420-1495). Agricola, a Hollander, after getting his master's degree at Louvain in 1461, finished his education at Paris, Pavia, and at Ferrara under Guarino. On his return, in 1479, he strongly influenced Hegius, who had his school of St. Lebuin at Deventer. The teachers in this school were chiefly members of the Brothers of the Common Life, although Hegius himself was not a member. Agricola passed on to Heidelberg in 1484, at the invitation of Dalberg, the Bishop of Worms. Although he died only a year later, at the early age of forty-two, and had done but little writing, his vigorous personality and genuine scholarship did much to turn German thought toward the new learning, especially to the study of Greek. He was intensely Catholic in his ideals of education.

A still more important person than either of these in the Classic Renaissance in Germany was the distinguished priest, Jacob Wimpfeling (1450-1528) of Schlettstadt in Alsace. He studied and taught at Heidelberg, and was rector there in 1482. Whilst he was at Speyer, in 1497, he published his first treatise on education, Isidoneus Germanious, in which he drew largely upon the excellent Catholic manuals of Barzizza. Four years later, he urged the city authorities of Strassburg to found a school in which education would be conducted on the new lines; the school over which Sturm was to preside, a generation later. But the Teutonic mind responded very grudgingly to these new ideas. The progress of the Classic Renaissance in the Germanies was slow.

Johann Reuchlin (1455-1522) was the foremost of the German laymen who took an interest in classic studies. He taught Greek at Heidelberg under Bishop Dalberg, in 1496. His chief distinction is that of having introduced into Germany the study of Hebrew as one of the learned languages. He was always a sincere Catholic and tried, though unsuccessfully, to win over his grand-nephew Melanchthon (Philip Schwarzerd, 1497-1560) from adherence to Luther. The University of Heidelberg, after the death of Bishop, Dalberg, was unable to maintain its early leadership in classic influence. It was to Tubingen, Erfurt (under the scholarly Eobanus Hessus), Wittenberg, and Leipzig, that German humanism owed most of its growth. Desiderius Erasmus (1466-1536), the greatest figure in the northern Renaissance, was a Catholic priest, born in Roterdam. But in his aims and in his life he transcended nationalism, and hence cannot be considered a German humanist. Although he bitterly satirized the abuses flagrant in the Church, and directed much of his writings toward the reform of these, he was too intelligent to be caught by the mingled frenzy and chicanery of the Protestant Revolution.

Erasmus, with the Frenchman Bude and the Spaniard Vives, formed the triumvirate of letters of the northern Renaissance. Of the three, Erasmus was the most forceful and effective writer, but Vives the most thorough going educator.

Juan Luis Vives (1492-1540), after his early education at his birthplace, Valencia, in Spain, studied at the University of Paris for five years, whence he proceeded to Bruges, in the Spanish Low Countries, in 1514. Henceforth, although he travelled about much, he looked upon Bruges as his home. Erasmus welcomed him enthusiastically at Louvain, where he wrote, lectured in the University, and tutored. His treatise, In Pseudo-dialecticos, written when he was twenty-six years old, sharply criticized the debased Scholasticism of the period and advocated inductive methods of study. More, who admired him greatly, introduced him to the English Court, where Queen Catherine employed him as tutor to the Princess Mary. From 1523 to 1528, Vives divided his life between his tutorship to the Princess, a lectureship at Oxford, and his writings in Bruges. He published numerous educational works, the most important being his De Tradendis Disciplinis (1531), which Foster Watson reckons "probably the greatest educational work of the Renaissance." Vives was an excellent Catholic in his principles and in his life; a fact which Watson offers as one of the reasons why his name has been obscured in later ages.[24]

In France

France, through its naturally close relations with Italy, was early aware of the new educational development. Italian scholars visited various French centres of learning, and taught classes in Greek at Paris as early as 1458. But the Classic Renaissance did not take strong hold upon French minds until after the Italian campaigns of Charles VIII and Louis XII. In particular, the French Court at Milan, 1498 to 1512, became a channel for the spread throughout France of interest in the new learning. The foremost French leader in the new education was Guillaume Bude (1467-1540), the friend of Erasmus. Francis I welcomed him home from his studies in 1522, and made him royal librarian. Bude was a first-rate Greek scholar, and did much by his writings to promote that zeal for the study of Greek which became so notable in France. He was a sound Catholic, and in his many educational treatises manifests clear Catholic ideals of education. But because he was hostile to the dominance of Scholasticism at the University of Paris, and proposed that the new studies be put upon an academic equality with the chairs of philosophy and theology, the Scholastics accused him of Calvinist leanings: a charge from which he was completely exoncrated only after his death. He was largely instrumental in persuading Francis I to found the College de France. During 1517 and 1518 Bude tried to secure the services of Erasmus as first rector of the College, but unsuccessfully. Hence the establishment of the College lagged for some time, but was finally accomplished in 1530. Bude's most important work on education was De L'Institution du Prince, written in French in 1516, but not printed, through fear of comparison with a similar work by Erasmus, until 1547, seven years after the death of Bude.

II. EDUCATION IN THE SCHOOLS

Its limited connection with the Renaissance in general

Some histories of education naively assume that the large educational theories of a period, often the more or less original work of a few individual writers, are put into complete practice in the schools. It cannot be too often repeated that this assumption is not founded in fact. There are, and always will be, two great obstacles in the way of reducing educational theory to school practice; the very limited competence of most teachers, and the essential immaturity of their pupils. The result is that schools tend to drag everything they touch down to the low level established by these inevitable limitations. Renaissance treatises on education present splendid theories;

Renaissance schools, with a few exceptions, show a drab practice which differs from that of mediaeval schools chiefly in the relatively unimportant point of mere curriculm. Almost all the Renaissance educational treatises follow the lead given by the best Italian writers, and whilst laying the intellectual and aesthetic foundations of education in the study of classic literature, insist strongly upon physical, moral, and even religious education, upon harmonious development of the whole individual. Yet even a cursory study of pedagogic writings makes it evident that this ideal of education was not new. It is to be found just as clearly expressed in scores of mediaeval treatises.[25] One can read these theories admirably put by John of Salisbury, for instance, at the very time when the existing schools were already hardening into mere logic-chopping machines. In just the same way, the Renaissance schools, in spite of this renewed and excellent theorizing, promptly became grammar-chopping machines. The Renaissance ideals, like so many other 'revolutions' in education were largely another case of parturiunt montes; and the schoolboy mouse of which they were delivered was pitifully similar to other schoolboy mice of ages preceding and following. There is no lasting magic in a change of curriculm. Only a great teacher makes a great school; and even he demands, for more than mediocre success, conditions which are not always at his command.

The Inspiring Exceptions

However, there were great schools during the Renaissance, and they deserve study. It is true that a great many men whom history considers important in the Classic Renaissance confined their efforts to writing about education, and carefully shunned the schools. Erasmus, for instance, could never be tied down to a school. But some, especially of the early leaders in the movement, although attached to courts or universities, turned to actual teaching in schools, either to augment their scanty incomes, or from a generous desire to promote education in practice as well as in theory. such men were great teachers, whose teaching work was of value, not merely to their pupils, but as an example to other less gifted teachers. Barzizza was such a teacher; so too were Vittorino da Feltre and the two Guarinos. The greatest of all seems to have been Vittorino, whose work cannot be passed by even in so condensed a book as this without some brief notice.

Vittorino da Feltre

Vittorino de' Rambaldoni, called generally da Feltre from the town in which he was born in 1378, studied under Barzizza at Padua, learned mathematics from Pelacani da Parma, and Greek from Guarino da Verona. In 1422, when he was forty-four years old, he succeeded his old master, Barzizza, in the chair of rhetoric at Padua; but resigned after a year, because he found the students wild and unmanageable. He then set about opening a school at Venice, but in that same year, 1423, was invited by the Marquis Gianfrancesco Gonzaga to come to Mantua and engage in the education of the Marquis' children. Vittorino accepted the invitation, with the stipulation that he be allowed to open a formal school and take other pupils besides the children of Gonzaga. He was given a villa for his school, the name of which he changed to Casa Giocosa, the Pleasant House. Here, in charming surroundings, without financial worries, he carried on a small, select school for twenty-three years, until his death in 1446. His pupils, in addition to the Gonzaga children, boys and girls, and the children of some of his friends, included a number of poor children. The basis of studies at Pleasant House was Latin and Greek literature, but genuine attention was paid also to history, mathematics, drawing, music, and such natural history as the times afforded. Everything reasonable was done to make study attractive. There was little punishment, plenty of recreation excellent care of the health of the children. Games played an important part; though Vittorino aimed more at physical hardiness, health, and the moral control acquired in play, than at mere athletic skill. The children heard Mass every day, received the Sacraments every month.

Vittorino left no writings; but his pupils, who loved him as much as they admired him, spread his fame through the world as an excellent teacher, a model of the Christian gentleman and scholar. His school, which seems to have been even a finer piece of work than that of Guarino at Ferrara, is often hailed as the great pedagogical glory of the Classic Renaissance. Every discussion of the Renaissance brings it in as an instance of school work of the period, often with the implication that it was a 'typical' Renaissance school. Nothing can be farther from fact than to call the schools of Vittorino and Guarino 'typical'. They were, as Burckhardt is careful to point out,[26] quite simply "unique of their kind." They had advantages which no ordinary school can expect to have: in the unusual character of their teachers, in their physical and financial position, in the selection of their pupils. And it is to be noted that, with all its excellence, Vittorino's school turned out such a man as Lorenzo Valla, the mocking voluptuary.[27] This is not to belittle the school of Vittorino, but merely, for the sake of historical perspective, to indicate again the limited influence of even the best sort of school. A thousand schools like Vittorino's might have changed the whole character of the Renaissance; a single school merely lends to the Renaissance a fictitious glory.

The Brothers of the Common Life

Less excellent in individual quality than the schools of Vittorino and Guarino, but more influential because more numerous and more widespread, were the schools taught by the Brothers of the Common Life, a distinguished Catholic religious community founded about 1381 by Geert de Groote. De Groote was born at Deventer, in Gelderland of the Low Countries about 1340. He came of a wealthy burgher family, studied medicine, theology, and canon law at Paris, taught for a few years in the chapter school at Deventer. About 1364, still quite a young man, he was sent on a mission to Pope Urban V at Avignon. On his return he received two rich benefices, taught theology at Cologne, lived a foppish life; until in 1374, through conversations with a devout friend, he came to change his ways. He gave up his house to a community of nuns, and spent some years in religious meditation. About 1380, having been ordained deacon, he got license to preach throughout the diocese of Utrecht. His sermons, in the vernacular, produced great effect; young men in numbers flocked to him. He encouraged them to study, set them at copying manuscripts, helped them to form sincerely Christian characters. One of his disciples, Florentius Radewyn, suggested to him, about 1381, that these young men should pool their earnings from copying manuscripts and should live in common. Gradually there was developed a permanent organization; without vows, but pledged to practice poverty, chastity and obedience according to each one's conditions of life; forbidden to beg, obliged to maintain themselves by work. De Groote's attacks on the vices of the clergy resulted in the withdrawal of his license to preach. He appealed his case to the Pope, but before any reply could be received De Groote died of pestilence contracted whilst ministering to those ill of the plague. He was only forty-four years old at his death.

The educational work of the Brothers of the Common Life began with their care for the moral and physical well-being of poor scholars; whom they lodged in hostels, supplied with work as copyists, and tutored when they were ill equipped for the established schools. Their tutoring succeeded so well that many of them were asked to teach in the schools. Here again their success led to their taking full charge of the schools or opening new schools. The basis of that success was Christian character as well as scholarly accomplishment. By 1470, Buschius, one of their pupils, reckoned that they conducted more than fifty schools in Flanders, France, and Germany. In

1500 the school at Deventer had more than two thousand students. As these schools were intensely Catholic, the Reformation broke up most of them. The best account of one of the schools is given by the Protestant Sturm, in his report to the magistrates at Strassburg in 1538.

The Brothers of the Common Life successfully adapted the new curriculum of the Renaissance to the Catholic ideal of education, their aim being expressed in the phrase pietas literata. They added to the study of Greek and Latin some mathematics, history, and geography. They divided their schools into two sections: elementary, for reading, writing, grammar, arithmetic; classical, for the languages, history, rhetoric, etc. They introduced a careful disciplinary organization, arranged classes into decuries under charge of monitors (a detail afterwards adopted by the Jesuits and others), offered prizes for good work. Their students gave performances of plays by Terence. Had the Brothers of the Common Life escaped the devastation caused by the Protestant Revolt, and continued their school work through the sixteenth and succeeding centuries, the history of the Jesuits might well have been quite different from the actuality. As it was, the influence of the Brothers was felt, not only in the eminent men they trained, such as the great Cardinal Nicholas of Cusa, Rudolph Agricola, Alexander Hegius, Sturm, and Pope Adrian VI, but even more in their wider spread of sound educational practice. The schools of following ages owe much to them.

Universities in the Renaissance

Almost without exception, the leaders of the Classic Renaissance were men trained in the universities; and their work was primarily a revolt against the universities. It was inevitable that the universities should be hostile to the Renaissance. The new learning was a terrifying threat to the established traditions which are always sacrosanct in an organized institution. It made its way, at first, outside of the universities: at courts, in writings. It had to batter at the university walls for entrance, or creep in with the sapper work of individual converts amongst the university lectures. But in the end the result was a gradual, slow surrender of the universities, scarcely completed before the seventeenth century. However, the universities had their revenge. A precious formula of the Scholastics was, quidquid recipitur ad modum recipients recipitur: when the formalized universities admitted the new curriculum, they promptly set it in a mould. The universities, together with the lower schools, succeeded in rendering futile the great educational dreams of the Renaissance leaders; they made of the new learning, in a short while, merely a change from Aristotelianism to Ciceronianism. It is both amusing and tragic to observe the fiery zeal of Pierre de la Ramee 28 against the wooden Aristotelian dialectic of the University of Paris, and to note that the end of his campaign is an even more mechanical system based upon Cicero. Both his friends and his foes called his system, Ramism; and fought about it fiercely for a hundred years.

Other Renaissance schools. It is often shallow and dangerous to speak of a 'type'of schools; since there are such constant differences in schools even of the same period. Yet a summary account is forced to consider rather the things in which schools agree than those in which they differ; and it must be confessed that the agreements are more numerous than the differences. The chief thing common to schools during the long time in which they were under the controlling influence of the Classic Renaissance was the general use of Latin and the Greek literature as the foundation of their studies. Most of these schools also borrowed a common stock of ideas about school organization from the schools of the Brothers of the Common Life. A third common quality they all soon acquired: the melancholy one of being dull, narrow, inflexible in academic routine. Some of the schools were already old when the Renaissance curriculum began to affect them; such as Winchester, which was founded in 1379, and Eton, established on the same model some sixty years later. Some were newly organized on the basis of humanism; such as Colet's foundation of St. Paul's in 1509, or Sturm's gymnasium at Strassburg in 1538. Some had masters, such as William Lilly and Johann Sturm, who were really eminent scholars and eager educators; some had to be content with bread-and-butter men who made no more mark in teaching than they would have made in any other profession. Sturm himself, for all his high qualifications, became a follower of the overelaborate Petrus Ramus, and developed in his Strassburg gymnasium, which he governed for nearly forty years, as narrow a sort of humanist school as can be found anywhere. A notable cause of the dull lifelessness of Sturm's school, as of most others, was the obvious fact that the approach to Latin and Greek literature was made upon an interminably long and winding road over the sands of grammer. The vast majority of the pupils never got out of the sands. In the course of time, the masters quite simply took this sand-trudging to be the essential school education. When they were reproached for this attitude, they fell back for defense upon some theory of 'formal discipline.'

Numbers and influence. On this most important point it is extremely hard to get compact and helpful information. The badly troubled times of the Protestant Revolution, coming so swiftly on the heels of the Renaissance influence in schools, naturally affected both the number of schools and their effective influence upon education. But the Renaissance seems to have brought about some real increase in the number of schools. Further, it helped the organization of schools, since it led to a gradual sharper distinction between elementary and secondary schools by emphasizing the curriculum of the latter. When, however, we consider that the change in schools due to the Renaissance was chiefly a change in curriculum rather than in method, we may reasonably doubt that the

Renaissance schools in general were more efficient than those which preceded them. Schools continued, by economic law, to be the privilege mainly of the wealthier classes.

Conclusion

The Classic Renaissance was a challenge to existing ideals of education. It was stimulating, it prodded Europe out of a rut; and therefore it did a real service to education. It is a truism to say that routine is hostile to fine human development. The Renaissance broke an old routine; that is to its credit. But it ended in establishing a new routine; that marked its essential limitation.

Between the limits of the old and new routine, in the energetic ferment of the Renaissance, many great social and educational forces were set at work; the influence of which persists to our own day, and is likely to persist much longer. Some of these forces were beneficial, such as the wider tying together of the remote past and the present, the developing sense of the human continuity. Even through the fog of grammer, that development has tended to widen the vision of schools, and certainly has stretched the horizons of general thought. It could not bring classic beauty into the schools, if only because immature students can have little appreciation of beauty. Some of these forces were not beneficial, chiefly the reformation of pagan ideals of life. Some hang in the balance, may be used for good or ill; and by that very fact would seem to indicate that they are of very great importance. Perhaps the most significant of these last is the new emphasis laid by the Classic Renaissance upon the individual.

The earlier semibarbaric ages, often called the Dark Ages, were strongly individualistic. Such organizations as existed during those ages, the Catholic Church, the religious orders, the various feudal societies, were comparatively loose in structure. Cluny gave the lead to organized stability, first in its own monasteries, then in the society which surrounded it.

The great revival of learning in the twelfth century turned more and more to an organization of truths and opinions, to systematizing all human relations. Indirectly, it led to the development of national organizations, the various modern States. System became in time the fetish of the schools. In the fourteenth century, the schools sickened, and nearly died, of an overdose of system. The Renaissance was, in great part, a revolt against that oppression of too much system. Individualism, at times a wild and hysterical individualism, marked the Renaissance movement.

Now, every society recognizes instinctively that individualism is close kin to anarchy. Every society, so long as it has the physical power to do so, restrains the individual. Theorists are forever contending, and rightly, for a balance between the two: between individual freedom and social restraint. But the balance is hard to come by, and is never stable. Ever since the recrudescence of striking individualism in the Renaissance, every society, Catholic or Protestant, ecclesiastical or civil, school or family, has been wrestling, in varying degrees of poor success, with the problem of asserting itself against the individual and of granting to the individual such measures of freedom as he must have for his true growth.

Hence, in political societies, we can trace the gradual extention of the franchise, and the growth of political skill by which governments render the franchise as nugatory as possible; in the Protestant churches, we see a successive surrender of authority, in the hope of placating individual members, and of retaining them within the shadow of a pulpit without doctrines; in the Catholic Church, with no surrender of authority, we observe an increased considerateness of discipline;[32] in the schools, we have attained the amazing concession of 'elective curriculum,' the dominance of paid athletics and the charming insouciance of youthful philanderings in coeducation.

To blame the Classis Renaissance for all the vagaries of this struggle between the individual and society, would be absurd. If we must strike a balance of praise and blame, history seems to show that the Classis Renaissance, for all its defects and limitations, gave a real impetus to vital education, from which later ages profited. Many good results came from that loosening up of educational garments which had grown too tight for the peoples of Europe. But the Classic Renaissance did an irreparable harm to Western civilization and education by enlisting men of force and influence in the service of pagan ideals, and by tending to establish those ideals in the minds of young and old at a time when the weakness of religious leaders had left the people without adequate guidance from Christian revelation. The pagan of today will see nothing to blame in that fact; the Christian, with an outlook beyond this present life, is forced to conclude that the Renaissance took away from its own and succeeding generations immeasurably more than it gave.

Finally, it must be remembered that the forces of the Renaissance were scarcely in full swing throughout Europe, when all European society was shocked and twisted by the cataclysm of the Protestant Revolution. We must consider the educational effect of that Revolution in the next chapter; but we must note here that it did not do more than momentarily halt the ultimate work of the Renaissance, for good and for evil.

Topics for Discussion

1. The Doctrinale of Alexander de Villa Dei, and its influence through three centuries.
2. The educational work of Cardinal Nicholas de Cusa and Cardinal John Dominici.
3. The light thrown on schoolboy life by the Colloquies of Vives.

4. The position of women in Renaissance education.
5. An estimate of the educational writings of Erasmus.
6. A comparison of Erasmus and Vives on education.
7. Varying effects of the Renaissance in town and countryside.

REFERENCES

1. In the matter of school education this prominence of individual becomes very marked in the eighteenth and nineteenth centuries. Rousseau, Pestalozzi, Herbert, Froebel, Hors Mann, exert an influence which is nothing short of astounding.
2. Discorsi, lib. I, c. 12 (translated by N.H. Thompson, London, 1883.
3. Money, except by the mentally unbalanced miser, is always valued only for its power to procure fame and pleasure.
4. Burckhardt. *Civilization of Renaissance*, 3d ed., Vol.1, 173 sqq.
5. Pastor, *History of the Popes* (English translation), Vol. 2, pp. 115 sqq., cites instances of this curiously disordered craving, leading assassinations.
6. Pastor, *History of the Popes* (English translation), Vol. 1, pp. 15 sqq. Valla was about twenty-three years old when he wrote this book. The year following 1431, he was ordained priest. He became a great scholar, denounced the Donation of Constantine in 1440, was important secretary under Pope Nicholas V. and died at the age of fifty, a Canon of the Lateran.
7. Owen, *The Sceptics of the Renaisance,* London, 1893, pp. 141 sqq., 153 sqq. Cf. also W.B. Skaife, Florentine Life during the Renaissance, Baltimore, 1893, pp. 131 sqq.
8. See Rebelais, Gargantua, lib. I, cap. 57, for satiric discussion this.
9. J. Burckhardt, Civilization of the Renaissance in Italy (Middlemore's translation, 1898), p. 161.
10. L. Pastor, *History of the Popes* (English translation), Vol. 1, p. 15.
11. See C. Bishoff, Studien zu P.P. Vergerio dem Alteren, Berlin and Leipzig, 1909.
12. D'Ancona, Sacre Rappesentazione de' secoli XIV, XV, e XVI; 3 vols., Firenze, 1872.

13. P. Vigo, Una Compagnia di Giovinetti Pistoiesi a principio del XVI, Bologna, 1887.

14. Renaissance architecture was imitative; its sculpture had only the originality of being dissociated from architecture.

15. Eugene Muntz, Histoire de I'Art pendant la Renaissance, 3 vols., Paris, 1889-95, Vol. 1, pp. 232-73.

16. E. Rodocanachi, Les Corporations ouvrieres a Rome depuis la chute de i'Empire Romain, 2 vols., Paris, 1894, Vol. 1, pp. 75, 99 sqq.

17. C. Bianchi, La Compagnia della Misericordia, Firenze, 1855. In Florence alone there were about 1500 seventy-three religious associations.

18. Carlo Piazza, Opere Pie di Roma, Roma, 1679, pp. 391 sqq., 429 sqq., 462., 546, 549.

19. W.B. Skaife, Florentine Life during the Renaissance, pp. 180 sqq.

20. Ulysse Chevalier, Repertoire des sources historiques du moyendge, Paris, 1877-83. For the fifteenth century alone, he gives references for *over eighty* Italian saints and blessed.

21. F. Fabri, *Evagatorium*, edited by Hassler, Stuttgardiae, 1849, Vol. 3, pp. 393 sqq.

22. Cf. also Burckhardt, Civilization of the Renaissance, Vol. 1, p. 243, for instances of humanists in the pulpit, political announcements etc. Often the pulpit was used least of all for religious instruction. It might be interesting to compare the Renaissance pulpit with the American Protestant pulpit of today.

23. C. Cantu, Italiani illustri, Ritratti, 3 vols., Milano, 1873-74, Vol. 1, pp. 201 sqq., gives a general description of the low state of the clergy. It is notable that much of the best work done in Christian education during the Renaissance was done by laymen.

24. *Cyclopedia of Education*, New York, 1913, Vol. 5, p. 739. See also estimate of wide influence of Vives in later pedagogy by K.A. Schmidt, *Encyklopadie des gesammten Ersiehungs-und Unterrichtiwesens*, Gotha, 1876-87, Vol. 9, pp. 843-51.

25. See the excellent, and unheeded, criticism of Peter of Biois (who died in England about 1200) on the unbalancing of education by a craze for metaphysical subtleties. Epist, 101; Migne, P.L., 107:311. For John of Salisbury, see the Metalogicus, iib. I, c. 24, and lib, II, c. 9, in Migne, P.L. Vol. 199.

26. *Civilization of the Renaissance* (Middlemore's translation, 1898), p. 213.

27. Cf. G. Voight, Die Wiederbelebung des classischen Alterthums; 2 Bde., Berlin, 1880-81, Vol. 1, p. 470.

28. More widely known as Petrus Ramus. He was born at Cuth in Picardy, 1515; was a university lecturer and principal of seven colleges; published fifty-two treatises. The two most important were Araistotelicae Animadversiones and Dialecticae Institutiones, in 1543. He saw the evils of pedantry, but he could not get away from it. He became a Calvinist in 1561, and was killed at Paris, in the St. Bartholomew massacre in 1572.

29. Leach says that a moderate estimate of grammar schools for England in 1535 is three hundred; most of which were swept away under Henry VIII and Edward VI. *English Schools at the Reformation*, pp. 5, 6.

30. The introduction of new grammars in place of the old Doctrinale of Alexander de Villa Del, which disappeared with amazing rapidity after 1520, and the wide use of the Dialogues of Erasmus and Vives do not indicate after all, any serious change in school method. The aim of schools continued to be chiefly the ability to read and write. Latin, even though now they aimed more at Clceronic Latin than before.

31. Clear historical records show beyond question that the Protestant States, which ranked their churches as governmental departments, were as severely repressive societies as any in history; in spite of the theoretical principle of 'private judgment.'

32. See a stimulating and suggestive article by Archbishop Alban Goodier, in the *London Mouth*, Vol. 152, No. 777, pp. 193-203, March, 1929.

8

Universities in the Middle Ages

The university is a product of the Middle Ages. The university, like Gothic architecture, parliaments, and constitutional monarchy was a product of the later Middle Ages. It arose and established its character in the twelfth and thirteenth centuries. The earliest universities—Salerno, Bologna, Reggio, Paris, Montpellier, and Oxford—were established in the twelfth century, and Cambridge was founded in 1309. The thirteenth and succeeding centuries added other universities to the list, so that eighty, at least, are said to have been established before 1500; and every land in western Europe-from Hungary to Spain and to Scotland, and from Italy to Scandinavia-had its university or universities. Many of them are flourishing today, after centuries of vigorous and fruitful activity. A very large share, indeed, of the most distinguished living universities were founded before 1500.

NATURE OF UNIVERSITIES

Forces which determined the character of the medieval university. The university was the institutional expression of the intellectual flowering of the Middle Ages. Growth of cities, increase of wealth, the conquest of areas—long held by the Arabs—which gave western Europe easy access to much of the learning of antiquity, the growth of strong governments with consequent tranquillity, which was favourable to the arts of peace, and the patronage of princes, all furnished conditions highly conducive to the study of the liberal arts and sciences, and of the professional disciplines. Wealth and the learning of antiquity had, however, been present in ancient Rome when higher teaching declined. The explanation of the university's growth must, therefore, be found in some other factors. These factors were: (1) The unity of western Europe under the Papacy; (2) The respect, amounting to deification, with which learning was regarded in the twelfth and thirteenth centuries; and (3) The development of a body of scholars and scholarships in western Europe.

It must be remembered that the unity of Europe in the thirteenth century was a unity of the spirit, which admitted of individual self-expression. There were groups, to be sure, outside of this unity: Albigensians, Waldensians, and later, the Lollards; but for the most part Europe aligned itself willingly with the Holy See. The Popes gathered power into their hands largely because necessary governmental functions were being neglected, or because rulers and people dreaded above all else to be outside the fold of Christendom, deprived of the offices and fellowship of the Church. We shall see how this unity of Christendom gave direction and character to the medieval university.

The vital force of any university is scholarship. The course of the development of scholarship in the twelfth and thirteenth centuries was traced earlier but nothing was said there of the reverence in which it was held. In view of the Middle Ages, nothing could exceed the dignity and significance of learning. By learning we arrive at the truth-the very truth of God himself. Learning, it was believed, admits men to the secrets of the divine will, invests their utterances with divine sanctity, and supports their decrees by giving sanctions. The universities became the special custodians and interpreters of truth. Princes and Popes deferred to their opinions on points of theology and of law-civil or canon. Cities deferred to them; "Bononia docet" adorned the coins of Bologna.[1] As custodians of learning in an age in which learning was esteemed as at almost no other period in the world's history, universities enjoyed enormous prestige. It was said in the Middle Ages that Italy had the Papacy, Germany had the Empire, and France, the University of Paris: and this saying was meant to range these great powers far above other institutions. With what deep seriousness the medieval scholar took his work may be judged from the following extract from the paragraph with which a Bologna doctor of the law about 1250 closed his course of lectures:

> Now, gentlemen, we have begun and finished and gone through this book, as you know who have been in the class, for which we thank God and His Virgin Mother and all His Saints. It is an ancient custom in this city that when a book is finished mass should be sung to the Holy Ghost, and it is a good custom and hence should be observed.[2]

It is clear, however, that important as respect for scholarship is, it alone does not suffice to create learning and the institutions of which learning is the vitalizing interest. The status of learning, at any period in the world's history, depends upon the relation in which learning in that particular age stands to the scholarly tradition. The scholar is sustained by the living intellectual environment with which he is in contact. This environment is, at any moment, conditioned by its past, and especially by its immediate past. The scholar is a child of his time who can show an intellectual pedigree extending through many generations. The essential conditions of the rise of universities were furnished by the twelfth and thirteenth century scholarship. University courses of study and methods of teaching, moreover, were as they were, largely because of certain movements and characteristics of twelfth and thirteenth century scholarship, and because, thanks to extrinsic forces, Arabic influence predominated over classical Greek influence in the scientific movement of the period, and the humanistic studies were crushed by dialectical and professional interests.

The scholarship of western Europe in this time was Latin and Christian. It was preoccupied by theology to an extraordinary degree and affected by the ascetic outlook of the clergy, who made up almost the whole body of scholars. It was hampered by superstition, and as the twelfth century advanced, it was further limited by a narrow utilitarianism which predominated among students. Scholarship was, however, invested with real dignity and was held in high esteem. Extrinsic forces which strengthened these tendencies in medieval scholarship were: (1) The development of ecclesiastical and governmental bureaucracies; (2) The better publicity received by scientific works translated from the Arabic than by those translated directly from the classical Greek;[3] (3) Ecclesiastical and feudal domination of learning; and (4) The triumph of the Dominicans-the Preaching Friars-in the universities. Bureaucracies offered preferment to the legalistic type of mind. Now most of the obvious justification of the universities is the fact that they offer professional preparation. But the way to the professions through the study of literature was long, and pure science seemed to offer no direct return of a practical nature. The grammars of Donatus and Priscian were difficult. The age produced, therefore, two grammers, the Doctrinale of Alexander Villedieu (1199) and the Grecismus of Evrard de Bethune (1212), which were in rhyme so that they might be easily memorized. These grammars were tremendously popular. Before 1588 no less than 267 editions of the Doctrinale had been printed.[4] Popular or not, these rhymed grammars represented just the sort of surrender to the demand for quick results that is always fatal to scholarship. The popularity of logic was due to the same demand for easy success in the professions; as a result, the liberal and humanistic scholarship of the twelfth century gave place to the formalism of scholasticism, which dominated western scholarship for the next two centuries.

The predominance of Arabic influence over the Greek in

the scientific Renaissance of the twelfth century also contributed to shape the spirit and method of medieval universities. As Professor Haskins points out, though the Latin world could have got a large part of its science directly from the Greek, it did not.[5] Despite the fact that there were treatises of Galen and of Euclid and dialouges of Plato which had been translated into Latin directly from the Greek, of which there were no Latin versions through the Arabic, and despite the further fact that, where there were translations both directly from the Greek and from the Arabic, the former were "more faithful and trustworthy"[6] than the latter, western Europe in the Middle Ages preferred to take its science at second hand. Arabic texts and commentaries, for the most part, were the medium through which Europe knew Greek science in the high Middle Ages. Even Aristotle was seen through the eyes of Moslem scholars, of medieval scholastic theologians of the Greek Christian Church, and of the redactors of later Imperial Rome. The spirit of Arabian scholarship, of Byzantine scholasticism, and of Christianized imperial Rome-not that of the Academy, the Lyceum, and the schools of Alexandria under the early Ptolemies-gave tone to medieval science. Now the science of ancient Greece was liberalized by the richest humanistic tradition known to the history of thought. Arabian, Byzantine, and later Roman culture brought no such tradition of humanism to medieval Europe as could have been imbibed at the foundation of Greek classical literature. A fearful limitation was imposed upon the universities of the Middle Ages when scholars of the twelfth and thirteenth centuries willingly accepted translations as the basis of their work. By contrast, from the fifteenth to the early ninteenth century all aspiring scholars were taught Greek, and were perfectly able to appreciate the advantages of a translation made directly from the Greek over one made from a Spanish version of an Arabic redaction of a Greek work.

The neglect of the humanities to which the influences

already noted contributed was powerfully reinforced by the ecclesiastical control exercised over universities and by the dominant position which the Dominicans, or Preaching Friars, held in them. The antipathy to literature and history of a majority of professional scholars in the later Middle Ages marks a great point of difference between the medieval flowering and the great Renaissance. Professor Haskins, after describing the work of translators from the Greek in the twelfth century, says:

> The absence of the classical works of literature and history from this list of translations from the Greek is as significant as it is from the curriculum of the medieval universities. We are in the twelfth century, not the fifteenth, and the interest in medicine, mathematics, philosophy, and theology reflects the practical and ecclesiastical preoccupations of the age rather than the wider interests of the humanists. The medieval translations were not regarded as belles lettres. They were a means to an end.[7]

Not only did ecclesiastical interests predominate in medieval universities, but the legalistic point of view and theological preoccupations triumphed among churchmen. The commanding position held by the Dominicans is at once an evidence of the victory of dialectic over experimental and humanistic studies and a reason for its being carried on to such completeness. The Dominicans had been organized to combat heresy by the use of reason. Their methods were, therefore, those of contraversy, and their field of interest was polemical theology.

The general character of the medieval university. The university could have been created by no other culture than that of Latin Christendom at the time of its greatest flowering-the twelfth and thirteenth centuries. The ancient world had no true universities. There were, to be sure, centers of higher teaching and of productive scholarship in classical antiquity-

Athens, Alexandria, Rome, Antioch, Pergamon, and Constantinople are notable examples-but classical antiquity did not develop the university. The democratic Greek states could not have produced an institution so universal in outlook and cosmopolitan in membership, while neither the despotisms which followed Alexander the Great in the Greek world nor Roman imperialism could have endured any such state within a state as the university was. The university was a creation of these two centuries, and its salient features were those of its age.

Three features mark the medieval university. These features were: (1) Its corporate character; (2) Its special privileges and immunities; and (3) The protection which teaching and scholarship enjoyed in it by virtue of its one great right- the right to grant to its graduates, license to teach anywhere in orthodox Christendom (jus ubique decendi). The features of the university were interrelated and were closely conected with, or even dependent upon, distinctive characteristics of the institution. A special characteristic of the medieval university was its virtual lack of buildings or equipment. This lack of material possessions, while it imposed limits upon the university's work, conferred upon it the great blessing of independence. No university was bound to its city; it was this independence which enabled it to maintain its liberties in many a hard-fought struggle. For the university was, to give Pasquier's oft-quoted phrase, "built of men," so that, in times of persecution it could retreat before its foes and still carry on its work though with but the most scanty equipment. Another characteristic of the medieval university was its aim-professional training. There were three higher professional faculties; the faculty of theology, the faculty of law, and the faculty of medicine. There was also the faculty of arts, in which youths customarily studied before entering upon the work of one of the three higher faculties. Another characteristic of the medieval university was its internationalism. Its language was Latin; its students and teachers were drawn from every part of Latin Christendom; its most significant loyalty was to the Church; and it never hesitated to appeal to the one great international power-the Papal Curia-when in need of a defender of its liberties and immunities. These features of the university cannot be considered in isolation from each other, but may be discussed under the heads of the three features which, while no more distinctive of the university than were the others, actually constituted it; these were the university's corporate character, its autonomy, and its power to grant the license to teach.

The Corporate character of the medieval university.

The word universitas was applied in the Middle Ages to any aggregate of persons recognised as a unit, and in its legal and technical sense meant simply a corporation. In the twelfth century the term was applied to associations of various sorts-to corporations of municipalities and to guilds of tradesmen, as well as to guilds of teachers and of students. The usage by which the noun universitas came to denote first a society of teachers and scholars, universitas societas magistroum discipulorumque, and then the impersonal institution which employs professors and teaches students, evolved through centuries. The early guilds of students had no monopoly on the term which was later to be used exclusively of institutions devoted to productive scholarship and higher instruction. In many instances the teachers of various faculties and students from various parts of Europe belonged to different guilds-Bologna, for example, had a number of universities; that is to say, of masters' guilds and of students' guilds. The advantages to be gained by federation of the guilds, led in time to the development of one government for each of the universities.

The guilds were little states within states, organized for the maintenance of common interests, for mutual aid of members, and for the cultivation of fellowship and community of understanding and feeling between them. There was need of such associations. Centuries before the universities began, Roman imperialism had gradually rendered the people who lived under it incapable of local self-government and of local self-defense. The inroads of the barbarians having destroyed the imperial government in western Europe, chaos was for centuries Lord of Misrule from the Mediterranean to the Rhine, and from the Balkans to Wales. Gradually, a measure of local authority and of order was imposed by feudal lords-both spiritual and temporal-and something was done in the way of local defense. As serfs were emancipated and as commerce and the crafts developed, the interests of feudal lords did not at all coincide with those of townsmen; consequently, the latter organized their own associations-guilds and leagues-to protect and advance their business and fortune. These associations gained rights, both by the sanction of custom and by charter from some acknowledged power-as that of the Pope or Emperor. It is important that the student of the history of universities remember that customary associations were recognized as having a corporate character and vested rights; for the earliest character to some of the older universities were not granted until they had been recognized for decades as centers of general resort for higher studies (studia generalia). Rashdall points out[8] that voluntary associations in medieval Italy enjoyed legal status as corporations, "without any special authorization of the State." He shows, further, that, owing to the fact that the breach of an oath in the age made the perjurer liable to proceedings in the ecclesiastical courts, voluntary guilds held real legal power over their members. It is clear, therefore, that the actual founding of universities may antedate their earliest charters.

The rise of student guilds of masters was after the following fashion: Governments in the Middle Ages were capable of imposing order locally only, but scholarship was international. Students ranged from Scandinavia to Naples, and from Prague to Oxford, but no secular government could protect the civic rights of its sons beyond the limits of its own borders. No English consular official was at hand, for example, to see that the citizen of London who studied at Bologna was given equal justice should become involved in the toils of the law while he was in Italy. The German at Prague, the Italian at Paris, or the Picard at Oxford was in like case. Even within the Empire there were many small, semi-autonomous states; and passing from one of these to another left the citizen himself virtually without civic rights. Feeling the need of protection and of mutual aid, masters and teachers formed associations. The statutes of the German nation at Bologna illustrate very well the purposes of such associations of students or of professors. The objects of the guild were set forth as "fraternal charity, mutual association and amity, the consolation of the sick and the support of the needy, the conduct of funerals and extirpation of rancour and quarrels, the attendance and escort of our doctorandi to and from the place of examination, and the spiritual advantage of members."[9] Threatened by real or fancied injury from without, the guild had recourse to force, to argument, or to appeal to rights guaranteed under some charter granted by the Pope or by a secular ruler, as best suited the particular case. There were separate guilds of students and masters in Italy. At Paris and at Oxford the students belonged to the university, but all power was in the hands of the masters. At Bologna the students' guilds exercised most university functions.

At Bologna there seem to have been four student universities, originally: the Ultramontane, the Lombard, the Tuscan, and the Roman. By the middle of the thirteenth century there were two universities, the Cismontane and the Ultramontane, each of which was divided into clubs, called nations from the fact that each association was made up of members from a particular region. Each nation elected one or more Councillors, who with the rectors, "formed the ordinary executive body of the university."[10] Each university at Bologna had as its head a rector-a student, who was elected to office biennially. The electors were ex-rectors, newly elected councillors, and certain special delegates. No layman was permitted to exercise jurisdiction over an ecclesiastic; the rector was, therefore, required to be a cleric. The office was an expensive one, for the rector was expected to maintain the dignity of his office by living in considerable state and by entertaining extensively. It may be said here that, in the course of time, all rectorships were combined into one, and that the power of the student rector was gradually reduced, until in the sixteenth century it was a mere shadow. The semblance of student government was, however, preserved in Italian universities until the nineteenth century.

Whereas at Paris and other northern universities both students and professors of all faculties were members of a single body,[11] doctors and masters at Bologna were not members of the universities of students, though subject to the student rectors. There were, however, guilds of professors; there was certainly one of professors of law, and there was another which included both doctors of medicine and masters of art. The associations of masters controlled graduation and so entrance upon the profession of teaching at all times. The municipal authorities of Bologna, however, exercised a very considerable degree of control over the choice of professors to fill salaried positions in the city. This power of the city magistrates seems to have been invoked to prevent professorships from being the monopoly of a few professorial families. The external control over membership of the teaching faculties at Bologna contributed to the loss of a closeknit corporate life of the scholars there. Lack of unity was, however, inherent in the division of the students into various universities, in the separation between student guilds and guilds of masters, and in the attempt to create a select inner circle of masters who controlled remunerative appointments.

The fact that all members of the university at Paris or at Oxford were under a common government enabled these universities to deal strongly with inner disaffection and with threats to their liberties from without.

The liberties of universities. A second feature of the medieval university was the enjoyment by its members of special privileges and immunities and by its officials of special powers in their dealigns with officials of secular governments and with private citizens. *The Authentic Habitat* of the Emperor Frederick Barbarossa (1158), granted his special protection to scholars within the Holy Roman Empire. It further permitted any student against whom a lawsuit was brought to choose as the judge before whom his case was to be tried either his professors or the bishop of the city in which he was studying.[12] Charters protected students of particular universities or students residing in particular cities in specified ways. Examples are numerous. Scholars were exempted by various rulers from being cited to appear in courts away from the particular city of their residence. Special orders of kings and of the Emperor exempted students from taxation. Municipalities granted poor students the right to beg. Prices charged by dealers for books and food, and by landlords for lodgings were, under privileges granted by the charters of some universities, to be fixed by the university authorities. The university as a corporate body was granted the further right of enforcing its decisions against the officials of either state or municipality by suspending its lectures, and even by removal to some other city or country. A bull of Pope Gregory IX, granted in 1231 to the University of Paris, conferred upon the University the privileges of suspending its work as a means of enforcing its right to fix the prices of lodgings for its members, and of compelling redress for injuries received by its members. On occasion the Papal Curia went further, and invoked the ban of the Church against persons who had wronged some university.

The License

A third feature of the medieval university was its prerogative of presenting candidates to the proper ecclesiastical authority- the Archdeacon at Bologna and the Chancellor of Notre Dame at Paris-who, as representative of the Church's authority, conferred upon the candidate the right to teach anywhere in Christendom (jus ubique docendi). The license is not to be confused with the mastership (magisterium), which was conferred by the university at Paris and at Oxford.[13] The license had as its basis the conviction, universally held in Latin Christendom, that teaching is at once the special duty and the peculiar prerogative of the Church. Christ said to his disciples, "Teach all peoples." This, churchmen believed, meant that the Church must teach and that no one may teach anything against the authority of the Church. It is, therefore, they believed, proper for the Church to send out teachers and to see that only those persons teach who can and will teach what is true and right. In medieval Europe this position of the Church was scarcely disputed for the idea of Church unity was one of the most powerful in Latin Christendom. On every hand it was thought that there should be but one fold and one shepherd-the Holy Roman Church and its Head on Earth, the Pope-and that the one Shepherd should say with what spiritual food the sheep should be fed. Heresy-the holding or teaching of any opinion contrary to the teachings of the Church-was everywhere regarded as a fearful offense against God and man. With great care, therefore the Church spoke through her Councils, announcing just which opinions were approved and which were forbidden. Those who taught in Her name-priests and teachers-were rigorously examined and carefully watched, to prevent any teaching by any accredited representatives of the Church contrary to the body of accepted Catholic truth. The practice of licensing teachers grew up in connection with this effort to safeguard teaching. The practice evolved so gradually that it is not easy to describe in a word, but it may be said that, in general, candidates for the license were presented, by the professors who taught them, to a church official (the Chancellor of Notre Dame at Paris and the Archdeacon of Bologna are examples) who was empowered by the Pope to grant to proper persons the license to teach everywhere. It was presumed that between them, the professors and the ecclesiastical official who granted the license had guaranteed the quality both of the candidate's scholarship and of his orthodoxy.

THE RISE OF UNIVERSITIES

Universities built by the free activities of scholars. There was long a tendancy to attribute the origin of each of the great medieval universities to some particular event, or to the influence of one great personality: the writings of Constantine the African are supposed to account for the "founding" of the medical faculty at Salerno; the discovery of the "lost" Roman law resulted in the rise of the law faculty at Bologna; a strike at Paris accounts for Oxford; Abelard built the University of Paris and so on. Such views made much of the new exploded theory that the revival of scholarship and the growth of cities in the eleventh century were due to the release of the Europe from the fear of the end of the world expected in the year 1000-those who have recourse to this explanation being strangely oblivious to the fact that releasing a man results in constructive effort only in case the person released is possessed of vitality, a cultivated skill, and intelligence, and has a social environment deeply rooted in a long and continious cultural tradition. Professor Rashdall, discussing the rise of the University of Salerno, sums up the case as follows:

> It is no doubt at first sight tempting to trace the medical knowledge and skill of Salerno to contact with the Saracens of Southern Italy or Sicily; but it appears to be well established by the researches of Henschel, Daremberg, de Renzi, and their successors, that no external cause can be assigned to the

beginnings of the movement, any more than to the somewhat later revival of dialectical and literary culture north of the Alps, or to the revival of law in the Lombard cities. The medical traditions of the old Roman world lingered on midst the material civilization of Magna Graecia, just as the traditions of legal culture lingered in the freer and more political atmosphere of northern Italy.[14]

The truth is that universities were not built by patronage or by chartered privileges, or even by single great leader. They grew because scholarship is essentially an activity of strongly individualized personalities in interaction. The wrecking of the ancient Roman Empire had deprived men of the institutions upon which they had long depended. The centuries which intervened between the collapse of the ancient world and the twelfth century flowering allowed opportunity for the development of selfreliant individuals of great creative power. Many such men turned to scholarship as an outlet for their restless genius, but scholarship is a social activity; so scholars formed associations and took the medieval name of corporate associations- universitas. Chartered status and elaborate organization came later. The university arose freely and later was organized and formalized; just as scholarship and literature arose as a product of free spirits in the eleventh and twelfth centuries to be formalized, institutionalized, and exploited in the following centuries. Universities were the creations of scholars in the twelfth: scholars in the fifteenth and sixteenth centuries revolted against them. But the universities of the fifteenth century were no more the universities of the late twelfth or early thirteenth than the scholarship of the twelfth century was that of the Dominicans of the age of Erasmus, Colet, Tyndale, and Sir Thomas More.

Where and how *universities* began. The medieval universities had as their function the training of men for higher positions in civil and ecclesiastical administration, for the practice of medicine, and for the profession of scholarship itself. The basis of university studies was furnished by the Seven Liberal Arts.[15] The Compendium on the University of Paris aptly indicates the place of the liberal arts in the scheme of the medieval university. Describing the constitution of the "Large Faculty of Arts," the Compendium says:

> The remaining faculty, far more numerous than the others, is called the famous Faculty of Arts, the basis, mother, and nurse of all the others. For this faculty has for its dean the Rector who is head of the whole University. He is chosen and confirmed by the Faculty of Arts alone...[16]

But though the liberal arts furnished the basis for all university studies, these studies culminated in the work of the professional faculties. Two types of interests then combined in the medieval universities-interest in liberal scholarship and in the practice of the professions of the medicine, law, and divinity. The real node about which an early university grew was its professional schools: medicine at Salerno, law at Bologna, and theology at Paris. The growth of later Studia-even that of Oxford-was so greatly affected by established patterns of teaching and government that the influence of the learned professions upon them is obscured; but practicing theologians at Paris, practicing lawyers at Bologna, and practicing physicians at Salerno and at Montpellier supplied the crucial activities which led to the development of universities. At each of these places, lecturers on the body of scholarship pertaining to the respective professions attracted scholars who formed a studium, the nucleus of a university. Salerno never achieved chartered form-indeed, it declined just as other universities were receiving official sanctions for their organizations- but it was, nevertheless, a university. Let us turn to consider briefly the rise of the great mother universities-Salerno, Bologna, Paris, and Oxford- and of Cambridge, Montpellier, Naples, and the Papal University at Rome-each one of which illustrates certain important facts respecting development and character of university scholarship.

Salerno

It will be remembered that Southern Italy was the Magna Graecia of antiquity; that for much of the Middle Ages part of the region-notably that under the rule of the Counts of Salerno-acknowledged the authority of the Eastern Emperors; and that the Greek language flourished there for almost nineteen hundred years-that is, from the planting of the Earliest Greek colonies there in the sixth century B.C. until the thirteenth century, when it was displaced by the rising Italian tongue. Balsilian monasteries, repositories of Greek books, were to be found in Sicily and southern Italy; monks from Italy traveled in the Byzantine Empire, and their numbers were recruited from the east. Bronze doors, the product of Byzantine craftsmanship, ornamented palaces and churches in southern Italy, while the enterprise of Amalfi merchants enriched Italy by a constant flow of objects of use and of art from Syria and Constantinople.[17]

Among the Greek survivals in Southern Italy none was more significant for the rise of science than the tradition of Graeco-Roman medicine, which lingered at Salerno, to find a voice in the writers and translators of the eleventh and twelfth centuries and so to become the fountain of the stream of medical scholarship which was one of the great forces in the intellectual life of medieval Europe. Salerno, located about thirty miles southeast of Naples, was a center for the practice of medicine as early as the ninth century. Early in the eleventh century Garipontus, first of the medieval writers at Salerno of whom we have knowledge, produced a compilation in the Graeco-Roman tradition. About the middle of the same century the most famous of Salernan translators, the monk, Constantine the African, brought out Latin versions of works by Greek, Graeco-Roman, Arabic, and Jewish writers on medicine which were soon to be prescribed as textbooks in the medical faculties of universities, and "formed the ars medicinae of the Middle Ages."[18] A succession of writers on medical subjects extended the fame and influence of the school, so that it was, undoubtedly, the most important early center of medical scholarship in western Europe.

Salerno never developed a university organization. It received the first official recognition only in its decline, when, in 1230, Frederick II issued a decree giving to persons examined at his court by masters of Salerno and certain other officers a monopoly of the practice and teaching of medicine in his Kingdom of Sicily. During the great period of the school's work, it seems to have been a sort of voluntary and self-perpetuating association of practicing and teaching physicians and of teachers of the arts. Students were required to spend three years in the study of the liberal arts before taking up the study of medicine. Five years were devoted to the study of medicine itself. The society of doctors seems to have had a head, called at first a praeposius and later a prior. The significance of Salerno, therefore, lies solely in its contribution to scholarship and to the growth of the scientific spirit. There is no trace of any contribution made by the school to academic organisation, or titles, or degrees, or dress, or student customs. Salerno, "The City of Hippocrates," as the Middle Ages called it, is notable for having built up the medical curriculm of the medieval universities and for having furnished the early textbooks and professors of medicine to Bologna and Montpellier.[19]

To the question "Why did Salerno develop into a medical school of higher grade, while other tenth-century centers of the teaching of medicine in western Europe-Chartres for example-had no such development?" it may be answered that not one reason but many must be assigned for this development. These reasons were: (1) the survival there of the Graeco-Roman tradition of medicine, (2) the fact that at a crucial time the Count of Salerno acknowledged the sovereignty of the Bysantine Emperors, Greek continued to be a vernacular tongue there, and there was much travel and other communication between the Salerno area and Constantinople; (3) the presence in Sicily and southern Italy of Arabic physicians and of Jewish doctors who practiced among the Moslems; and (4) the happy circumstance that Salerno attracted some men (notably Constantine the African) who wrote on medical subjects. Salerno was not a center of practice and teaching merely. Other forces, such as the presence of monasteries, may have helped in the progress of studies, but the meeting of scholarly traditions and their assimilation by productive scholars were the determining forces in the creation at Salerno of the medical faculty of the university.

Bologna

In the eleventh century a political development took place which was unique in the Middle Ages: this development was a medieval revival of the city state. Pavia, Venice, Pisa, Bologna, and other northern Italian cities made themselves felt as political forces. At Bologna, during the later Middle Ages, the bishops, feudal lords, and the municipal corporation struggled for ascendancy in the government of the city. At times one, at other times another, of these parties was dominant. The ecclesiastical and municipal authorities found that their interests coincided in many raespects and were served by Roman institutions. They therefore had constant recourse to Roman law in attempts to find support for their claims agaionst the secular lords.[20]

Both Church and municipalities supported schools, those of the municipalitaies being "the direct descendants of the Roman schools." The struggle between the contending parties-bishops, feudal lords, and municipalities-operating in the midst of and upon medieval ideas and institutions, produced effects of the utmost importance for the growth of liberty and of scholarship. These effects were the university corporation, the revival of Roman law, and the creation of canon law as an organized and exact body of knowledge. The institution about which these great developments centered was the University of Bologna.

The University of Bologna resulted from the growing together of three educational institutions which had long existed side-by-side in the city. These three were the system of monastic schools, which developed the canon law as a field of scholarly endeavor; the Cathedral, which brought to the growing university the study of the liberal arts; and the system of municipal schools of rhetoric and of law, which contributed the scientific study of law not only to Bologna but to the world.

The vital force in the University's growth is not to be sought in some external influence, but is to be found in legal scholarship, which developed there in the eleventh and twelfth centuries. Great masters of the law went beyond compendiums of their subjects and even beyond codes, to study the opinions of ancient jurists; the crux of the revival was the return to the Pandects or Digest of Justinian.[21] The Code and Institutes were not, of course, neglected in the revival; but the emphasis shifted, after centuries during which epitomes and summaries were depended upon, to the study of the decisions of the great jurists of antiquity. Once more as in the great days of the making and study of Roman law, the entire Corpus Juris Civilis was covered systematically by students. The emphasis upon the study of the Digest developed lawyers with a grasp of the principles of jurisprudence and consequently with the capacity for independent thinking. The revival was an intellectual one.

The manner of the revival was as follows. Citizens of the renascent city-states of northern Italy awoke in the eleventh and twelfth centuries to an intense consciousness of their political rights and liberties. The rise of commerce, the great schism in the Church, and the protracted struggle between the Papal Curia and the Emperors of the Holy Roman Empire had combined to place the Lombard municipalities in a strategic position; they were courted on the one side by the Emperors and on the other by the papal party, which was also the party of Italian nationalism. Constitutional issues entered into the political disputes of the period. The lawyers of Ravenna, a center of imperial jurisprudence, supported the cause of the Empire. The papal and national forces, therefore, put their lawyers forward. Matilda, Countess of Tuscany from 1075 until 1115, requested Irnerius to renew the books of the Roman law. Even before the accession of Matilda, the legal revival had made considerable progress in Rome, Pavia, and Bologna. The rise of commerce created a demand for the services of lawyers which reinforced the demand for their services in political and constitutional cases. Early in the twelfth century the teachers of the law were a recognized force at Bologna. The revival was fruitful of practical consequences. It was lay and secular in spirit, as contrasted with the theological interest of the University of Paris. This does not mean that there was more of freedom of inquiry or of resistance to dogma in Italy than in France. There was rather more of intellectual independence and rebellion against obscurantism at Paris than at Bologna. The intellectual character of the whole university movement must not, however, be discounted. The legal revival was closely connected with resurgent Italian nationalism, with revived Italian commerce, and with the vigorous life of the renascent city-states of Lombardy. The revival was fruitful for the regulation of human relations, but the heart of it was the vigorous pursuit of constitutional law. The movement was both utilitarian and intellectual in its significance.

The Iranerian revival of the civil law was paralleled by the development of ecclesiastical or canon law. From time to time, for centuries, decrees of councils and other authoritative statements of ecclesiastical bodies or officers respecting faith and conduct had been compiled and published. About 1140, Gratian, a monk who taught in the monastic school of San

Felice at Bologna, brought out a synthesis of canon law, commonly called the Decretum. This book, which its author called The Harmony of Discordant Decrees (Concordia Discordantium Canonum), was one of the most important textbooks ever written. It gave a powerful impulse to the cause of papal absolutism[22] and established canon law at once as a subject of study in the studia generalia just then being established in Europe. So important was this book that Gratian is commonly spoken of as the founder of the science of canon law. Gratian was a profound student of the Roman civil law and of scholasticism. Now Roman law had affected not only the development of the administrative principles and structure of the Roman Church but also of its theology. The revived study of the Roman civil law, therefore, enriched the content of canon law and of theology. Canon law lent itself, moreover, to the method of scholasticism as developed by Abelard as did no other subject. Not even theology and civil law are as complete within themselves and consequently so perfectly adapted to dialectical treatment as is canon law. Abelard's method of balancing authorities in seeking an answer to any question never gives more perfectly the illusion of impartial intellectual inquiry arriving at truth in support of dogma than when the field of inquiry was itself created by the authorities who approved the dogma.

The Decretgum is divided into three parts. In the first section the principles and grounds of canon law are presented, with the offices of the clergy and other religious persons; the second part treats of church property, which ecclesiastical jurisdiction, with penance, and with Christian marriage; and the third part discusses the liturgy and sacraments of the Church.[23] Almost at once this textbook became authoritative. The written word enjoyed a prestige in the Middle Ages which it has enjoyed in no other period of the history of western Europe. Gratian's work took its place beside the writings of Aristotle and Peter the Lombard as an authoritative basis of thought and action.

Irnerius and Gratian were great teachers-as were certain of their predecessors and successors at Bologna. Students flowed into Bologna, therefore, from all parts of Latin Christendom. At a very early date, certainly before the issue in 1158 of Frederick Barbarossa's Authentic Habita, the doctors or teachers of the law at Bologna formed colleges or guilds. Later other faculties organized. Owing to a series of circumstances, this guild never became the University of Bologna, but it is important to remember that the work of scholars and teachers of the law went before the formation of a university.

Foreign students at Bologna, feeling the necessity of mutual protection and of association for fellowship, formed themselves into guilds, called universities. Just how early this was done no one can say with certainty. A Bull of Pope Clement III, issued in 1189, recognized the existence of an organized body of students, or of bodies of students. At one time there seem to have been at least four of these universities, but in course of time they combined. Since the university was organized to afford travelling students protection primarily against the citizens of Bologna, citizens of that city were excluded from membership in it; so it came about that the professors of the city, who were citizens of Bologna, were excluded from membership in the university. This strange situation then arose: despite the fact that the essential functions of any university are academic, the University of Bologna—the guild of students-possessed no academic authority or functions; these functions all pertained to the doctors' guilds. Teaching, scholarly authorship and the admission of candidates into the learned professions were not activities of the University. The University busied itself with the regulation of the price of lodgings, with passing upon the quality and price of books offered for sale, with controlling rates of interest on loans made to students, with controlling the movements and other activities of professors, with maintaining the rights and dignities of the University against the municipal authorities of Bologna, and with composing quarrels within their own ranks. The University of students reached its greatest development in the thirteenth century and quickly declined in power and in influence. In the fifteenth century it was but a shadow of its former self.

Paris

The theological university. The University of Paris had its origin in an intellectual movement of which Peter Abelard was the ablest and most conspicuous representative. The central aspect of this movement was the dialectical development of theology. This development had results of the utmost importance for European scholarship, for in it the theological interest predominated over both the humanistic interest and the interest in the natural sciences; while logical elaboration of the pronouncements of the Scriptures, of the Fathers and Doctors of the Church, and of the Roman Hierarchy predominated over experiment religion.

In sharp contrast with Bologna-where a municipal school of rhetoric which had developed the teaching of the Roman civil law, a monastic school specializing in the teaching of canon law, and a cathedral school of the liberal arts attracted the students who formed the University of Bologna-the schools which drew students to Paris in such numbers that a studium generale evolved there were all ecclesiastical in character. These schools were: (1) the cathedral schools of Notre Dame of Paris, presided over at the beginning of the twelfth century by William of Champeaux; (2) the schools conducted by the collegiate church of Sainte Genevieve-a foundation not subject to the Bishop of Paris, the chapter of which in the early part of the same century was composed of secular clerics, and (3) a school, opened in 1113, by the canons regular of St. Victor. This last institution was prominent only for a very brief period, but for a short time it did add to the luster of Paris as a center of higher studies.

In the later part of the twelfth and the early part of the thirteenth century, the studium at Paris evolved the characteristic features of an autonomous university. Since certain features of the ecclesiastical schools just listed gave direction to the development of the studium and contributed to the distinctive organization of the University of Paris, it is necessary to consider what these features were. They were three in number. (1) The respective chancellors of the Cathedral of Notre Dame of Paris and of the autonomous collegiate church of Sainte Genevieve were privileged to issue the licentia docendi. (2) The members of the schools, both teachers and pupils, were clerics. (3) Long before the university was formed the custom had grown up of requiring each beginning teacher to have a master, who directed and sponsored him. The crime first charged against Abelard was not heresy, but that of teaching without a master.

The ecclesiastical character of the schools from which the studium evolved at Paris had an immediate consequence for the masters and students of Paris: their privileges were those of the clergy. Whereas the guilds at Bologna secured their rights and privileges by treaty, winning concessions from their opponents and gaining support from their allies, the members of the University of Paris were clerks and took their place in the governmental scheme of the Church. The liberties of the universities were secured principally because of their alignment with the Papal Court. It is not surprising, therefore, that masters and scholars -all members of the clerical order and all looking to the distant Papal Court for support and encouragement-should have formed a single body. Whereas at Bologna there were a number of guilds of masters and other guilds of students, masters and students at Paris were a single corporation. It is not surprising either, that since members of the university were clerics, they should have formed a hierarchy, not a republic, and that the masters should have dominated the corporation. The dual relation in which pupils stood at Paris had important consequences, moreover, for the development of the autonomy of the university. Students looked for the licentia docendi to the chancellor either of Notre Dame or of Sainte Genevieve, but they could be admitted to the society of the masters only by the masters themselves. The masters could not deprive a person licensed by the chancellor of the right to teach, but they could refuse to have anything to do with him or to recognize his students. We shall see that the masters retained and extended their control over teaching and study at Paris and became, under the Pope, an autonomous power.

How the studium at Paris developed and gained university status. About 1100 the schools of Paris came to enjoy a splendid reputation. The liberal arts, theology, and perhaps medicine, were taught there, and a little later civil and canon law were taught in the city. A succession of great masters, among them William of Champeaux and his pupil Abelard, who eclipsed him, attracted hundreds of students to the city. Paris became a city of teachers, and there seems to have been a society of masters.[24] Before the close of the twelfth century, it is said, Louis VII granted to the masters of Paris the right to suspend lectures as a measure of retaliation and protest in case of any injury to any student or master.[25] In 1208 a violent riot took place in Paris, in the course of which there were many fights between students and the townspeople. Following this riot a charter was granted, a provision of which was that any scholar arrested by royal officers should be turned over to the ecclesiastical authorities. The personal property of scholars was protected against seizure except by authority of the ecclesiastical court.[26] The Provost of Paris was required to swear to respect the privileges of the scholars of the city. By the year 1210 the society of masters of Paris had a set of written statutes. A few years later Innocent III recognized the existence of the university as a corporation by authorizing the election of a proctor, who should represent it at the Papal Court. He further recognized the society of masters by sanctioning the readmission to the society of a master who had been expelled from it for a breach of its rules.[27]

Between 1210 and 1230, a struggle of the utmost importance to the University of Paris took place. The chancellor of the Cathedral of Notre Dame attempted to compel all masters of the city to swear obedience to him. A dispute ensued which resulted in a great victory for the masters. The chancellor was required to grant the license to candidates recommended by the masters and he was stripped of any disciplinary powers over the university. As time went on, the masters of arts of the university organized into groups called nations. Each nation had a head or Proctor. By 1225 there was a seal of the entire university, and by 1246 the right of the university to a seal was conceded. The teachers of arts, law, theology, and medicine were organized into faculties-the teachers of the three higher faculties being excluded from the nations. Each faculty had its head. By the middle of the thirteenth century the head of the faculty of arts was recognized as Rector of the entire University and was so addressed by the Pope in 1259. All bachelors of arts were required to swear obedience to him, so that his supermacy was established over the entire university.

A great riot of 1228-1229 resulted in the killing of some students of Paris by soldiers. The masters suspended lectures in an effort to secure redress of injuries, and when this measure was not effectual, they dissolved the university of a period of six years.[28] Masters and students left the city. The reigning Pope, Gregory IX, intervened in the quarrel. He secured the punishment of the offenders against the university, and succeeded in healing the breach between the city and the university. He issued a bull giving his sanction to certain privileges of the universities. The prices of rents for the lodgings of students were to be fixed by a committee composed of two masters and two townsmen; the Bishop of Paris and the Abbot of St. Germain-des-Pres were to respect the privileges of the University; the right of the masters to strike in defence of their rights was expressly recognized.[29] In 1245 Innocent IV granted to the scholars of the University of Paris exemption from being cited to appear in ecclesiastical courts at a distance from Paris. The next year he instituted a Court of Conservation the duty of which was to protect the university. Later the faculty of arts secured the right of electing the conservator; the university had attained status in the papal government that made it independent of local civil and ecclesiastical officials. The Rector and Regent masters were the equals of secular lords and of the great abbots and archbishops of the Church.

The origin of Oxford University. Between the years 1167 and 1190, a studium generale evolved with great rapidity at Oxford in England. There had been schools at Oxford for a very long time before 1167, and they appear to have won considerable reputation before the middle of the twelfth century; but late in that century, as many bits of evidence go to show, the little city on the upper reaches of the Thames became the center of scholarship in England.[30] It is hard to say just why Oxford, rather than the capital or some great cathedral city, should have become the site of the earliest university in England, but its location in the heart of rural England is highly significant. For England was, until very recently, rural: the country and parish furnished the bases of its social and economic life. Oxford was easy to access from all parts of England, but few cities of the country could have been further removed from the foreign influence which were drawn to the courts of the King and of the great princes of the Church. Medieval Oxford was enfolded and nourished by England. It was born of England. No medieval university aligned itself more closely with the aspirations of the nation in the midst of which it was located than did the oldest university of the English-speaking world.

The studium generale at Oxford appears, moreover, to

have received its first impulse to growth from a nationalistic movement. Henry II, as a measure taken to check the activities of the sympathizers with his enemy, Thomas a Becket, in the year 1167, ordered all clerics who derived their income from English churches and who were abroad, to return to the country within three months, "as they loved their revenues."[31] There is some indication, moreover, that in that same year the King of France ordered all alien scholars to leave his realm. The supposition is that many English scholars transferred to Oxford. Certainly the studium must have been well developed by 1184 or 1185, when Giraldus Cambrensis read his book Topographica Hibernica before the scholars and "the Doctors of different Faculties" in the city.[32]

The first constitution of Oxford was borrowed from Paris before the French university had achieved its full development. Oxford became, like Paris, "a masters' university"; like Paris, moreover, it developed nations-each with its proctor-in the faculty of arts; and, to an even greater extent than at Paris, the faculty of arts at Oxford predominated over the higher faculties. The officer who presided over meetings of the faculties at Oxford was the chancellor. This official was at first the representative of the Bishop of Lincoln and was appointed by him. He was thus an extra university official-not a member of the masters' guild. The proctors, therefore, discharged many of the academic duties which might well have been within the jurisdiction of the presiding officer of the university. The nations were eliminated at Oxford in the thirteenth century, but the proctors continued. In the course of time it became the custom to have the chancellor elected by the masters. This official, therefore, gained status within the guild of teachers; but the proctors and masters continued to exercise prerogatives secured while they stood apart from the university.

The first written statutes of the masters at Oxford were published in 1253. The following year a papal bull was addressed to the "masters and scholars sojourning at Oxford in the diocese of Lincoln."[33]

A striking feature of the university organization both at Oxford and at Cambridge is the prominence there of resident and teaching corporations-constituent members of the respective universities-known as colleges. These institutions developed in the Middle Ages of the hostels established and endowed by the charitable to provide lodging, care, and supervision for scholars. The colleges were endowed, while Oxford and Cambridge had almost no endowment in the Middle Ages, with the result that the colleges gradually took over most of the teaching and disciplinary functions from the two ancient English universities. This made possible the development of an exceedingly strong corporate life at Oxford and at Cambridge-a feature which makes them almost unique among universities of the world.

The Imperial University of Naples

The universities so far considered grew up spontaneously, as scholars first did hightly significant work and then received wide-spread appreciation. The teaching and authorship of the great scholars drew other scholars to the centers where they flourished, and these all formed voluntary societies for mutual protection and assistance. The Emperor, the Pope, and various kings issued charters and decrees, conferring rights and privileges upon these voluntary associations and sanctioning those they already enjoyed. Universities thus became factors in the policies of monarchs.

In the thirteenth century an innovation took place: monarchs began to found universities where none had grown up. The first instance of the founding of a university by a royal charter occurred in 1224, when the Emperor Frederick II chartered the University of Naples. He established it as a measure of retaliation against the university cities of northern Italy, so that it was not the creation of free scholarship but of political action. Frederick forbade his subjects to resort to any other studium. The institution was subject in all matters to the political authority, being until 1947 under the supervision of the royal chancellor. It thus lacked, throughout the period under consideration, the freedom essential to scholarly work. Created to furnish bureaucrats for a despotism, the contributions of the University of Naples to the spiritual and intellectual progress of the Middle Ages were negligible.

The University of the Roman Court. Unique among the universities of the Middle Ages was that founded by Pope Innocent IV about the year 1245. The university specialized in civil and canon law. Theology flourished there. The University of the Roman Court was, moreover, one of the five universities (Bologna, Salamanca, Paris, and Oxford were the others) at which, by direction of the Council of Venice in 1312, the Greek, Arabic, Chaldee, and Hebrew languages were to be taught.[34] There is, moreover, evidence that some attention was paid there to philosophy and medicine.

The University of the Roman Court did not, of course, conform to the pattern of the typical medieval university of students and masters. The cardinal chamberiain was its chancellor, and it was governed by a college of doctors. It is, however, of peculiar interest, since it reflects the place which higher scholarship, especially in the fields of civil and canon law, had in papal policy. The development of constitutional law and government and of the papacy were inextricably mingled in the Middle Ages.

WORK AND LIFE IN A MEDIEVAL UNIVERSITY

University degrees

The status of any higher teacher or other professional man in the Middle Ages depended on the one hand upon his being persona grata to the Church, and on the other upcn his being accepted by his professional colleagues.

In the age in which the universal form of association of merchants, craftsmen, and professional men was the guild, this last meant acceptance into a guild. Entrance to any guild was controlled by its members. As teachers formed guilds of masters-called colleges at Bologna and universities at Paris and Oxford-they developed the practice of receiving new members into their ranks by a regular ceremonial. Oaths were administered to the candidate, a book was given the newly created master at Bologna, and at Paris he received the book and scholar's cap. This reception of new members into the ranks of masters was called inception.

It will be recalled, moreover, that from the very early period of the history of the Roman Church there existed in every typical chapter of cathedrals and collegiate churches an official called the scholasticus or chancellor, who exercised general supervision over teaching. One of the principal duties of a chancellor was to license teachers, under powers vested in him by the ecclesiastical hierarchy. This formal sanction of a teacher by the officials of the Church was called the conferring of the licentia docendi. As studia arose, the Roman hierarchy was represented at each by an official empowered to license teachers and those entering upon the practice of law, medicine, or divinity. The Archdeacon of Bologna, the Chancellor of the Cathedral of Notre Dame of Paris, and the Chancellor of Oxford University-first appointed by the Bishop of Lincoln and later elected by the Oxford masters themselves-conferred the license at their respective universities. Efforts of kings to control the license at certain universities were, on the whole, unavailing. The real power in licensing candidates came, in time, to rest with the university faculties. At Bologna the archdeacon and the guilds of doctors worked, save for the period of one brief quarrel, in harmony. The Archdeacon appears to have been content with the revenues and dignities attending his right to confer the license, and to have left the actual control of examinations to the doctors of the university. At Paris, on the other hand, the Chancellor of Notre Dame and the University engaged in a long struggle which resulted in the reduction of Chancellor's power over the university almost to the point of extinction. A papal decree required the Chancellor to license all candidates properly presented by their respective faculties-a requirement which, in effect, made the university the degree-granting authority. At Oxford the Chancellor always owed his position to the university, and when at length he became an elective officer of the university, the masters' guild had all academic masters fully within their hands. Inception and license thus became so closely associated to be almost indistinguishable.

The first degrees were simply the license to teach or to practice medicine or law. Teachers might be called doctors or masters, and, as degrees arose in the thirteenth century, there was, for a long time, no distinction between masters and doctors, who were also called professors. In course of time, the title master came to be used of members of the inferior faculties and that of doctor of the superior faculties of medicine, law, and theology. Gradually these license came to stand for status: they were degrees. In course of time scholars were admitted, in a limited way, to guilds of masters. Since such a student could not, because his privileges were quite limited, be called a master; and since, furthermore, he was just entering upon his new status he was called a bachelor (baccalaureus)- which means a beginner. Like the titles of master and doctor, the title bachelor was first used quite informally, but came, as the thirteenth century advanced, to be regarded as a degree.

Requirements for degrees were not at all standardized in the Middle Ages. In general it may be said, however, that candidates of the various degrees were rquired to have attended lectures on prescribed books and to have undergone examinations. Candidates for the baccalaureate were commonly expected to have attended and participated in a given number of disputations. Prospective masters and doctors were required to give a prescribed number of lectures before being admitted to examination for their degrees.

Academic exercises

The work and ritual of a medieval university were no less highly organized than was its governmental structure. The principal exercises by which learning was carried forward were four; the lecture, the repetition, the disputation, and the examination, and all were conducted according to well defined and recognized principles, and with much formality. The lecture might well involve first the reading of a text, then its full exposition, next comment on passages of special interest, and finally the raising of problems for discussion. Lectures were expected to confine their remarks to the text before them, avoiding digressions and especially avoiding trespassing upon the ground of other faculties. A teacher of the law of thirteenth century Bologna stated the plan according to which he proposed to conduct his course as follows:

"First, I shall give you summaries of each title before I proceed to the text; secondly, I shall give you as clear and explicit a statement as I can of the purport of each law (included in the title); thirdly, I shall read the text with a view to correcting it; fourthly, I shall briefly repeat the contents of the Law; fifthly, I shall solve apparent contradictions, adding any general principles of Law (to be extracted from the passage), commonly called "Brocardica" and any distinctions or subtle and useful problems (questiones) arising out of the Law with their solutions, as far as the Divine Providence shall enable me. And if any Law seem deserving by reason of its celebrity or difficulty, of a Repetition, I shall reserve it for an evening Repetition."[35]

Comments made by lectures were not at random, but were in the accepted tradition of interpretation of the texts before them. These accepted interpretations were preserved in written commentaries called glosses read to classes by lectures, following the reading of the texts themselves. Repetitions were simply detailed discussions of lectures which had been given—they must have been much like a modern interview between a tutor and the student with whom he meets. Lectures were classified as ordinary and extraordinary. An ordinary lecture was that given by a doctor or master; an extraordinary lecture was that given by mere bachelors or even, students of a certain standing. Lectures given by bachelors and other advanced students were regarded as learning exercises, by which the lecturer benefited principally, rather than as teaching exercises for the benefit of the student. Success in them, as in disputations, might, moreover, gain a great reputation for a young scholar. Bachelors, therefore, in some instances paid students to attend lectures which they were giving. The disputation was the one university exercise most distinctive of scholasticism. The disputation might be conducted by either of two methods. In the first a single reasoner alternately presented the arguments in support of the two sides to a question, ultimately showing the preponderance of evidence in favor of one side of the argument or the other. This was the method of the Sic et Non of Abelard. The false impression of objectivity and freedom which this method gave resulted from the complete discrediting of a thesis presented as the only possible alternative to the position which the expositor believed before he began to frame the disputation. With positions chosen and terms defined by a person committed to a fixed idea, the results of such an argument were a foregone conclusion. The second method was that of debate between opponents-one proposing, the other defending a thesis. This method was the more likely of the two to result ina genuine inquiry. The course of the disputation was rigidly prescribed. First, the question was stated; next the affirmative argument was presented; the presentation of the affirmative argument was followed by the presentation of the negataive argument; objections to arguments were then made, and the objections were themselves attached in an attempt to refute them; finally accounts were cast up and a conclusion reached.

Students disputed with each other as learning exercises. Doctors engaged in public debates which excited widespread interest in the highest quarters. Frequently a public disputation was inaugurated by the posting, by some doctor, of a set of theses he was prepared to defend. Martin Luther thus launched the debates which led first to his excommunication by the Roman Hierarchy and then to the open division of Christendom.

Examinations were not a feature of the work at medieval Oxford and Cambridge, but on the continent of Europe, public and private examinations were used to determine the qualifications of candidates for degrees. These were oral and were conducted with great ceremony and care in the observanced of forms. At Bologna a candidate for a degree was presented by the consilarius of his nation to the rector, who was requested to admit him to private examination. The candidate took an oath that he had complied with all the conditions laid down in the statutes, that he would obey the rector and would make no gifts and give no entertainments (in excess of the value prescribed in the university statutes) to the persons upon whose decision success in the examination would depend. Before the private examination could be held, moreover, the candidate was presented to the archdeacon by a doctor, who had previously satisfied himself as to the candidate's fitness for a degree.

On the morning of the examination, the candidate, after first attending a Mass of the Holy Ghost, presented himself to the college of doctors in which he was preparing to take his degree. He was given selected passages for study and was permitted to retire, with the doctor who presented him, to his own house, where he prepared for the final trial. Later in the same day the candidate came before the examining doctors and the archdeacon, who presided at the examinations. The doctor who was sponsoring him-his promotor-introduced him to the archdeacon and examiners. The candidate then discussed the selected passages assigned to him and was examined on them. After the completion of the examination, a ballot was taken and the fate of the candidate determined by the majority of votes cast by the examining doctors. The public examination at Bologna, essentially the inception of Paris and Oxford, was simply the ceremony attending the conferring of a degree. The candidate lectured in the cathedral and was presented to the archdeacon, who after making a complimentary speech, conferred to degree. The candidate's promotor then invested him with the insignia of his new rank, and the newly-made doctor was seated in the professional chair and handed an open book, and a gold ring was placed upon his finger.[36]

Buildings and Equipment

Medieval universities were not housed and equipped as are those of the modern world. Professors frequently lectured in their own houses or in rented halls. Irnerius is said to have lectured from a pulpit placed at a street corner. Convocations were held in churches. Books were few and libraries had but few volumes. Equipment was most scanty. There were no laboratories. Pupils sat about the lecturing professors on rude benches or on rushes of straw on the floor. Buildings were scarcely heated at all.

University Studies

The medieval student in pursuit of his university degree read, or had read to him, a number of texts and the glosses or commentaries which contained the accepted interpretation of them. Independent investigation was not dreamed of by the medieval university student; he mastered the content and meaning of the books which constituted the canon of literary and scientific learning in the Middle Ages by hearing them read and explained, by participating in discussions and disputations on points in them, and by conning over them with care. In the course in theology, the Bible and the Sentences of Peter the Lombard were the basic books. The works of St. Thomas were approved for members of the Dominican Order. In medicine the works of Galen, Hippocrates, Avicenna, and Bartholornew the Englishman were prescribed at Montpellier in 1340. At Paris the texts of Avicenna and Averroes and of their European followers were also used. Gratian's famous Decrtals was the foundation of the course in canon law; but the body of the canon law was constantly receiving accessions as popes and councils issued decisions and decrees. The Corpus Juris Civilis furnished the content of the course in civil law. In the arts course, logic or dialectic was the subject most studied. The classics of Greek and Roman antiquity were neglected. Priscian's vast compendium of grammar was studied, but the Prior Analytics and Posterior Analytics of Aristotle furnished the student the formal framework of studies. The Ethics, Politics, and Economics of Aristotle, and his works on natural philosophy and on metaphysics made up the very heart of the medieval arts curriculum. The books of Boethius, Gerard of Cremona, Euclid, and Sacrobosco also were read in courses on music, astronomy, and matematics respectively.

The length of time prescribed for study for the various degrees varied so greatly from one age to another and from university to university that it is not worthwhile to attempt a generalization about the matter. At Paris in the fourteenth century a candidate for the degree of Bachelor of Arts was required to be twenty years of age and to have studied from five to six years. For the doctorate in theology at Paris eight years of study were prescribed until the reforms of 1366, when sixteen years were prescribed for this degree. The earliest statutes at Paris prescribed six years of study for license in medicine for those students who had not been previously licensed in arts; students licensed in arts could receive license in medicine in five and a half years.

Colleges. In the very early period of university development in medieval Europe, students who were pursuing their studies away from home made private arrangements for board and lodgings in the university towns. Singly or in groups, they lived in rented houses or rooms. At Paris groups living in hired houses took on a stable character and became in effect societies. Save in the case of very wealthy students, who lived, each with his private tutor, in his own house, each house occupied by students was presided over by a master. Paris thus became the inaugurator of the collegiate system. Direction was given to the development of the collegiate system by a very ancient institution of Europe-that of the hospital. A medieval hospital was a guest house, at which travellers, the sick, the aged, children, and the poor, were gratuitiously entertained or permanently cared for. Poor students were regarded as proper objects of such hospitality. At Durham, in 1190, places were provided at St. Cuthbert's Almshouse for three poor students of Durham school. They were to be housed and fed at the expense of the foundation. Ten years earlier, however, Joyce of London had endowed a room for poor scholars at Paris, and this foundation developed into the first of the endowed colleges there. Other benefactaors established similar halls of residence for poor scholars at Paris and elsewhere. The religious orders built houses for their members at university centers.

Residential halls or hospices for students came to be called colleges. The term collegium was originally equivalent to universitas—it simply meant a corporation. Gradually the term university came to designate the entire studium; while the word college came to mean a residential institution.

Very different collegiate systems developed in the south of Europe, in German lands, and in France and Great Britain. There were small residential colleges from the thirteenth century onward in Italy and from the fourteenth in Spain, but the colleges of those lands were never of great importance.

They continued to be merely halls of residence. The college of Spain, perhaps the most important medieval college of Bologna, was planned to care for only thirty students. The colleges of the German universities were intended primarily for masters, and secondarily, if at all, for students. In France, Scotland, and England, on the other hand, both masters and students lived in colleges. At Paris a college consisted of a group of students presided over by a master. At Oxford and Cambridge a college was a corporation, governed by its head and senior members-the head being elected by all the members of the foundation.[37] As a result of the development of colleges in which both masters and students lived, collegiate teaching developed a system which reached its fullest development in the tutorial systems of Oxford and Cambridge. In the German universities and in the south of Europe, on the other hand, a professional system developed.

Women in medieval universities

The universities of the Middle Ages were men's institutions. Later research has discredited earlier traditions of the medical women of Salerno.[38] There were however, learned women in university cities, some of whom held recognized positions as public teachers. Rashdall notes that a married woman of Florence was, in 1304, listed among the lay teachers of Latin in that city, and that Dona Beatriz Galindo of Salamanca was summoned by Isabella the Catholic to be her teacher in the Latin language. So few and scattered are the references to women with any pretensions to literary or scientific learning in the later Middle Ages, however, and so limited are the scholarly attainments of those women who are counted as authors or scholars that these very references afford melancholy evidence of the exclusion of women for centuries from literature, science, and the learned professions.

Student life

In age, students of medieval universities ranged from

young lads to men entering upon middle life, and in dignity from street gamins and beggars to archbishops and even to cardinals. Some of them were vagabonds, wandering from university to university, and begging at the doors of the charitable for their daily bread. The wilder of them initiated new students into their ranks with rough horseplay and feasting at the neophyte's expense. A body of student songs grew up. Of recognized amusements and games there were, however, few. Lacking outlets for their spirits in recognized ways, many students turned to poaching, to drinking, to brawling, and even to highway robbery, in their search for excitement. The pageantry of university life and the disputations and discussions, however, furnished excitement which seems to have been much to the medieval taste. Letters of students reflect zest of life and preoccupation with the student's perennial problems—finances and studies.

The achievements of the medieval universities. The universities of the Middle Ages achieved a form of organization and a place in society in which scholars enjoyed autonomy in the pursuit of their academic tasks, and under which, standards of academic work could be elevated and maintained. Some logic was the one approved method of scholarship, learning was of necessity limited in range; literature was almost excluded from universities, while medicine and the natural sciences were studied in a relatively profitless way. The study of law and of theology, however, flourished, and the achievements of the scholastic philosophers in these fields were enormous. Deductive logic itself was refined; the meaning of terms was fixed; and scholars were trained to close and exact reasoning.

Two points stand out in this discussion of universities. The first is the central role played by pure scholarship in the creation of universities: a phase of this point is the importance of the humanities in maintaining the tone and direction of scholarship. A second point is this: freedom of study and of speech is the essential condition of higher scholarship. Not even the patronage of Frederick could create a university at Naples under the control, in all masters, of a despotic bureaucracy.

REFERENCES

1. Schachner. Nathan, *The Medieval Universities*, pp. 3 and 4. London: George Allen and Unwin. Ltd., 1938.
2. Here quoted from Odofredus. C.H. Haskins, *The Renaissance of the Twelfth Century*. p. 204.
3. Haskins, C.H., *op. cit.*, p. 301.
4. *Ibid.*, p. 138.
5. *Ibid.*, p. 302.
6. *Ibid.*, p. 208.
7. *Ibid.*, p. 300. Reprinted by permission of the President and Fellows of Harvard College.
8. Rashdall, H., *The Universities of Europe in the Middle Ages*, Vol. I, p. 152.
9. Rashdall, H., *op. cit.*, Vol. I, pp. 159-160.
10. *Ibid.*, p. 183/
11. *Ibid.*, p. 233.
12. Norton, A.C., *Readings in the History of Education: Medieval Universities*, pp. 82-87.
13. Rashdall, H., *op. cit.*, Vol. I, p. 282.
14. Rashdall, Hastings, *The Universities of Europe in the Middle Ages*, Vol. I, p. 77. New Edition, Edited by F.M. Powicke and A.B. Emden. Oxford: The Clarendon Press, 1936.
15. D'Irsay, Stephen, *Histoire des universities francais et cirangeres*, Vol. I, p. 99. Paris: Auguste Picard, 1933.
16. Burke, R.B. Translator, Compendium on the Magnificence, Dignity and Reliance of the University of Paris in the year of Grace 1317. Philadelphia: The University of Pennsylvania Press, 1928.
17. Haskins, C.H., *op.cit.*, pp. 141-142.

18. Powicke F.M. and Emden. A.H. Editors, Rashdall's *The Universities of the Middle Ages,* Vol. I, p. 86. See also pp. 78-81. See also D'Irsay, Op. cit., Vol. I, pp. 104-106.

19. D'Irsay, *op. cit.,* Vol. I, pp. 108-109.

20. *Ibid.,* p. 78.

21. Rashdall, Hastings, *op. cit.,* pp. 98-101, 112-114, 120-125.

22. Rashdall, Hastings, *op. cit.,* Vol. I, p. 126.

23. After the article "Gratian," The Columbia Encyclopedia, p. 749.

24. Rashdall, *op. cit.,* Vol. I, pp. 289-291.

25. *Ibid.,* p. 291.

26. *Ibid.,* p. 295-297.

27. *Ibid.,* pp. 300-302.

28. *Ibid.,* pp. 334-339.

29. *Ibid.,* pp. 337-338.

30. Rashdall, *op. cit.,* Vol. III, pp. 12-16.

31. *Ibid.,* pp. 13-14.

32. *Ibid.,* p. 25.

33. *Ibid.,* p. 55.

34. *Ibid.,* Vol. II, pp. 30-31.

35. Rashdall, *op. cit.,* Vol. I, p. 218.

36. *Ibid.,* pp. 224-229.

37. *Ibid.,* pp. 513-514.

38. *Ibid.,* p. 85.

Index